Thunder on the Prairie

Enjoy!

Ferne Carter Chapman

Thunder
on the Prairie

REFLECTIONS ON PRAIRIE LIFE *in the* 20'S AND 30'S

Ferne Carter Chapman

"Hold on to your hat and hitch up your britches! Here's a slice of life as it really was on the North Dakota Prairie during the Depression. No fancy trimmin's—just a well told, often hilarious and heartbreaking tale written by the woman who lived it, Ferne Carter Chapman, a 'natural born' writer of great stories."

—Linda Mihalic

ON THE COVER:
The cover is an original oil painting by the author, depicting the Carter Homestead as it appeared in the 1920s and 1930s.

DEDICATION

This book is dedicated to the memory of my husband of forty years, Jack, whose love, kindness, and support lives on; and to the memories of my parents, William Harlow Carter, Sr., and Lillian Blanche Walters Carter; my sisters, Blanche Mae Carter and Maridelle Annette Carter Stallone; and my brothers, William Harlow Carter, Jr., Cameron Earl Carter, and Duane Willard Carter.

I further dedicate this work to my brothers and sisters, Eugene Albert Carter, Marian Murriel Carter Holmes, Shirley Ione Carter Zimmerman, Winfred Leal Carter, Gladyce Lucille Carter Erling, and Yvonne Gloria Carter Laporte.

ACKNOWLEDGEMENTS

My thanks to son, Jack, for his assistance, encouragement and enduring patience through my many alterations to this book; to my daughter Lynda for her criticism and advice; and to my son-in-law, Larry for many hours of computer work and photography.

I am very grateful to my good friends, Darcea Schiesl and Linda Mihalic for their invaluable contributions, as well as their unlimited encouragement and inspiration.

My gratitude would not be complete without mentioning my sister, Gladyce Lucille Carter Erling, for her many hours of typing, and my sister Shirley Ione Carter Zimmerman, for her offer to share additional family background from her book, Carter Coat of Arms.

Last, but certainly not least, I would like to thank all of my brothers and sisters for contributions of their personal stories to this work.

TABLE OF CONTENTS

IV. **Around The Farm**

Prologue

Many forms of thunder exist on the prairie: the thundering of horses' hooves attempting to elude the cowpokes' lariats; the hoofbeats of frisky cattle as they gallop through the lane; and the pounding feet of a spooked herd of sheep as they attempt to evade a hungry coyote.

And it is quite possible that the reverberation of the armies, like that of General Sibley's less than seventy-five years before us, had left it's own kind of thunder.

Out on the prairie, the sights and sounds of thunder and lightning were frequent occurrences. But when there was silence in the heavens, the thunder of my scattered thoughts and overwhelming emotions howled, cutting a passage through my consciousness.

Pa claimed that we lived "at the end of the last outpost to nowhere"; while Ma repeatedly declared the Dakota territory to be "a Godforsaken place." During the early 1920s and 1930s, Earl, Lillian and us Carter kids were caught on the abyss of raw open country. Much like those on the battlefront of General Sibley's army, we were confounded at every attempt to control our lives and tame this wilderness.

What we didn't know while living such a precarious existence was that the challenges and hardships we endured were only introductions to those yet to come. It took all the fortitude and stamina we could muster as we grunted and groaned to tackle life from all angles to accomplish our objectives. My family weathered physical injuries that ranged from minor to severe. We struggled with the tragedies of loss and hardship that are inherent to life on the prairie. But just as thunder and lightning clear the way for calm weather, so too, do the challenges of prairie life.

It's strange how lightning always precedes thunder in an electrical storm. As the electrical intensity of the lightning increases in magnitude, the thunder follows its path in

1

mind-shattering peals. So it was with myself on both the emotional and physical levels of my life. The calm before the storm could not compare to the exhilarating feelings of inner peace and joy that followed a thunder and lightning storm. The air was electrically charged with a new freshness.

Like the "Sons of Thunder" in the Scriptures, through it all Pa and Ma had the innate comprehension not only to be great, but to do great things. The legacy they left me cannot be duplicated. They instilled in me the values of working hard, thinking big, choosing well, and persevering. They taught me that a cultured society does not produce honesty and integrity, it does not make me virtuous, nor does it stimulate my dormant faculties. This challenge would be mine, alone.

My parents, William Harlow Carter, Sr., and Lillian Blanche Walters Carter, suffered many trials and tragedies in raising twelve children in the tortuous Dakota Territory. They withstood adverse conditions brought about by the smallpox and influenza epidemics, and the Stock Market crash of 1929. They weathered the invention of the automobile, the airplane, the electric age, the mechanized age, the synthetic age, and the age of technology. They endured and persevered!

I realize now that I could have profited more by paying greater attention to the remarkable love, faith, and sacrifice they gave each one of us. My intention in writing this memoir is to provide a journal of my experiences and reflections, to document my family's heritage, to record a brief history of our immediate region, to encapsulate a genealogy, and to recount memories shared with my brothers and sisters.

Thunder on the Prairie, in all its forms, assaulted me with fear, sorrow, pain, tears, and agony. Finally, in due season, a new joy and zest for life emerged. This is my story.

Dakota Territory and Acquistion of the Homestead

The Dakota Territory — My Pa and Ma fought innumerable odds raising their family of an even dozen kids and trying to scratch out a living from the barren soil of the North Dakota prairie. Their story would not be complete without a brief history of the region.

Until the late 1840s, white settlement in the region of present-day North Dakota was largely limited to areas along the Missouri River. In 1848 the discovery of gold in California brought many hopeful prospectors through the territory on their way to the gold fields. Because of the influx of people to the region, land companies were formed. By early 1861 hundreds of settlers had migrated to ~~the~~ this part of the country.

On March 2, 1861, President James Buchanan signed an act establishing the Dakota territory, which included all of North and South Dakota, as well as large portions of Wyoming and Montana. The territory was named for the Dakota people, one group of which were the Sioux.

To protect those living along the Missouri River and the migrants and settlers travelling through the area on their way to the Pacific Coast, the government built many military posts.

Although the Homestead Act of 1862 granted each person who was head of family and 21 years of age or older, 160 acres of land, the first claim filed under the act was not filed until 1868. Each homesteader was required to live on the property, build a house, dig a well, and farm the land for five years.

Those desiring land and citizenship had to file at the General Land Office located in their county seat. The filing fee was $5.00 to $8.00 per homestead entry. All plots of land were filed by numbers in a process known as "blind filing". All entries granted carried the official seal of the General Land Office.

In 1863, under the command of General Henry Hastings Sibley, 4,570 soldiers, scouts, and civilians, followed the Sioux to the Hawk's Nest region, northwest of my family's homestead, then on to the Big Mound, where a bloody battle ensued. The conflict came to an end on July 4, 1863 at the Battle of Big Bend on the Cheyenne River, southwest of Lisbon, North Dakota. In its wake, buried beneath the heavy, rich loam, rest the Sioux warriors, many white soldiers, and the army doctor.

In 1864, the U.S. Congress provided land grants to help build the Northern Pacific Railroad from Minnesota all the way to Washington State. The railroad arrived in Dakota territory in 1871, crossed the Red River in June of 1872 and reached Bismarck, N.D. one year later. As late as 1870, there were no more than 2500 whites living in the region of present-day North Dakota.

However, in response to railroad advertisements and letters from relatives, hundreds of people immigrated from the Eastern United States, and from Northern Europe in the late 1870s and early 1880s. In the 1890s large numbers of ethnic Germans, Ukrainians, Czechs, and others from Central and Eastern Europe came over to start wheat farming.

With the arrival of the railroad and more expedient access to markets in the larger cities, the population of the region grew. My ancestors and a stream of immigrants poured into the area. It became a melting pot of Russians, Germans, Canadians, Norwegians, Poles, Swedes, and Danes. Because of the ethnic diversity , the settlers took on different customs from each culture, and often spoke in the regional vernacular.

In 1864 the state of Montana was formed from the western portion of this land, as was Wyoming in 1868. By 1889, the remaining area became the states of North and South Dakota.

Acquisition of the Homestead — My Pa's sister, Emma Jane, nicknamed Doll, and her husband, Ernest Campbell, filed for the original homestead plot. At the time, it was unbeknownst to anyone that circumstances would one day place the homestead plot into my Pa's possession as a lease rental.

In the early 1900s the Campbells built the original four room farmhouse of prairie rock and sod. The house was half under ground nestled into a small rise in the center of the homestead. The above ground portion was prairie rock with a sod roof. A wooden roof was later added. The structure was approximately seven feet by ten feet, and it stood about four to four and one-half feet above ground. The prairie stone had to be hauled to the building site by stone boat, a sledge drawn by a team of horses. Mortar was used to cement the stones together to form walls.

The Campbell family worked the farm for many years, and by 1924 they had added more buildings to the homestead. By the time their children had grown, the Campbells had become disillusioned with scratching out a living from the soil. They packed up their worldly goods and left for the green, rich land of Tacoma, Washington.

My paternal grandfather, Josiah Carter, purchased the homestead from the Campbells. At that time, the property included the stone farmhouse, a machine shed, a granary, a well, a sagging barn and a little house called the "privy".

5

My grandpa had purchased the farm so that his paralyzed son, Richard—we called him Gordon—would always have a home. Gordon had been shot accidentally by his brother, Albert , while the two were hunting gophers.

Gordon was a congenial, good-looking guy. Probably because of his injury, he kept to himself lots of the time. One day a new teacher arrived in town. She came to the Carter place to seek room and board. Her name was Mary Halverson, and she taught at the Chase Lake School. After living at the homestead for a time, she and Gordon fell in love and later married.

When Grandpa Carter passed away, the farm came into the possession of my Pa's brother, Uncle Joe — Josiah, Jr. It was presumed that Joe helped Gordon out financially, so Gordon gave the farm to Joe in payment. Gordon and Mary continued to live on the farm.

By the time that Grandpa passed away, the William Harlow Carter household had been blessed with six children. My Pa, William Harlow , or Earl, as everyone called him, needed more space to house his "young'uns" and more land to "scratch out a living for his brood". It was decided that my family would move into the Carter Place with Gordon and Mary.

The house was divided, not quite so equally, between Gordon and Mary, and the eight members of my family. We were given the kitchen, the dining room, a loft-like upstairs, and the big back porch. Of course, the back porch wasn't really useable because the cream cans, milk separator, washing machine, wash boilers, and extra milk pails were all stored there. The porch faced the dilapidated barn, the privy, and the featureless countryside.

In spite of it all, it was far better than the Carters had ever had. My folks had graduated from a one-room sod house, where laundry was done using a washboard and lye soap, and where they read by the light of kerosene lanterns.

During the move, from the Simley place, my folks had taken a load of furniture over to the homestead, and when they returned with a second, they found that a fire had destroyed most of the furniture from the original load. Later, it was established that a disgruntled neighbor had set fire to their possessions. Our transportation, too, left a lot to be desired. We traveled by "one hoss shay" and an old lumber wagon.

Mary was real pretty, and us kids were in awe of her, but Ma said she had too many "big city ideas", and that she wouldn't "set well with farm life at all." Looking back, I can only imagine what Mary was feeling about our having moved in with her and Gordon.

Not only were there six of us kids running around getting into mischief, but we snuck peeks into their part of the house every chance we got. I'm sure it was very disconcerting to her. I imagine her life at the homestead didn't turn out like she had wanted.

Mary, I'm sure, stuck it out as long as she could without going mad from deprivation, overwork, worry, and anxiety. The Carter clan was a close-knit group. Two brothers had married two sisters, making my Ma and Mary the outsiders. Ma told me, "We always felt left out of decisions that were being made."

Mary was different from the others. For one thing, she had a myriad of whimsical ideas that our caliber of folks had never come across. She insisted that Gordon buy her a new Model T with shuttered windows. The concept of a beautiful car like that was quite unheard of by those of us who were still traveling in old lumber wagons.

One time she told us that she was going to start raising chickens for food and to sell in town. She demanded that Gordon have a new chicken house built. Looking back, I expect that Uncle Gordon didn't have much income for that kind of "tomfoolery", so he perhaps borrowed, once again, from his older brother, Joe.

After my Grandpa Carter passed away, Gordon hired a worker to do chores around the farm. The hired hand had migrated from the south, searching for work and a place to live. Not long after he was hired, he and Mary skipped out, leaving all of us to wonder what on earth she was thinking.

Later, she and the hired hand came back to the farm in the middle of the night to steal our chickens. Everyone knows chickens are easy to steal when they're roosting. You just whip them off their perch and put them in a gunny sack. We hadn't counted on Mary and him stealing *all* of the chickens. She knew full well that the chickens were our livelihood not only for our own food, but for the sale of the eggs. Ma said it had been rumored that Mary and the hired hand had intended to steal our possessions, too, so Pa sat up in the hayloft with a shotgun for a couple nights—just in case! I'm not sure losing our possessions was as much of a concern as losing all the chickens. My family had very few nice possessions—but those we had we needed.

I felt sorry for Gordon. He was heartbroken to think that Mary just up and left him like that. But he busied himself with hobbies and crafts, and any other activities that could be accomplished from his wheelchair.

The Carter Clan

My Pa, William, Earl Or The Gentry — Grandpa Josiah Carter, Sr., was born in Beacons, Cambrian, Wales, a township at the base of the Cambrian Mountains, which still exists today with a population of 7,802. He emigrated to Central Mines, Michigan where he later married Annie Everett on December 31, 1878. During their marriage, they moved to a new home in Jamestown, North Dakota, which sat on a knoll, overlooking the roundhouse of the Northern Pacific Railroad.

My Pa, William Harlow Carter, was their sixth child in a family of nine. He was brought into this world on June 18, 1890. His brothers and sisters were: Josiah Henry (10-18-1879 to 3-21-1948), Emma Jane (7-08-1881 to 3-15-1971), James Alfred (8-21-1883 to 4-9-1975), Eliza Ellen (12-12-1885 to 10-31-1956), Libbie Lewesa (4-29-1888 to 7-12-1929), Albert Everett (10-31-1892 to 10-17-1954), Richard Gordon (4-18-1895 to 6-3-1930), and Julia Annie (7-20-1897 to 9-16-1897).

Shortly after the birth of her daughter, Julia, Annie passed away. Since Josiah worked on the railroad and was gone for long stretches of time, the brothers and sisters were left alone to care for themselves.

Around the time my Pa was born, in 1890, many important events were taking place, some more positive than others: Idaho and Wyoming became states, the first movie was shown in a theater in New York, and the first steel framed building was erected in Chicago. On the negative side, the global influenza epidemic ravaged humanity.

Judging my Pa's personality, I think I would say he may have become a proverbial cocky street kid, partly because of his upbringing, and partly because of his inherent virtues and capabilities. If cloning had been in vogue when my Pa was in his mid-twenties, the British actor, Hugh Grant, could have been Pa's clone. He was handsome and debonair. His courage would have allowed him to charge a prairie fire with a syrup pail full of water. His rectangular face, square jaw, wide set eyes, and brawny build gave the impression that he stored more knowledge than his fourth grade education had allotted him. Pa's arched brows could not hide the fact that something more than mere physical genetics was at work.

Even though Pa's real name was William, he was better known as Earl, but Ma and us kids referred to him as *The Gentry* when we were feeling real sarcastic. When he took to his whims, he could be pretty arrogant.

Paul Tillich says in his book, *The Courage to Be*, "...nothing in man is merely biological, as nothing is merely spiritual. Every cell in his body participates in his freedom and spirituality, and every act of his spiritual creativity is nourished by his vital dynamics." Today, I believe that the dynamics of Pa's very own soul governed him, although it wasn't obvious to us kids while we were growing up.

In photos taken on my parents' wedding day, August 14, 1912 , my Pa wore an English derby that teetered on the back of his head, surrounded by a mass of charcoal black hair percolating from an off-center part. No doubt about it, Earl was a swashbuckling member of *The Gentry* who aroused curiosity wherever he went.

I believe Pa was the type of person you could have called a contradiction in terms—he was made of flint and steel, but also of putty. He was generous to a fault. Sometimes giving away possessions to a friend in need, even though keeping the item would have best suited his family If a jovial mood struck Pa, he would lift his hat in an elaborate bow and salute.

My Ma, The Beautiful Face of Lillian — My Ma, Lillian Blanche Walters, was born September 20, 1893 to Alfred Eugene Walters and Mary Anne Lutz of Shakopee, Minnesota. She was a second generation American of English, Holland Dutch, and Scotch-Irish descent, with a grandmother that was one-sixteenth German. My Ma had two brothers and two sisters: Alfred, Archie, Emma and Genevieve.

Considering the time in history, my Ma's early rearing was a fairy tale existence compared to the hardships of her later years. In the mid-1800s, her father helped establish and inspected flour mills in and around the Minneapolis-St. Paul area. After traveling for several years, and living in seven or eight places around Minnesota, the family moved to Medina, North Dakota, where her father purchased his own mill. The Red Starr Mill rings a bell with me, but my sister, Shirley's account named the Diamond Flouring Mills Company as his employer.

During summer vacation from Purham High School, Ma worked at Aunt Adelaide's summer resort on Lake Pulaski (Loon) Lake. She and her cousins tidied the rooms for vacationers and helped in the kitchen. After dark, they all marched down to the shores of the lake to spear frogs for the next evening's exclusively elegant frog leg banquet for the guests.

Among its many attractions, the resort boasted a roadside stand. Behind the counter, the young employees spun yarns, pulled taffy, and sold maple syrup to vacationers for twenty-five cents a gallon. Aunt Adelaide and Uncle George had a perfectly natural sugar product, gathered directly from their own maple tree orchard. The maple sugar industry was important early in the history of agricultural development. In the pioneering days, the Indians, too, collected maple sap under the spring "sugar-making" moon. Ma told us that the maple sap was an ugly brown color, halfway between that of dark molasses and sorghum. She would regale us with tales of sap-collecting and taffy-making during her summers at the resort. She told us about hanging kettle type buckets from the tree branches, or from fork type poles. Later the sap would be collected by placing metal spouts into the tree trunks. She said the sap was cooked to a soft ball stage. If a ball formed in cold water, the sap was cooled a bit, then pulled by hand. Ma recounted, "We pulled 'til our arms ached. We sold so much of it that our feet hurt and the soles of our shoes had worn through from all the runnin' back and forth on the dirt floor behind the candy and souvenir counters."

No doubt about it, I thought my Ma had the face of a person with dramatic ability. Comparing her wedding picture back then with one of Jane Seymour today, Ma could have been Jane Seymour's twin. She was shy and not prone to making public speeches, but she did manage to "cue up" in several stage plays for the country school programs. She could also vocalize in perfect pitch. In later years, her dramatic abilities were suppressed. Why—I do not know.

Courtship And Marriage of Earl And Lil — Ma often talked of her and Pa's courting days. "We met in 1910, she would say, "I was in high school, and your Pa was employed on the railroad. Every girl in town was after him—but I got him! We dated for two years, and after I graduated from high school, we were married. He courted me while we were on hayrides, in the surrey with the fringe on top, while we played "shinny on the ice" (a forerunner to hockey) and while we danced at folk dances—and there were plenty of them!" My Ma would hum the tunes of her courting days. In full voice, she would sing *Comin' Through the Rye*, *Girl of My Dreams*, and *I Want a Girl Just Like the Girl That Married Dear Old Dad*.

Earl chose his bride well. Lillian was definitely easy on the eyes—slender, with a near "Twiggy" waistline and medium height. She stood erect, and looked quite composed as she rested one beautifully sculpted hand on Earl's right shoulder, as they posed for the wedding snap. My Ma's chocolate brown hair was loosely enfolded on top of her head, intertwined in a soft crown-like bun. A few spiraling wisps of curl broke free and dangled carelessly about her well-shaped ears, calling attention to the creamy transparency of her complexion. Her brown eyes sparkled beneath high naturally arched eyebrows. The look of her full youthful lips made me think they were created by her verbosity. When Ma talked, others listened. After all—she was the educated one in our family!

She talked of the dowry Pa had for her. "He bought a team of horses, six cows, and a set of furniture which included a table and chairs, a sideboard, stove, bed, and dresser." She told us of her own dowry—a hope chest filled with linens she had saved since she was young. As it turned out, the contents of the hope chest remained in the trunk for some forty years awaiting a home nice enough in which they could be displayed. As far as I know, the only time the bedspread and pillow shams saw the light of day is when she took them out of the chest to air them out, and one time when her father visited the farm. Ma guarded the nubby cream-colored bedspread as if it were a delicate piece of porcelain.

Ma's Wedding Dress —"My wedding dress was a lightweight batiste with tiny overlapping pleats in the bodice," Ma said. "It was form fitting to halfway between my thighs and knees, then billowed to the floor in the back. I'm glad I got married when I did," she chuckled, "because the Gay Nineties wedding dresses resembled the Flapper Era. They had lots of gewgaws, ruffles and flourishes, brilliants, bangles and beads drippin' from every available space. Far as I'm concerned," she said, "the Roaring Twenties styles drastically changed." She chattered on, straightening her spine to its maximum height from a sitting position, "Mine was the color of whipped cream with a dash of vanilla. Your Grandma Walters insisted that my dress be high-toned lookin' like the Victorian Era dresses from back then. My dress had a high neckline and was trimmed with fine expensive lace. I wore your Great Grandma Lutz's cameo brooch."

"A thought just came to mind," she told us. "Grandma's friend from Ladysmith, Minnesota, hand made the fringe that draped from the three-quarter length sleeves. It was just long enough that it traveled down my slender arms, leading everyone's eyes to the shiny new gold band your Pa gave me. I was so proud and happy that day. I don't remember who all was at the wedding," she mused, "but, I'll tell ya one thing, those "high-steppers" that used to hang around yer Pa wasn't there. Right after the ceremony, we left by team and wagon for our first home. It was a sod hut with dirt floors."

Pioneer settlers constructed sod huts by putting a framework together, and stacking cut sod against it to insulate the hut from the elements. This type of housing actually began during the Stone Age, and was used in temperate climates. Hundreds of years later North Americans adopted the same shelter style construction—and Voila—sod huts for American homesteaders.

"After the wedding, times were tough," she recalled. Us kids watched her face, questioning how times could possibly have been tougher than nowadays. She explained, "It was a time when America was beginning to slide into a pre-Depression mode. But in those days we were happy and hopeful." I noticed that her tone of voice denoted a sense of failure. "You kids were being born, so we had to move to a shack that was a little bigger than the sod hut—the Johnny

Johnson place. With crop failures and all, we couldn't afford to winter over the livestock and feed you kids, too. So we sold off most of the stock. Our sod hut was upgraded to a tarpaper shack," Ma recounted. "In fact, we lived in the tarpaper shack when the flue fire started. There wasn't enough water handy, so yer Pa and me had to douse the fire with a brimmin' full chamber pot." There wasn't much to lose. The cubbyhole of a house was a repository for barnyard crates, animal mash barrels upended for lamp tables, and mismatched dishes and cast-off cooking utensils from an old hotel."

Besides the wedding of my parents, several other notable events occurred in 1912. The railroad opened, and trains began to run through nearly every town or within close proximity of a town's grain elevators. It was very sad and ironic that the "unsinkable" SS Titanic sank on her maiden voyage after colliding with an iceberg. One of the 1,513 passengers who drowned was Pa's second cousin.

My Grandpa Walters — I remember only one of my grandparents, crusty old Grandpa Walters, our maternal grandfather. After our Grandma Walters died, he came to the farm just once. But once was quite enough. Judging by the friction between them, I would say he was not my Pa's favorite person. And after Grandpa's lengthy stay of several months, us kids understood Pa's feelings very well.

As I recall, having a grandpa around for a while was enjoyable. But then, having anybody around, that wasn't immediate family was fun and different. Us kids thought visitors were one of life's unexpected pleasures that broke the monotony of our ho-hum existence.

Grandpa Walters was tall and lanky. His chiseled features were accentuated by a white totemic Edwardian mustache and thick, coarse white hair which was combed back from his face. In Grandpa's day, the designer look was bib overalls, just like all the other menfolk of the farms. He

15

always carried a cane of some sort—maybe a whittled diamond willow stick, named for the diamond-shaped knots in the tree trunk—or maybe just a sturdy scrub branch. His huge cane quite often made painful contact with our little legs when he wanted to move one of the us out of his way. Since Grandpa had not been in the service during World War I, and had not been exposed to the noise of cannons, guns, and the like, I wondered why he always had to cup his palm to his ear every time someone spoke to him. Ma cleared that mystery up in a hurry, "He's like yer Pa—he only hears what he wants to."

One thing that stayed in my mind was that Grandpa got the only partitioned room in the whole house that had its own door. It was located at the head of the stairs, and to us kids, it was always locked. No, not by key—but because of my Pa's say so. Grandpa's room was beautifully appointed with all of Ma's best things. Her best wedding day bedspread was finally taken out of the cedar chest. A pretty hooked rug she had just completed, a beautiful wood toned two-drawer commode with a polished marble top, and the most beautiful handpainted china pitcher and basin that I had ever seen, graced his room. Sitting next to the basin was a colossal white shaving mug that looked big enough for a us young'uns to have used as a chamber pot. He was also given our best "slop jar" with its very own lid.

I recall one time when Grandpa took his daily walk down the meandering dirt path toward the garden, and us little kids snuck upstairs to steal a peek into his room. Each kid lurked in the dark landing, not only waiting for his or her turn to peek in, but watching for Grandpa's return. The landing was always dark and Grandpa was old—we knew that we could easily escape into another bedroom before he could hobble up the steep staircase. Not long after his visit, Grandpa passed away.

My Brothers, My Sisters And Me — To get a true perspective of the challenge that Pa and Ma had in raising us young'uns, I guess one would have to be informed of the quantity and quality of the children. Since I'm an expert on my own personality—and only have my perceptions and observations on which to base the stories of my brothers and sisters—I'll start with myself.

Fern Ladelle Carter — I was born on November 22, 1923, on the old Simley place in Chase Lake District. Even though the news had just reached Ma and Pa that there was a birth control clinic in New York, I escaped into this world to become the middle kid in the even dozen of the Carter clan. It just goes to show—God had a plan, and it was carried out through Lillian and Earl.

It seemed the world came near to exploding the year I was born: a horrific earthquake hit Tokyo and Yokohama, Japan, and killed 120,000 people; the Dome Oil scandal hearings took place in Washington, D.C.; the scientific community discovered the structure of the atom; and the Old Age Pension was introduced in Nevada and Montana.

In the late 1920s and the early 1930s, parents frequently psychoanalyzed the middle child by using a tool called the razor strap, but by the late 1950s, the middle child was being carted off to the psychoanalyst for behavioral problems! Pa's razor strap was a highly visible tool, which hung by the mirror over the dry sink. Its mere presence was enough to keep me in line!

My badge of honor was not awarded for predictability. Neither did I excel in readin', writin', or 'rithmetic. The three *R*s, to me, meant rascality, rebelliousness, and run-like-heck. Being a tomboy, I excelled in sports. I ran relay races in school competitions. Ma said, "You at least ran true to form."

Unless *A*s could be mistakenly turned into *F*s, I was a straight *F* student by the time I was in seventh grade. I was usually given spirited parts in the school plays—probably because of my tremendous amount of unbridled energy. My body certainly did not fit a chair comfortably for long periods of time. Pa said I was just fidgety. Ma said I was a d$#n fool. As I saw it, the problem was in the choices I made to utilize the overabundance of energy. I would rather have used it to expedite matters of conflict, than to foster far more advantageous adventures. A pencil, to me, was meant for chewing on while I cogitated, and for making holes in the paper—not for doing my studies. Anything that resembled schoolwork was unacceptable to me. I much preferred a more active method of creating, like a hammer, nails, saws, and wrenches. My larger-than-life, long range plans were usually snugged up in a couple months, depending on how much work they would entail. Perhaps my overabundance of energy and my reluctance to study were the reasons that I didn't finish my high school courses. I finally graduated in 1967 with my youngest child.

What's In A Name—I'm sure I wasn't the only person in the Universe who was less than satisfied with their name.It was years after my school days that I finally decided to change my run-of-the-mill Fern to Ferne. It all began when an acquaintance, Dr. Berkabile saw me struggling to cope with one illness after another. He gave me many helpful suggestions, one of which was to add an *e* to the end of my name. He said, "It will help lessen some of the shocks to your life." I contacted Ma and told her all about the suggestion. I asked her if she would write to Medina, North Dakota to get it changed legally. Ma chuckled, "Maybe the *E* is like a blunt cut on wood, it catches everything." With that, we both laughed. Ma complied with my wishes and wrote to Medina with the change. When Ma signed the name change from Fern to Ferne on my birth certificate, she chuckled again, but wrote the reason for the change as *Vanity.*

Years later, I discovered in the scriptures that when individuals became persons of substance, the name was changed—as in Genesis 17, Sari to Sarah, Abram to Abraham; in Acts 9, Saul to Paul; and Peter received his name from the Greek word Petros, meaning rock. So who's to say whether change is good —for vanity reasons, or simply by choice.

Ma And Me — On the North Dakota prairie farm in early spring and summer, attendance at Sunday School was often deferred in favor of working in the fields. It was alright with me, since I felt intimidated and ridiculed because we were poor country folks. Even if my countenance could measure up—my clothing and outward manner couldn't.

There were a few times in my young life that I'd had brushes with my Lord, such as the time in the Presbyterian Sunday School Summer Camp. I had been touched to excitement—enough so that I walked two feet above the ground. But Ma said, "A few days in the wilderness of the hayfield will take that out of ya!" Sure enough! Just like the Old Testament said, the locusts had eaten all my gains. The gains were partially restored some sixty years later when I became Ma's care giver. We had occasion to share old memories, old hardships and old times, in general.

Today, I feel that God had ignited me in to service on several occasions. But back then I didn't know what I know today! It becomes very clear in I Corinthians 13:11, "When I was a child, I spoke as a child, I understood as a child: but when I became a .....woman, I put away childish things."

There were few times I ever felt that God had tickled our spirits, in an attempt to bond us as mother and daughter. One of those special times was when she and I appeared on stage together in a school play. I hammed it up, ad-libbing and improvising to fill in the gaps of my crazy part. Soon, Ma jumped in. She and I completely strayed from the script, but we had a hilarious time doing it.

Another time that I felt our relationship might be improving was when I saw a worm crawling across Ma's salad plate. I pointed it out to her, telling her that I was near regurgitation. Ma just picked it up, looked at it, and said, "That's okay, he didn't eat much!" Needless to say, I couldn't contain my laughter nor could I eat the rest of my salad. She and I sat and howled. We belabored worm and sheep tick stories until our eyes watered and our voices caught. I believe it was the most laughter we had ever shared.

Blanche Mae Carter — My sister Blanche, was the first born of Earl and Lillian. She came into this world on the Johnson place, March 13, 1913, the same year the Panama Canal and the Rockefeller Institute opened. It was also the year that the United States allowed immigrants to enter from Southern and Eastern Europe. Enticed by the Homestead Act, 10.5 million immigrants came to the U.S. between 1904 and 1914.

My sister Blanche, was born a "preemie", long before medical science had coined the word. She weighed only two pounds, eight ounces, and fit snugly into a shoebox. The warming oven was used as her incubator. Country folks treated their newborns just as they treated baby chicks, lambs, and runt pigs: they were placed in the warming oven of the kitchen range, and fed warm milk with eye droppers or nippled bottles. Blanche was similarly fed first with an eye dropper, then later from a nippled beer bottle. Ma said, "A teacup-sized hat would just fit her tiny little head."

Ma recollected that her own hatred for cats had its roots in a bad experience with the baby. Ma had been out working in the garden, and had gone in the house to check on the sleeping infant. She found "Tom", our cat, straddling Blanche's cheek with its nose pressed up against Blanche's nose. Ma said the cat was trying to take the baby's breath away.

My memory of Blanche is hazy, to say the least. A seven year old doesn't pay too much attention to a person who is old enough to be her mother. All I know was that she was much older than me, and Ma put her in charge of all us younger kids. I do remember that she was fun to be around. Bea, as we called her, was kind and gentle, and viewed the world with rose-colored glasses. She was not quick to rile with anger, and if she was ever moody or distraught, I don't remember it.

She used to let me help her gather wild flowers, particularly wild pink roses, to make rose petal perfume. She also passed the time by making trinket dishes from old phonograph records that she had heated in hot water then formed into bowl shapes. She clipped paper dolls for us younger girls, and copied recipes for Ma. She made belts of folded colored paper, then preserved them with shellac. Blanche made pretty pictures from milkweed pods. The pictures were made using the ivory fluff that exploded from the ripened pods as a background, then tiny dried flowers were added. The last step was to paint a silhouette on convex glass, which was mounted over the floral portion. They were hung in pairs, and we thought they were beautiful.

Blanche was average in height, and had tiny hands and feet. She was blessed with heavily-lidded big brown eyes. Her manner was soft-spoken even when disciplining us little kids. She had fine warm brown hair that she kept marcelled or waved with flaxseed wave set. To curl her hair, she would suspend the iron in the chimney of the lighted kerosene lamp until it was heated to the proper temperature. Sometimes, if the wick of the lamp hadn't been trimmed, the curling iron would leave soot in her wavy locks.

Although her health was failing, she was able to accomplish many basic chores. She watched us little kids, fed the chickens, and helped Ma with the housework.

21

Blanche had developed Diabetes Mellitus, commonly known as sugar diabetes, early in her life. It is interesting that literature from the earliest times contains references to the mysterious disease which was accompanied by the passage of large amounts of sugar in the urine. An English physician, Thomas Willis, discovered through the most rudimentary of experiments, the tasting method, that the urine in the disease was "wonderfully sweet, as if it contained honey or sugar." It took another hundred years to carry out additional scientific experimentation. In *The Universal Home Doctor*, R. Scott Stevenson wrote, "We obtain this sugar which we know as dextrose or glucose from the carbohydrates or starchy foods eaten."

I don't know how my parents got the money to buy her medicine, but they handled it the very best they could. My brother, Eugene, and Pa would drive her to Canastota, South Dakota, in Uncle Gordon and Aunt Mary's new Model T for treatment. Ma was irritated with Mary's ways, but as she was remarking that the Model T was "another thing Mary just had to have," she was silently thanking heaven for the convenience. Ma told us kids that one day she had come in from working in the fields to find Blanche on the floor eating from the slop pail. Us kids told Ma that it was too gross to talk about. But Ma explained that Blanche's diabetes was very serious, and when her blood sugar level was thrown off like that, she could go into a coma. We all felt bad for Blanche.

She lived until age 22 with a severe case of diabetes for which there was no adequate treatment back then. She passed away on March 17, 1935. My sister Blanche's untimely death came within days of a tragic and devastating time for my family. We lost two brothers, and our sister, Blanche, within less than a week of each other.

I was just eleven years old. I could find no way to express the fear and grief of losing so many loved ones in such a short span of time. I couldn't tell where the heartache from losing my sister left off, and the heartache over the loss of my brothers began. I felt like I had fallen out of a tree, and got the breath knocked right out of me. It was as if my family's hearts and minds shifted to another place to escape it all. We just seemed to drift—each of us alone yet somehow connected—from day to day. It seemed to me that Blanche just turned out the lights of her mind, and left us.

I'll always remember Blanche for more than her rose petal perfume, her dietary logs, and her frailty. She was a creative, beautiful person, who persevered. She was a loving and kind-hearted older sister.

My sister, Gladyce, recently gave me Blanche's little gold-leaf dietetic logbook which is approximately seventy years old. It contains many recipes that Blanche had collected and recorded in her beautiful script handwriting.

William Harlow Carter, Jr. — My oldest brother, Bill, was born February 2, 1915 in Sharon, North Dakota. He was nicknamed Kaiser Bill because of the Kaiser's reign in Germany. At the time, he was "tow-headed," Ma said. But later, Bill developed a beautiful thatch of thick charcoal hair that he kept coifed with the popular pomades, hair tonics and lanolin of those times. His finely chiseled features were suggestive of a Roman soldier.

Several great world events took place the year Bill was born. The First Zeppelin was raised in Paris; Prohibition gained ground in twenty-four states; the Germans blockaded England; the first German submarine attacked; WWI began; and German airships bombed East Anglican ports. It was a time of turmoil.

Ma said, "Bill was a real scamp." He grew up being Pa's little sidekick—that is until he grew up and exercised his right to disagree with Pa. He worked hard and loved his family dearly. But like Pa, he found it difficult to express his feelings. Indeed, his snappy brown eyes seemed to hide his inner feelings. He was "toughened" into suppression of his emotions, like the generations before him. He was a kind and giving man.

Little Kaiser Bill was also a rough and tumble kid, like William Harlow, Sr. had been. His escapades were, in every sense of the word, bombastic. He jumped at every chance to break wild horses shipped to buyers from the West. He and his friends pulled other shenanigans like tipping over people's privies or removing them from their moorings altogether. Time and again Ma would shout at him, "You're getting to be a hellion, just like the kids across the lake."

As Bill got older he became creative and innovative. He carved beautiful pieces from wood and gave them to each of us kids for Christmas. He learned leather tooling, and often made Ma beautiful wallets, purses, and belts.

In the CCCs (Civilian Conservation Corps), Bill learned stone masonry. When he came home from the CCCs, he helped Pa out on the farm, building retaining walls and other works of stone masonry.

I recall Bill coming home from the CCCs with sturdy government-issue clothing. He dyed the clothes with black dye and wore them for dress-up for many years. He always looked very sharp in his original form of dress.

Bill had been a cook in the CCCs and later made his living as a chef. He also sold Guardian Service hammered aluminum cookware for several years. Bill married and had four children. He resided in Illinois for many years, until he passed away in 1997.

Eugene Albert Carter — My brother Eugene was born July 17, 1917 in Peterson Township, North Dakota. He was the third child born to Pa and Ma. Other great events besides the birth of the Carter's third child were: Woodrow Wilson propounded his Fourteen Points for World Peace and Germany and Austria agreed with Wilson's demands to retreat to their own territory before the Armistice was signed.

We called Eugene "Gents", and Pa called him "Wooden Foot". As the story goes, Gene and Bill used to wrestle. One time, according to Pa, Bill was winning for a minute. As he began to walk away, Gene picked up an extra long board that he could hardly swing. He was just quick enough to catch Bill behind the knees and give the term "buckle up" a whole new meaning. Pa thought it was so funny, that the story often bore repeating.

Eugene was taller than Bill and Pa—about six foot one. His sandy-colored hair was thick and handsomely styled. He had, and still has, a soft voice and quiet, honest nature. He is definitely *not a chatterbox.* He is as trustworthy with other people's property as he is with his own. Any fears my brother Gene may have had, were well hidden from us kids. If Gene had an Achilles heel, it took an extreme amount of pressure to reveal it. He withdrew from problems until he had time to work them out in his mind.

He was a super student, graduating from the eighth grade at 12 years of age. He could probably add a column of figures in his head faster than I could using a calculator. He was a methodical thinker. He had a quiet and gentle personality, though his unassuming manner is not to be construed as that of a shrinking violet.

Like Bill, Gene went into the CCC to earn money for the family. I remember a few Sunday dinners when Ma sliced up one ring of bologna to go around for the family. Lots of potatoes and perhaps some slivers of salt pork and beans accompanied the bologna.

One day, Gene and Pa took Blanche to the clinic in Canastota. Gene said that Pa was so excited because at 30 mph, Mary's car had passed up everyone on the road. Back in those days cars had to be hand cranked. They often kicked, leaving the "crankee" with a broken arm. A good jack and steep hills were both instrumental in taking the place of the crank. Sometimes the car would be jacked up, then pushed off the jack and allowed to roll down a hill to get it started.

Mary and Gordon's model T fascinated Bill and Gene. They would jump into it and garland our dirt yard with "wheelies". They'd push up the spark and gas levers, get the car going to the full speed of 30 mph, cramp the wheels to run in a circle, then jerk the steering wheel right off its post. Their shenanigans certainly upset the animals. The chickens squawked and went airborne, the ducks waddled around flapping their wings, quacking their displeasure, and our pet Collie dog backed his butt up under the porch, as if to protect himself. Us little kids would watch from the porch, squealing with delight at the sight.

Another time, the boys borrowed Mary's car and came up over the rise where the hill dropped sharply into a huge mud puddle at the bottom. The car jack-knifed, hitting the mud hole. The impact ripped the tires right off the front wheels!

Gene and Bill were both proficient in carpentry and machinery repair, and were ingenious at creating workable tools. It seemed that the urge to create machinery and find new methods to replace outmoded methods around the farm was in their blood.

Eugene was a "gun-toting hombre". Although the military hadn't trained him, he became an expert marksman. When it came to using his gun, he was right up there with the best of them.

I recall an incident when Gene had to protect his sheep herd. Some animal was stalking the sheep at night. Gene had related to us that seventeen of his sheep were killed in one night. The next night, twenty-one sheep lost their lives in a savage manner. The third night, Gene stayed up all night with his shotgun under his arm, waiting in the haymow above the corral. "When I spotted the reprobate, I began pulling the trigger and didn't stop until the culprit was sure-enough not moving," says Gene. The culprit turned out to be a huge wild dog from the surrounding area. Its death put an end to the killing of sheep. Episodes like this were common on the plains. My brother Eugene and his wife Edna, have two sons and reside in North Dakota.

Marian Murriel Carter — The fourth Carter child was born August 13, 1919 on the old Lundgren place. As she grew older, she was nicknamed Bobbi and Booba. As the story goes, she had a thatch of coal black hair which had been blunt-cut, like a bob. Marian progressed from hiding behind Ma's apron when company came to appearing on the school stage wearing only a homemade toy drum. She was three years old at the time.

Marian seemed taller than her 5'5" height. She was attractive. Her snappy sparkling eyes were always filled with excitement and enthusiasm over a new idea or creation. She was a good organizer, and excellent at rationalizing. She was creatively motivated.

Marian attended Valley City Teachers College. She taught school for several years, but later became a beauty operator. She owned her own beauty shop and ceramics business. While teaching ceramics, she won many awards for creativity and innovation.

Though she says its difficult to carry a tune, the children she taught won first place in singing at the Play Day celebration. Our sister, Gladyce, was her pianist. Marian quit teaching "Because," she said, "I could kick a cow, but I couldn't kick a student." My sister, Marian, and her husband Billy, still reside in North Dakota.

Shirley Ione Carter — The fifth-born Carter child came into the world September 15, 1921, just before the family moved to the homestead. Besides Shirley, the year brought a multitude of events—some good, some not so good. The not so good included WWI casualties, approximately 8.5 million dead, 21 million wounded, 7.5 million prisoners, and many missing. Total shipping losses: 15 million tons. The U.S. paid 179 million in war pensions to 646,000 pensioners, and the world-wide influenza epidemic struck, which took nearly 22 million lives.

One of the very good things that happened that year was the day Shirley was born. She was a delicately formed child and grew into a beautiful young lady. Her hair was taffy-colored, and her blue-green eyes seemed to hide more than they revealed. Her facial features were aristocratic and delicate. Shirley was not a noisy sister, but studious and brilliant—her mind methodically clicked every minute with reading, studying and planning.

There came a day when the floor needed mopping, and a healthy argument ensued between Shirley and myself. I forget the circumstances, but one thing was for certain, when Ma shoved the dirty, manure-infested mop in our faces, we soon decided to end the scrapping. Shirley was far stronger than her petite stature suggested. She could stand more intense work for longer periods of time than most of us.

I remember Shirley making gorgeous strings of beads from a simple salt, flour and water mixture which she colored with bluing, red ink, beet juice, and the dye from crepe paper. Once she molded the beads, she put holes through the damp dough with a needle. Old hat pins made excellent skewers and held several beads at one time. Nowadays, Shirley puts her brilliant mind to work in creative writing. She has written and published several books. Shirley has seven children and lives in Ohio.

Cameron Earl Carter — Cameron, the third son of Earl and Lil was born January 5, 1926 on the old Carter place. We immediately tagged him with nicknames such as Short and Cammie. Besides Cammie's exciting birth, other important events that happened during that year included the discovery of treating anemia with liver extract. French psychologist, Emile Caué, authored *Day By Day In Every Way, I'm Getting Better And Better.*

Cammie and I were best of pals. We did everything together. We helped each other with chores and school work. He was a blonde, blue-eyed handsome boy. He was gentle and compassionate. And he loved all the farm animals. Short once said, "When God made blue, He meant blue is love. And He gave us a whole sky full of it."

We have one picture of him. He's wearing an old battered Tom Sawyer-Huck Finn style gray cap which is cocked "just right" over his uncombed hair. Cameron Earl died of food poisoning March 11, 1935 at the age of nine.

Gladyce Lucille Carter — The fifth girl to be born to the Carter family was Gladyce. She was born June 18, 1931, on the old Carter place. She was Pa's birthday present. Several other exciting things occurred the year she was born Trotsky was expelled from Russia, the Arabs attacked the Jews in Palestine following disputes over the Jewish use of the Wailing Wall; Frank B. Kellogg won the Nobel Peace Prize; and Ernest Hemingway was recognized for his novel, *Farewell To Arms.*

As Gladyce grew older, she became Gladdy. She was always happy go-lucky and giggly. Another name she was given was Pootsa, but I don't recall how or why she got the nickname. By the time she arrived on the scene, she had four older sisters to cart her around the house. No matter how old, or how big we were, everyone got to take care of the baby. With Gladyce, it was a pleasure, since she was a cute, chubby little baby. She had brown curly hair and huge brown eyes. She was a near replica of our sister Blanche in both appearance and personality.

When Gladyce was nearing age four, government agencies and medical scientists of the day were experimenting with the health issues of the American population. Their targets, of course, were the nation's underprivileged. They issued government food to families under the Poor Relief Act. The Poor Relief Act aided the poor, yet what was intended as help for our family, became our family's greatest tragedy. The government subsidized food was packed using an experimental process in tin cans. After ingesting canned tomatoes, three of my brothers and sisters died, and three more were hospitalized.

Gladyce survived the tragedy after being hospitalized for some time. The doctor told Ma that Gladyce's eyes had suffered damage and her eyes were to be bathed with boric acid every hour, or perhaps more frequently, I can't recall exactly. Ma sat up nights bathing Gladdy's eyes. The tragedy caused permanent damage to one of her eyes, but we were all tremendously relieved and happy that she had survived the ordeal.

Gladyce is brilliant, with a mind that travels into several subjects simultaneously. Her sharp mentality shows when her mind is piqued. When her mood turns to "upswing", she is happy and light-hearted. She is capable of switching from a bundle of nerves into a serious intellectual, who studies many things. She's a perfect example of "the mind is the easiest thing to change." She can be viewed as a complete blend of many women. She encompasses cleverness of speech and wit, with an active imagination, as well as great courage.

I recall, however, that she did not apply her courage when encountered by a buck sheep at Alderton, Washington. She would walk a block further than necessary to avoid him when she went through the pasture to milk the cows.

Winfred Leal Carter — Winfred was the eighth child born to Earl and Lillian. He was born November 28, 1928 near the Westman place in Medina, North Dakota. That was the year that the economic conference in Geneva was attended by fifty-two nations; the early starts of Black Friday, with the collapse of the economic system of Germany; Louis Bromfield's novel, *Early Autumn*, won the Pulitzer Prize; the first exhibition for space flight took place in Moscow; and the lower Mississippi River Valley suffered a great flood disaster.

Winfred was nicknamed Din. He was a blonde baby with a myriad of curls—trying to outdo Eugene's golden locks, I presume. He, too, resembled the Walters' side of the family. He is six foot plus in height and large boned.

Winfred appears to be an invincible person. All us Carter kids enjoy winning at our endeavors, but something inside us dies if we lose. Winfred served his church as a minister for twenty-five to thirty years. He enjoys a good joke, and should have been a stand-up comedian. His repertoire of comical stories goes on for hours—proof of his excellent memory. He is loyal, kind and helpful to everyone he meets.

Winfred is a paint contractor, well liked by his employees and the people he serves. He is a hard worker and perseveres through any problem. He and his wife, Ethel, have two children and live in Edmonds, Washington.

Duane Willard Carter — My youngest brother, Duane, was born October 22, 1933. This blonde, blue-eyed baby was so soft and cuddly, we nearly kissed a hole in his chubby cheeks. We bathed and changed him as if he were a little doll. Since baby food wasn't available to us, we mashed regular food and fed him.

High chairs were non-existent, so the baby had to be tied to a kitchen chair with a tea towel. On warm summer days, we would make a tent under the clothesline, then take Duane into the tent so his tender skin wouldn't burn. We would sit on a blanket and play with him for hours while Ma finished her chores around the farm. Duane Willard Carter died March 17, 1935 at age 17 months after eating tainted food.

Yvonne Gloria Carter — The sixth daughter in the Carter clan was born August 13, 1936 on the old Challman place. The year of her birth marked the presidency of Franklin Delano Roosevelt; the U.S. passing the Agricultural Adjustment and Federal Emergency Relief Act; the ratification of the 20th Amendment to the Constitution; and the making of the Farm Credit Act law.

Yvonne was another gift to our household, a fitting birthday present for our sister, Marian. Yvonne's nicknames were simply Vonnie and Doo-Doo. She was a beautiful baby with deep brown eyes. Her face was soft and gentle, but she could snap like fire when aggravated. Yvonne is energetic and gregarious, and not easily discouraged. She is a good organizer, business woman and leader. Anything she can't organize is not worth giving time to. She, like Marian, is good at rationalizing things.

Many times during our lives, us Carter kids seemed to be accidents waiting to happen. This seemed to be the case with Yvonne when she and the ax collided. We teased her that she was acting sillier than usual because she got in Gladyce's way when Gladyce was chopping wood. Gladyce swung the ax high over head. Much to the surprise of the two, Yvonne received a substantial rap on the head with the blunt side of the ax.

Yvonne went on to become an accomplished florist and ceramist. She has nine beautiful children and resides in Wisconsin.

Maridelle Annette Carter — Maridelle was the last child born to Earl and Lillian. She was born July 24, 1938 on the old Derrickson place. In 1938 Franklin Delano Roosevelt had just signed the Social Security Act into law; Robert E. Sherwood wrote the novel, *Petrified Forest*, the first sulfa drug for the treatment of streptococcus was discovered; and the Rumba became a fashionable dance.

My Ma was forty-five years old when she had Maridelle. None of us knew that she was pregnant because she was of substantial weight by then. We came home from school one day to find Mrs. Heagy, the midwife, just about to leave the house. Ma was sitting in a chair snuggling the newborn to her breast. All the Carter kids were nursed until they were two years old.

Maridelle, for some reason was tagged with the nickname Tootie. She was a petite tot. The fact that she was the baby of the house and so small, she innocently held a commanding hold on Pa's affections, and ours, as well.

My sister, Shirley, reminded me that Tootie, as a little girl, hated to wear her shoes and her bloomers, so she discarded both every chance she got.

Maridelle was only four-foot-plus at her tallest. Her voice was soft and mellow and her mannerisms were demure. She giggled at everything and her eyes sparkled with an inner glow.

Maridelle went on to become a beautician. She frequently changed her hair color from ash blonde to pink, black, and lavender. She later became a blonde. When Pa asked her why she changed her beautiful ash blonde hair, she said simply, "Pa, we have to keep up appearances, and we need to practice on each other. I wanted something different." Sometimes her hair color was very *different.*

We enjoyed Maridelle for the years we had her, but she and her infant son, Anthony Stallone, were killed in an untimely motor vehicle accident in the Pacific Northwest in 1963.

The Carter Homestead

The Homestead — My family's homestead was situated in a hollow surrounded, in part, by a semicircle of burnt rolling hills. The hills were parched-looking—burned by the searing heat of many summers, and the unbearable cold of many winters. Our eyes were often drawn to the limited boundaries of our naturally restricted circle.

The house was located forty rods, 220 yards, from the west gate, and approximately two miles from the east gate. The old wagonwheel-rutted dirt road passed through the dooryard, connecting the two gates. To the south of the house was a bog which was a watering hole for our animals, and on hot days, a splashing hole for us kids. North of us was Cobblestone Hill, named for its thousands of large, irregular rocks.

The entrance to the homestead was through an almost imaginary west gate, which was no longer a gate at all, but rather a tangled mass of rotted fence posts and rusted barb wire. I don't remember there ever being an actual gate, but the leaning corner posts on either side of the road paid tribute to where the gate had once stood.

Some of us kids would sit there by the hour just hoping to see passersby on the way to the town of Crystal Springs, thirteen miles south of us. Sometimes we would see two a week! We got really excited to see folks, because strangers, and visitors alike, were few and far between. We sat staring off toward Crystal Springs, knowing that when Pa went there, it was an all day trip, traveling by team, and we rarely got to go with him.

Down the slope, past a row of Poplar trees and the gooseberry patch, sat the homestead. It consisted of a motley group of wind and weather-beaten buildings, a few farm animals, an assortment of broken and patched farm equipment, and flocks of chickens, turkeys, ducks, and several geese.

In the 1930s, the farm was comprised of eight dilapidated structures and a root cellar: a two-story house, a deteriorated garage, the original stone house — now the hog lot, a chicken house, a barn, a granary, a machine shed, and a privy.

The two-story house had once been a yellow color, finished in lath and plaster. The front door of the house faced west toward the irregularly spaced cottonwood trees, gooseberry bramble, a field of gopher holes, and a multicolored bed of bachelors buttons.

The dooryard, which like the barnyard, was open to children and animals alike, was the main thoroughfare for all the livestock and farming equipment. It also served as the guest passageway to the house and to the east gate. When not digging holes at the fringe of the yard, gophers scurried around, scaring the mother hens and their chicks. Poultry, livestock, goat, and sheep excrement peppered the dirt and rock yard so plentifully that there was virtually no place to step without getting your shoes soiled. There was no sign which said *remove shoes before entering,* so us kids managed to track all the debris into the house, up the stairs, and into any room to which we were headed.

Aunt Mary's chicken house had been excavated into the northwest hillside, like a root cellar, and had a shingled roof jutting out above ground level, which sheltered it to the east.

The wind-blistered, bluish-gray barn to the northeast was on tilt when we moved to the homestead, and was even more so when we left. The haymow door faced our house and the privy, while the main barn door faced south, toward the granary located southeast of the house. The lane leading to the bog and open spaces to the south, lay between the granary and the tool shed—which also served as a sheep shelter.

Along one side of the barn was the milk cow stanchions, including the all-important trough to catch the excrement. The trough was supported with railroad ties below ground level. Inevitably, the cattle chose the exact time we were milking to fill up the trough. Us kids would frequently exit the barn looking more like the sides of a manure spreader, than human beings. The opposite wall of the barn was fitted with rough slab lumber for the horse stalls, and a feeding pen for newborn calves.

Up the knoll to the south of the barn, and located between the barn and the well pump, was the sturdiest building on our property, the original four room rock house that Uncle Ernest and Aunt Emma had built. It had now been relegated to serving as "hog heaven". The weakened crossbeams of its roof beckoned us kids to "come jump and dance on me." To us it seemed like "rubber ice"—and equally as dangerous. We knew you could get caught under the ice and drown—worse yet, you could fall through the "rubber" roof into the pig mire and risk getting bit by a startled hungry hog.

Farmers never had to make hog wallows—the hogs took care of that themselves. We fed the hogs a collection of corn cobs, corn stalks, spoiled garden rutabagas, turnips and any other food waste that was available. The clutter and stench looked and smelled like we had moved into the stockyard arena. The aroma was so rank that we had to pinch our noses, and try to remember that the hogs

36

furnished a great portion of our food supply and income. This appalling condition did not compare to the fact that the waste from the barnyard and the pig wallow drained toward our well—located down behind the barn.

Beyond the barn, to the east on the knoll, sat the pump and watering troughs for the animals. Ma said, "The well was a story in itself." At the time the homestead was procured, water dowsers were a dime a dozen. They tramped the property of new land owners, attempting to find underground water by using a mysterious method called dowsing. Some dowsers used twigs, others didn't care if their so-called rod was as simple as a turkey wishbone or a set of metal rods, and still others swore by applewood sticks. The procedure appeared almost electric. The dowsing stick actually seemed to fight the dowser to the point of twisting off the bark of the twig.

Adjacent to the hog lot, one side of the dilapidated granary stood lopsided on partially secured concrete and the other side was precariously perched on huge prairie rocks. The roof glinted mysteriously in the sun. I can recall thinking, *It has that put-your-eye-out shine like thousands of diamonds.* I knew it couldn't be diamonds, especially during Depression days! How mysterious could it be? The shine that consumed my thoughts was nothing more than the flattened tin cans my Pa used for patching the roof.

The same fancy never-wear-out patches adorned the floors of the house, the knotholes in our upstairs, and the numerous holes in the siding of all our out-buildings. Inside the granary were poorly constructed bins that usually housed more rodents than they did grain. The rodent population grew so rapidly that trapping them became impossible. So my brothers Bill and Gene, who trapped larger animals in the winter, simply got rid of the rodents by using them for target practice.

To the south and west of the granary stood the original Quonset style machine shed that now housed sheep. The elements had taken their toll on the shed. The front door that had once opened wide to allow the entry of farm equipment, was no more—only its rusty metal rigging dangled from the overhead crossbars. The equipment that was once stationed in the shed, was now piled in a twisted, tangled, rusted scrap heap out by the clothesline.

To the east of the house and a little bit north, was the famous two-holer—better known as the *privy*. For convenience sake it had been strategically placed equidistant from the house and the barn. This way, whether you were working in the house or in the barn, you had the same distance to cover to get there.

Beside the clothesline to the south, was a dual purpose facility, the root cellar. This was a good-sized cave dug into the side hill. A frame had been constructed that followed the contour of the side hill around the opening, to which two slab style doors were hinged. The root cellar was equipped with shelving to hold fruit and vegetables over the winter. It was built to allow enough space to act as an emergency shelter for the family in the event of a twister or cyclone. Sad to say, the most ferocious twister hit before we could escape from the house and get to the shelter.

The House And Furnishings — One can only imagine what shape our house was in. Afterall, there was a family of fourteen coming and going from the fields, the garden and the barnyard. With so much time devoted to the upkeep of the animals, the fields, and the garden, there was very little time left for the upkeep of the house. This was also Depression Era. There was no money for paint, carpeting, and finery that makes a house a home.

The Kitchen — We usually entered the house on the east side because that was where the barn, the well, and most of the other farm buildings were located. To enter our kitchen we climbed the rickety wooden steps of a four foot elevated porch without benefit of handrailings. Imagine, having to carry two buckets full of milk from the barn, or water from the well, located half a block away, up the steep steps, and across the kitchen to the dry sink. Let me tell ya, that was a chore! Us kids took turns carrying the buckets. Ma said carrying two at a time kept us balanced—balanced and worn out, is more like it!

The interior of our house was far from the benchmark of modern home decorating. But at least it was no worse and no better than anyone else's in the district during those hard times. To say the kitchen was utilitarian would be the understatement of the century. The "depression-times garbage disposal unit" stood directly inside and to the right of the back door, hidden behind a grimy paisley flour sack which had been suspended from an old screen door spring, secured on either side by a huge nail. Since we never had leftover table scraps to put in the slop bucket, it usually contained sour milk, corn cobs, dirty wash water, and a few potato peelings.

The only sink in the entire household was a dry sink. As the times and finances dictated, there was no indoor plumbing. For this reason, the dry sink had to take on the dual duty of kitchen and lavatory needs—such as washing dishes and brushing teeth. The sides of the dry sink cabinet were covered with old faded linoleum. A chipped, gray speckled enamel washbasin sat in the well of the dry sink. The basin was scum-laden from the hard water, as well as from the homemade lye soap. Beside it, on the right hand side, lay a dingy white saucer, dulled by hairline cracks and large chips, containing a boulder size chunk of Ma's homemade lye soap, glued by scum to the antiquated saucer.

Our washcloths and towels were flannel scraps, flour sacks, and even some torn bits of worn out ragged underwear. Ma always said, "It's okay, jus' cut out the crotch." Sometimes the good parts of Ma's cast off dresses found their way to the towel rack, too.

On top of the dry sink cabinet was the galvanized water bucket, its leaky spots patched with copper rivets. The battered tarnished community dipper was used by family and guests, alike. If the dipper handle fell into the bottom of the bucket, us kids would just reach in—elbow deep, if necessary—and retrieve it, no matter how dirty our hands might be.

To the left of the basin, in one of my Grandpa's old cracked shaving mugs, sat our toothbrushes—all three of them—stored bristles up. Even though us kids didn't have our own toothbrushes, we were assigned four kids to the orange one, four kids to the blue, and four to the green. Sometimes I would be sneaky and try out the orange one, instead of using the green one, like I was supposed to. I was pretty sure that my sisters and brothers were probably sampling different ones, too. It didn't matter which one I used, they were all well worn and tasted like salt and soda. With no money for the luxuries, like toothpaste, ours consisted of a mushed up mixture of salt and soda, stored in a stained dingy glass fruit jar near the water bucket. A dip in the water, then a dip into the *mush* was considered the antidote for "all types of hoof and mouth disease", so Pa claimed. We sometimes followed brushing with a mouth wash of mild vinegar water. No wonder us kids only brushed if absolutely necessary!

Pa's eight by ten inch shaving mirror, free of frame and one corner broken off, hung over the sink—just out of reach of curious children. Ma said that if us girls had a larger mirror at our disposal, she just knew we would "primp all day long!" As a reminder to all of us kids to watch our *Ps and Qs,* the razor strap hung right next to the mirror in full view of even the tiniest of tots.

Summer Kitchen To Winter Shed — Because of winter fuel shortages and poorly fitted doors and windows, we had to vacate the kitchen and turn it into a winter shed. All the kitchen furniture, including the range, was moved into the dining room, which was already occupied by my family's dated sideboard, dining table, chairs and benches. It took a whole lot of furniture to seat our big family. There was hardly a place to walk through, let alone room to play.

What had been our summer kitchen, now became a multiple use cold room, filled with dank, earthy stable odors. Our winter galoshes, brooms, mops, a stack of washtubs , boilers, pails and cream cans vied for space with piles of miscellaneous farm paraphernalia. Small piles of soft coal for starting fires and sacks of flour shared a portion of the room with small dead trapped animals waiting to be skinned.

At the first sign of spring, before the thaw, the pelts were sold, and the remaining contents of the room were removed so that we could scald the floor of the summer kitchen. We spent *hours* carrying water to fill the washboiler. The washboiler was considered by pioneer women to be a hot water tank. "The water's heated to the boiling point, be sure to open the lid away from yerself," Ma cautioned. As we filled each pail, Ma would add a bit of pure lye and some shavings from a bar of her homemade soap.

Every dilapidated old broom that we could rustle up was called into play. Brooms in hand, us kids began to do the kitchen swabber's broom-rumba. Ma said, "It's more fun if you play while you work." We *sloshed* pails of the disinfectant water over the floor in great swells, and swept it out the back door to drain away. Ma blasted the floor with a few buckets of scalding hot rinse water while she yelled, "Watch out! Here comes another bucket!" Then, it too, was swept out the door. I was in the mop brigade, it was our job to get the floor as dry as possible using our mops. The doors and windows were opened to provide cross ventilation for drying the already warped flooring.

A Monarch Amongst Us — No, there was no sovereign ruler or exalted one in our house that is, except for our Pa. The Monarch I'm referring to is the old Monarch wood and coal stove. It sat along the west wall of the kitchen, near the door leading to the dooryard and the dining room. Though the name would lead you to believe that it was fueled with wood and coal, it wasn't so at our house. Heck, there was much cheaper fuel—in fact, free fuel—to anyone who would cut it up and haul it away. It was called sheep manure! The "magic fuel" we used was a combination of dried corn cobs, cowchips, tree branches, pieces of railroad ties, and the dried cubed sheep manure.

In the winter, we banked the stoves with coal, if it was available. Sometimes we couldn't get coal because the snows prevented the train from running through the outlying towns. Or sometimes Pa just couldn't get to town to buy it—but mostly, we just couldn't afford it. If nothing else was handy, dried grass, old unsalvageable hunks of leather harnesses, paper, or corncobs soaked in kerosene were used as fuel. You never knew from day to day what kind of fuel would be available at the Carter household!

Much of the time Ma would mandate us kids to keep the fire going. With my limited attention span, this often proved to be a disastrous practice! My mind would wonder off, and before you knew it, the stoking process had been compromised, allowing the ovens to cool, then heat, then cool again.

I remember Ma often wishing she had a New Perfection stove. She'd lament breathlessly, "It's sure a fancy lookin' contraption!" Ma read me the advertisement, "Turn out runaway biscuits in the new Aladdin biscuit pan." It included special utensils like a pudding pan for cooking "English Monkey Cheese Pudding." I regret that Ma never did see the actual stove—only the picture and the advertisement. Whenever she started wishing for the newfangled stove, she would say, "This ol' Monarch warmin' oven was a real Godsend when Blanche was born. Guess I better jus' hang on to it."

The warming oven had also come in handy to incubate baby chicks and to keep baby lambs and pigs warm until they could survive outdoors on their own. We frequently had to keep newborn animals inside, and us kids would bottle feed them. We would make cushy beds in the corner of the kitchen for them using boxes lined with hay.

I have fond memories of the old Monarch keeping forbidden coffee warm for me and my sister Marian. When she and I had to do the evening dishes, we would occasionally sneak cups of coffee from the pot and lace them with cream and sugar. If we heard someone coming, we would thrust the cups into the old warming oven, where they would stay nice and warm until we could get back to them.

It seemed like everyday of the week the top of the stove was obscured by the old wash boiler, the ever-present sturdy gray enamel coffee pot, the ten quart soup kettle and various cast iron frying pans. Most of them were filled to different levels with fat cubes at varying stages of rendering. This motley group of containers upstaged everything else, except perhaps, the six glad irons—cast iron flatirons—which were frequently moved to the front of the stove to be quickly heated for ironing clothes. When we were ready to perform the task, which was a continuous job in a family our size, we simply clipped a wooden handle into the center top of the heavy iron, and away we would go—lickety split across the fabric!

In every home, a decorative wooden matchbox hung beside the range, safely out of the children's' reach. As revolting as it sounds, you could hardly tell the color of ours because of all the fly specks. Since our farm had no electricity, matches were indispensable. They were used to light our many kerosene lamps, cooking fires and candles. Sometimes, they were called upon to perform in the lighting of backfires to curtail massive prairie fires.

Beside the matchbox, dangling from a soiled flour sack string, was a pencil which had been whittled to a stub. Our provisions list was a scrap of school tablet attached to the wall, usually scribbled with waxy crayons. The name of the item we needed was near invisible because of the pencil lead trying to compete with the crayola markings. Some of the letters stood out rather boldly, so you knew that the pencil point had been placed in a mouth to make the marks show up better. We did the same thing when doing our schoolwork. Spit was good! It worked for washing dirt off clothing that we usually discovered right before going into the classroom. It made good spitwads with which to agitate our classmates, and it was an unlimited source for washing the blood from the wounds created by our aggravated classmates. Around the farm, us kids even used our spit and dirty sleeves to clean the animals' salt block in the corral, so *we* could lick it.

Some people might get the idea that us kids had no manners at all. But our manners were impeccable when guests were present. Our cow pasture habits mostly stayed in the cow pasture if someone other than family was around.

A Trip to the Woodpile — It was a monumental task, to consistently refuel the stove. I could get mighty lonely just gathering wood, because the woodpile was way out past the *two-holer* outhouse, beyond the chicken coop. The unstructured mound was the size of a national monument and furnished a rugged backdrop for the equally tacky hen house.

Our so-called kindling was a crude mess of collected rubble from the surrounding countryside, most of which was gathered from the Northern Pacific Railroad right-of-way. I swore we had pieces and parts of railroad ties left over from the driving of the first spike in the town of Pettibone in 1911! Strewn over a quarter-block square were such wonders as old sections of well-rotted fencing, parts of the beaver dam from down at the bog, and a collection of debris from old turkey roosts, broken wagon wheel spokes, and doubletrees with rusted hardware.

I would inspect the huge mound, searching for a few splinters and small pieces that would allow me to rest my chopping arm, but wood gatherers before me had come up with the same idea. Since the doubletree would not part with its rusted hardware, I painstakingly drag the entire contraption to the house—feeling very proud. Ma glanced at the armload, muttered something under her breath that could have been construed as *stupid,* then sent me back to the woodpile in search of more suitable pieces for the stove.

Finally, the fire laid and ready to light, the match ignited a pair of miniature overalls, axle-greased beyond salvage, dried cowchips from the prairie, and one armload of *cursed* wood chips. I say cursed—because I was known to take to profanity, like my Pa, when struggle and hard labor challenged me. In such cases, if I happened to be within hearing distance of Ma's ears, her homemade lye soap took on a dual role, of not only cleaning but also, " *relaxin'* the motor-mouth flow of profanities," as our matriarch would say.

The Heatin' Stove — At times, it became necessary to move the old heating stove from room to room to get adequate heat, and to protect us from the cold of the harsh winters. A couple strong menfolks were enlisted to assist Pa with this task. After lots of grunting and groaning, and a few bits of profanity, the job was completed.

When the stove was in place, Ma would remove the round metal plate from the chimney hole near the ceiling.

The pipe had to be pushed into the hole so it would fit snugly to prevent smoke from billowing and puffing back into the room. Most importantly—it prevented soot from falling into the room if a kid or two got a little rambunctious throwing objects at each other. It wasn't uncommon for the object to go flying over a kid's head and crash into the stove pipe. In fact, it was almost an impossibility to *miss* the pipe, since it meandered from room to room, only secured to the ceiling with several lengths of bailing wire that hung like cobwebs above the pipes.

Ma would holler, "You guys tryin' to burn the house down? Jus' remember you'll be the ones formin' a chain gang line of water buckets from the well!" Such threats made us practice a little more caution when roughhousing.

Besides coal and wood, the primary source of our fuel was compacted sheep manure that we had extracted from the wintering barn using a pick, a pitchfork, a sickle, a saw, and any other appropriate cutting devices. Once cut, the manure was manually loaded onto a stone boat or wagon, then transported to the hill at the south side of the house. The sections of manure were placed on the ground in a pyramid fashion to allow the sun and air to circulate around it. After basking in the sun for a week or two, each little pyramid of manure was turned inside out to allow the sun to dry the opposite side. When it was thoroughly dried, we took it to the shed by stone boat, and stacked it in rows like firewood, for later use.

Ma had to stoke the heating stove much of the time in the absence of Pa and the boys. She would try to shove heavy chunks of railroad ties and manure into the stove, and it took plenty of patience, precision and muscle to get the slabs wrestled into the fire box just right. That meant us kids had to breathe smoke-filled air for long periods of time while it smoldered before breaking into flame. As a rule, we would usually fuss about the smoke getting into our eyes and throats. We weren't smart enough to know that the lungs would bear the brunt of the clouds of black soot. Although us kids didn't have to stoke the fire on a steady basis, we did carry wood and cowchips at regular intervals. The fire was banked at night with lignite coal chunks. Embers from the original fire would smolder and start a new fire for morning.

Target Practice Or Cooking? — The Carter family's cooking utensils looked like they had all been used by the army for artillery practice. Small copper rivets blanketed the sides and bottoms of almost every pot, pan and container we owned.

We used copper riveting kits to patch all the household utensils. One patching method consisted of a small copper brad being slipped through a tiny washer, then pushed through to the inside of the utensil where another washer was placed. Then, the utensil was placed over the point of the anvil , and the head of the brad was pounded flat on the outside of the utensil, causing it to split apart on the inside. This process was used to fix holes, leaks, and splits in our overused and much abused pots, pans, washtubs and various other containers.

Our food was cooked in a bevy of battered aluminum pots and pans, most of which were lid free. I recollect an entire repertoire of kettle lids, yet, they seemed to fit nothing in our pot, pan, and kettle kingdom. Cast iron frying pans, and army sized bread baking pans were used, not only for rendering lard, but for baking bread, English pasties, and roasting meat. The huge pans were also used to sterilize jars, and keep them hot during the canning process.

Our #3 and #10 washtubs got the most workout, serving as vessels for such tasks as washing clothes, bathing, and hauling produce from the garden. We also used them for shelling peas, rubbing salt into pork bellies at curing time, and for cleaning the entrails and hogs' heads.

47

Folks that are familiar with cooking, can well imagine the great quantity and capacity of pots and pans needed for a family of fourteen. The big problem was usually where to store all of these huge containers. Well, at our house they were stacked on every available surface, shelf, and table. They were in the ovens, on the stove top, out on the porch—you name it. They were there—and not always clean. I remember Ma simply following the oatmeal leavings of breakfast, with the ingredients for the next meal without ever having washed out the pot. That's the way it was on the farm. No time, no more energy! Just start one meal right after the other, with hundreds of other chores in between.

Pestilence In The Pantry — By late summer, the fly problem had become like the plague both in the house and out by the hog pen and animal areas. Flies were everywhere. Screen doors were of little value on the farm, for several reasons: can you really expect a kid—let alone twelve of them—to close the door *quickly*; can you picture all the doors askew on their hinges with cracks big enough to allow gophers to get in; or do you think that all those little fingers couldn't accidentally poke holes in the screen? All of these possibilities were realities at our house.

The homemade fly-swatters did little damage to the pesky swarm clouds that swooped in every corner of the house. The kitchen, of course, was the hardest hit. Above the pantry door hung great lengths of sticky fly paper which would be bulging with flies within minutes of hanging it. We restructured our worn out fly-swatters from inner tubings precisely cut to the dimensions of the previously purchased wire portions, which hadn't worn out.

When all the other options failed, and the flies got the upper hand, we had no other recourse but to wage all out war with our flour sack tea towels. It took three people to do this job: two flailing away with the towels as flag wavers to scare the flies out the door, and one—preferably a small

48

kid—to push the door open like a flash, when called upon to do so. The two exterminator warriors began flailing their towels on the far side of the kitchen. Then a loud yell from Ma, "Quick! Shut the dining room door! They're goin' in there." Then another shout, "Open the back screen door, quick." Tiny legs would dive for the screen door, and thrust it open just in time to hear, "Hur'yup and shut the door! They're comin' back in!"

Such episodes became an almost daily activity for us kids. We thought about giving them some of Pa's Hundred Proof, thinking maybe they would just stagger on out by themselves. Ma didn't think that idea was real funny. As I recall, the same tea towels we used to snap at flies were also the same ones used to dry the next meal's dishes.

Our Table Finery — At our house, no stylish table settings graced the table, and the silencer pad was only a well-worn cracked oil cloth used daily until its backing showed through and the pattern had become a dull gray. Our flour sack tablecloth was sewn together in four sections, and barely fit the table, with no extra fabric to drape down the corners. Ma had appliqued a bouquet of flowers in the center and at each corner. It was used only when we had guests for dinner, or for special occasions. "It's the launderin', Ma would remind us, "I don't want to wear it out."

The cabinetry at our house boasted no Montgomery Ward breakthroughs. Our Hoosier wasn't an oak kit with multiple layers of country blue paint and fancy decals, like the ones we saw in the catalogs. It was a freestanding homemade veneer cabinet, replete of paint. Its doors were warped and smeared with fingerprints and fly specks. Some paraffin wax boxes, a few baking powder cans, the recipe box, baking soda boxes, and fruit jars were stored on the very top of the six foot high cabinet. The center door knobs were made from half of a wooden thread spool.

The handcrafted cupboard was loaded with stacks of mismatched, cracked and marred dishes and tin plates. Our china patterns consisted of early chip, crack, and second hand varieties, most of which had seen their full use by other families as poor as we were.

Various and sundry sauce dishes, cups, and jelly jars were used for drinking glasses. The coffee cups were anything from Grandpa Walters' old shaving mugs, to discarded earthenware mugs from the Buckwalter Hotel that Ma had obtained while working as a part-time cook. The milk pitcher was usually a large, dented tin monster that us kids couldn't handle by ourselves with any degree of control. Our much used sugar bowl and cream pitcher was referred to as the "odd couple", since it had never matched. Our silverware was a hodgepodge of mismatched, bent and well-worn varieties, as well.

Behind the lower doors of the cabinet were various sizes of dilapidated pie and bread pans. There were also some large metal bowls and a few cracked and faded hand-painted china pieces we had inherited from Grandma Walters. Nothing could stay new-looking for long in the Carter household.

The Sittin' Room —The sitting room wasn't frequented in the daytime during the summer months. But in the evenings it became a place where the family could gather around the fire in the potbellied stove and chatter about the day's events. If we became too boisterous, Pa simply pointed his forefinger at us, and the hilarity immediately subsided. With as many kids as there were in our family, it didn't take much to be boisterous.

Anyone entering our sitting room could see that it had obviously not been designed by an interior decorator. The furniture was lined up against the walls, and only the Heatrola sat in the middle of the room. Us kids were intrigued by the stove with its chrome trim and isinglass windows. Our favorite pastime was to poke our fingers through the isinglass windows. We didn't realize that our fun caused a catastrophe. There was no money to replace the isinglass. Like everything else around the homestead, it either got patched or stayed broken.

The old ebony diamond-tufted divan or lady's "fainting sofa", and an old marred black walnut center table sat by the north window. Ma's treadle sewing machine was even more a part of the room than was the black leather settee. I'm sure Ma must have treadled and pedaled a million miles while she sewed clothes for her brood on the machine.

The Wireless — No band of Americans approached the decade with more fervor than the radio industry. Between 1921 and 1922 the sale of radio receivers for home use began a boom resulting in the licensing of 564 broadcasting stations. By 1927, the radio was pretty much a standard fixture in most homes The Federal Communications Commission was established to oversee broadcast operations.

The wireless, to us kids, was a very exciting and impressive piece of equipment. We learned early on that it took some doing to get any kind of sound out of it. A thin black wire seemed to be the part that controlled the quality of noise the best. I remember that we did everything from stretching it across the room, to stringing it up on nails and pushing it out the open window , to even making one of the younger kids stand and hold on to it—anything to get better reception!

A bunch of us would pile onto the settee, and watch and listen expectantly, waiting for some blast from out in space somewhere. Sometimes, only a few words were audible, but that was okay with us. Any kind of diversion from the monotonous tedium of our lives was welcome.

Sometimes we picked up the Via Aquinia Quailla, The Republic of Mexico, with all the Mexican dance music. We

51

got goose bumps and giggled excitedly as we listened to the upbeat music of the mariachis on the air waves. I recall one time bragging about our wireless and telling others of all the good things we could hear on it. It wasn't long after that bragging session that one of Pa's distant cousins told her children, "Watch what ya say 'bout them Carters, they kin pick it up on their wireless." Me being such a *stinker*, I willingly confirmed the idea!

By the end of the 1930s, the voices of the *Golden Age of Radio* crackled into the homes of the very wealthy, into the tenements, into the camps of the Civilian Conservation Corps, and into run-down farm homes like ours, providing drama, light entertainment and documentary programming to the masses.

I recall Pa and his cronies listening intently, along with millions of other Americans, to President Roosevelt's *Fireside Chat*. With this broadcast, and the *New Deal* programs he established, President Roosevelt was able to keep the collective American psyche afloat during the hardest of times. When the President was on the air, us kids dared not make a move or a sound, shuffle school papers, or leave our seats. Pa insisted that, "All Americans should pay respect to the Presidency, rendering unto it, the rent owned for the space upon which we live in this world."

After dinner, when the chores were all done, the family would gather in the sitting room to listen to such programs as Lawrence Welk and his Biggest Little Band in America broadcasted from way out in Yankton, South Dakota. Precious hours were spent with George Burns and Gracie Allen compliments of our wireless. But towering above the world of radio programming was Ma's favorite, Will Rogers. He was one of America's greatest humorists. His humorous political commentaries were the delight of the common man. Rogers once said that the U. S. Congress was comprised of the world's best comedy writers.

The wireless was good, but I thought it also brought scary things into our household, too. In 1937, the Hindenberg zeppelin crashed. We heard about it on the radio. Orson Wells' broadcast in 1938, which was purely fiction, panicked the nation into chaos, thinking that the Martians were coming. It was the talk of the town in Crystal Springs. They talked about it in schools, and they even announced it at the town hall before the Bob Steele and Gene Autry films could begin.

Before we got our radio, we felt so remote from the rest of the world, out here on the prairie. The only way we ever got news was when Pa went to Crystal Springs and talked with the townsfolk. I don't think newspapers were delivered out on the prairie, but we couldn't have afforded one anyway. Our wireless brought us into a world us kids had never known existed.

Ma's Pie-Ano — Ma's most prized item of furniture was a newly acquired, but well used, upright piano which had been delivered from somewhere by team and wagon.

The piano fit snugly against the door jamb to the left of the front door. Its finish was a blistered black because someone had applied several coats of varnish stain before sandpapering it. Mildew or mice had munched the felts nearly clean, the ivory was missing from more than one key, and it was predominantly out of tune—but it was Ma's "pie-ano."

The bench had a compartment that held several dog-eared pieces of sheet music. It also held Ma, who was rather stout in those days.

A neighbor, Mrs. Tony Klieter, taught Ma to play Star of the East, and she practiced until she got all the flourishes, flares and moves. In the evening, Ma sat at the piano for hours while us kids listened to her play. We were all so proud of her music and told her so. While Ma was preoccupied with her music, us kids used that time to ham it up and be rambunctious. Six or seven of us smaller children lined up on the black leather divan, each with a bowl of popcorn or chokecherries. Some of us kept sliding down the pillow hump at one end. Then the giggling began, but when the popcorn spilled, Pa said not a word. Instead, all he did was point. We all knew what that meant, so we simmered down once again to listen to the piano.

Of course, the "pie-ano" was not off-limits to us youngsters. Ma allowed us to bang away for hours. I think Pa hoped that if we kept it up, a virtuoso would develop—right there in the back country. Somehow he scraped together enough money to buy a metronome and pay for music lessons for Shirley and Gladyce. I recall that I had taken music lessons for a short while, but Ma said, "I knew it wouldn't last 'cuz yer butt wasn't made for sittin' and yer fingers weren't made for twiddlin'."

The Old Upright Talkin' Machine — A precursor to the phonograph appeared in 1857 when Edouarde-Leon Scott deMartinville attempted to record and reproduce sound waves. His invention was called a Phonautograph. By 1877, Thomas Edison and Alexander Graham Bell had improved on the idea using indentations embossed into a sheet of tinfoil by a vibrating stylus, then wrapped the tinfoil. Bell then teamed up with a man named Tainter and developed and patented the Graphophone.

In 1887, a German-born inventor named Emil Berliner, improved upon Thomas Edison's invention by tracing sound grooves in a spiral on a flat disc, rather than in a helix on a cylinder. This resulted in what Berliner called *records*, which he played on a machine of his own invention, called a gramophone.

At one time we owned a machine with the Berliner patent that played the cylindrical type of records. To this day, I still don't know what happened to our gramophone.

My Pa, through bartering, had obtained an upright

phonograph for us. A mountain of records came with it. Some even came in their original sleeves. Us kids referred to the phonograph as our *talkin' machine.* The machine stood just inside Ma and Pa's bedroom door. We had to have permission to step inside to play it. The machine was so tall that I had to stand on a huge stack of records to be able to see into it and to wind the crank. The needle had to be replaced at regular intervals, but Ma or one of the older kids took care of that job.

Our records, stacked in piles on the floor, would have brought a fortune in the antique collectors' market by today's standards. We had such tunes as *The Whistler and his Dog, The Preacher and the Bear, Whispering Hope, The Blue Danube, Swanee River, Buffalo Gals* and many others.

We liked to play the John Philip Sousa marches for Ma. She told us that he was a great American composer and bandmaster, and was famous for about 136 military marching songs, including the *Stars and Stripes Forever, Semper Fidelis, Liberty Bell and the HMS Pinafore.* Ma was pretty patriotic, and she was impressed by the fact that he was so active in the U.S. Marine Corps.

Since most of the record sleeves had long since disappeared, and since us little kids had been using the pile of records for a step ladder, you can guess the quality of musical sounds our records had. If we wanted the one on the bottom or in the middle of the pile, we slid it out grating it across the grooves of the other records, creating sounds like coarse sandpaper over slab lumber. When a record became so scratched that we couldn't hear the words, we set it aside for future use. Remember—*nothing* in the Carter household was wasted or thrown out before its time.

Pa And The Spring-Action Doors — Although I was too young to remember, Ma recounted a story to me about Pa coming home tipsy one night. "Carter always took his own sweet time 'bout comin' home from town," she explained, "but I always had a hot pan of tea on the heatin' stove for him durin' the cold months. This particular night, the tea had boiled a long time, so I set it off the stove onto the hearth." Our hearth was merely a piece of tin that covered a one-inch deep, four foot square platform which prevented fuel box sparks from igniting the floor and Ma's hooked rugs.

"After Pa put the team in the barn, he was still a bit tipsy. When he came into the house, it seems he forgot the spring-action effect of the swingin' double doors. Yer Pa staggered into those doors and they sprung open with a vengeance. He was thrown into a spin, and as he spun 'round, he lost his balance—and *splat*—he plunged butt-first into the hot pan of tea!" Ma laughingly shook her head, "I never saw Carter move so fast in all the years we been married! If I didn't know better, I'd think the Man Upstairs let Pa have an off-balance twirl just to git his attention. If yer Pa ever had an angel on his shoulder, I wasn't too sure 'bout its color!" she chuckled.

The Commons — The upstairs portion of our house consisted of one common room, sectioned off into sleeping rooms by a curtain hung from a rope. The rope was strung from one end of the huge upstairs to the other. No—this was not a hospital room, but it resembled one. The privacy curtain, although it served its purpose well, was less than sterile, as were the beds and the surrounding area. The beds in each room consisted of old rusted bed springs and straw mattresses.

The soiled tan monk's cloth curtain sagged in the center and dusted the floor where it rested. Our breakthrough bedrooms separated the boys from the girls. In winter, the chamber pot with lid sat in the corner of the room. Piles of clothes lay everywhere. We had no closets. Each morning us kids sorted through the pile for *clean dirties.* Even if the clothing belonged to another kid, the rule of the day was—first come first served. If I got it first, it was my outfit for the day.

In winter, frost appeared on our bed covers and quilts made from woolen overcoat squares, old army blankets, pants, and any other fabric that would do the job. We didn't have a spiral staircase, but we had one that was built at a 90-degree angle, which means literally straight up. Our skylights were wide cracks between roof boards which sunlight, snow and rain couldn't resist. The snow and frost penetrated our bed covers in the winter, and in the summer, the rising sun directed its beam in our eyes. Who needed a cock's crow as an alarm clock?

Our four star armoire was not blessed with charm, doors or decoration—only open shelves made of rustic slab wood. Wall decor was Crayola drawings done in serpentine lines on linen-colored plastered walls.

I don't remember the bed sheets being changed at regular intervals. This may have been part of the reason why we had so many bedbugs. It was frightening to think that enough bedbugs infiltrated the coils of our bedsprings, that the entire bed could have marched right off. To sterilize the bedsprings, Ma poured boiling water through each coil separately. The boiling water ran right through the tightly wound coils and onto the floor. When the sterilization process was complete, we had to sweep up the dead bedbugs, then mop up the dirty water.

Our Private Bath And Spa — No particular time was set for baths, but they always took place before a school program or some other important event. The time would inevitably come for each midget to have a good *scrubbin'*.

Our bathing area would have been considered a true space-saver. It was a curtained stall draped with a dingy army blanket, sharing the tiny space behind the kitchen cookstove with our Pa's twenty gallon stoneware crock of homemade beer. Sometimes the crock did dual duty with a batch or two of hops, while the beer was being aged in bottles in our dank cellar. The odor of the fermenting crock was enough to make us tipsy before our splash in the spa was completed. Our privacy was guarded by several high-backed chairs lined up in a row, backs draped with flour sack material. In the middle of all this sat the old galvanized metal washtub.

Much to our dismay, us kids had to participate in not only the punishment of the bathing itself—but the punishment of hauling the water for the bath. It took six of us to carry enough water from the pump for Ma to heat on the stove top for bathing. Even though it seemed to us, at the time, that we hauled enough water to fill the Mississippi River, in reality, we only brought in enough to fill two wash boilers and several large canning kettles. After the water was heated, the #10 washtub was filled three-quarters full.

The beauty bar, as you might have guessed, was a lump of Ma's homemade lye soap securely tied in a rag. This comprised the bathing "muffy" for the entire family. The younger kids bathed together, while the older ones were afforded a bit more privacy. As each kid finished his or her bath, Ma would part the curtain and rinse them off using a small aluminum kettle filled with warm water. This act ended our bathing ritual—until the next important event that is!

Story Book Neighbors — The art of conversation was the hallmark of community life. I recall summer evenings when neighbors would gather in each other's front yards and discuss hard times, crops, animal breeding, stud service trade, food, the latest gossip, how to stretch the meager food supply for a large family, canning and preserving foods and the latest on birth and death.

There were some bright sides to our life in those days. In spite of hard times, us kids found much to giggle about. When one got going, it was contagious. Though Pa would point his finger and grunt, a command motion which carried ultimate authority, we couldn't stop. Ma said, "It's that kind of stuff that can finally make your Pa laugh." We giggled over all sorts of things, but mainly over nicknames given by us, or by someone else, to people around the lake.

My Pa and two Norwegian neighbors made beer together, drank together and spun yarns together. When they were halfway between being less sober and out-and-out obnoxious, they were hilarious. Pa called Gurney Sand, "High Pockets" because he was so long-legged and short-waisted. Good old C.G. Sand: The "C" stood for Cornelius, "Corny" for short. Pa nicknamed George Halverson "Slingshot" because of his log bowed legs.

Rachel and Guerney Sand were our neighbors, living to the north of us on the old Huggarude Place, which was the same homestead on which Aunt Libbie and Uncle Edgar Mell had lived.

The Sand's place was beyond the Bill Jenkins' farm, and up a fairly steep hill called Cobblestone Hill. The Sand family were cousins to the Halversons, who lived east of the lake. Between the two families, they managed to produce eight ruffians who terrorized us kids all the time—especially in the terror zone around the schoolhouse.

The homestead and surroundings of the Sand's place were much like those of everyone else in our community. The blue-gray, wind-scoured outbuildings were north of the old square, dilapidated house. A few gnarled weather beaten shrubs stood by the corner of the house lopping over the path. Two ancient chairs with most of the back spindles missing, stood on the broken down porch. My thought was that any self-respecting person would have splintered them for fire wood years ago. The Sand's farm had long ago been reduced to a garden, a few milkers, a few dozen chickens and two small fields along the hillsides.

Rachel and Guerney, like many married couples, made an interesting study in contrast. Ma would often say, "Rachel and Guerney Sand are mismatched." Guerney seemed to be a morose, bent man with a rugged thin frame. He spoke slowly and softly—if he spoke at all—in his thick Norwegian brogue. His voice and tone were soothing and sincere. Guerney was particularly slow—slow to the point of motionlessness. He was content to let others take the lead. I was never sure if Guerney did much work. I could see him ambling around the place, carrying a milking stool from time to time, or occasionally I'd sight him in one of their small fields. He looked too frail for physical work, if you ask me.

Rachel, on the other hand, was brusque and sharp-tongued, with sharp features and had a commanding presence. She was a tall slender woman—a resilient and weathered farm hand type. Rachel looked the way I imagined Sacagawea might have looked—tall and slender with sharp features and jet black hair. I decided that Rachel Sand had a heart that could have been hewn from an anvil. I was frightened by her hard-driving personality, harsh tones and the clipped off sentences of her thick brogue. I was secretly glad that she wasn't my Ma and Guerney wasn't my Pa.

Ma's views were usually limited to the clothesline, cowchips and cookstove. We knew Ma to have a sulky and grudging attitude from time to time. Mrs. Sand said Ma's body was plumb wore out and she should barter for some of them new pills just discovered called vitamins. Mrs. Halverson said Ma needed to get out from under her blue denim apron and go to Ladies' Aid Society more often. Ma's sullen excuses would run from one to another: It was either canning time, birthing time, or the rim needed to be soaked back onto the buggy wheel. What she really meant was that Pa wouldn't let her go, or that she felt intimidated, having to appear in scuffed stove-blacked sturdy shoes, and in the same old sponged blue dress.

One day Ma sent me on an errand to the Sand's place. As I came up the knoll toward the house, I saw Rachel walking slowly up the cow path leading from the barn to the house. Fierce summer winds whipped the long straight skirt of her shabby blue dress around her sinewy body. Her straight black hair was pulled back from a scraggly center part at the top of her head, and snugged into a frowsy bun at the nape of her neck.

I can see her now, as I saw her then, against a backdrop of blue-gray shacks and weather-beaten shrubs. She was carrying two big galvanized pails of fresh milk, which she set down on the dirt path littered with cobblestones, cow pies and chicken droppings. As I approached asking to borrow sugar, she took a rigid stance, shielding her eyes from the hot sun with her leathery palm cupped to her brow. She remained motionless for several moments, pondering the weather, I supposed. She mused, more to herself than to me, "Ha! Da vedder's goin' ta be gude." My look of amazement prompted her to say, "Dare ar signs ya know! Dat's vat aye alvays do, ta tell da vedder for tamarra." She picked up the two pails of milk and headed for the house. She called over her shoulder, "Come inta da house, and I'll fetch da sugar yer Ma asked fer."

Once inside, I looked around the familiar setting. The potbellied heating stove was in the middle of the huge living quarters. Beside the stove, on a hand hooked rug, sat an old fashioned rocking chair. Next to it was a basket of sun-faded rags, waiting for the time that Rachel could make another rug. I knew that once the chores were done, Rachel would sit and rest in the same way that I had always seen her. She would rock in her dated swing rocker with its faded handmade quilt padding, in front of the coal stove, humming familiar tunes until her eyes grew heavy with sleep. Then she would catnap.

Nothing was simple in Rachel's life—or in any of our lives—for that matter. Never ending household and farm chores took its toll on all of us. Working the hay fields under the excruciatingly hot sun was difficult, monotonous and time consuming. There was no shelter from what few rains we had, nor from the full hot sun. I expect that at times in her life, as in most peoples' lives at Chase Lake, things must have seemed utterly hopeless. With sheer determination and hard work, Rachel had a strength, probably not dictated by strict religious values. Innate in Rachel, my Ma, and many others in our community, was the ability to continue forging ahead to overcome problems that would have defeated most others.

Neither Rachel nor Ma displayed kittenish charms. Out on the prairie, their joy and anticipation for a new life had been sucked from them by poverty, like nectar was sucked from a flower by bees. They won nothing without a struggle. Even wash day on a hot midsummer afternoon would find them both with their arms half-in and half-out of hot soapy lye suds, looking like boiled lobsters. Their daily life, right down to such an insignificant thing as a fly drowning in a pail of milk, forced them to make a deliberate decision to "turn it loose, or put it out of its misery."

We overlooked many things on the farm, simply because everyone was too tired from having done the most important things first. We enjoyed a neighborhood of folks that stretched for miles around the territory. Even if we didn't visit them, they furnished us with *fodder for making fun of them.* It wasn't a nice thing for us to do, but it was the only outside activity we had in those days.

Another neighbor, Carsten Torgeson, made extra money by peddling liquor. He had a tub of old bottles inside the door of his machine shop, but the buried treasure was his liquor. When someone came to make a buy, Carsten would leave the house and walk down around the trees and yard. Then he would come back, lift a wash tub by the kitchen door and bring forth the moonshine to continue the deal, as if he had had the bottles stashed a great distance from the house.

Pa occasionally asked Albin Rosselle and old John Trowbridge to help us out around the farm or with the haying. Albin had the physical brawn of Hercules, yet an underdeveloped mental capacity which prevented him from flourishing in the community. One time, I remember Ma inviting Albin to stay for supper. While partaking of Ma's chokecherry sauce, instead of putting the chokecherry pits to one side of his plate, he simply chewed them to mush. I could see that Pa was straining the corners of his lips to keep from laughing, but when us kids began to titter, he pointed at us in displeasure and grunted a warning. This gesture had long ago been defined as the signal to "shut up." Ma, like most people, had opinions and criticisms concerning others, but she discouraged us from doing so saying, "Jus' be glad that ain't you. Besides, maybe Albin is too polite to spit the seeds into his spoon."

Pa, too, had his opinions and prejudices mixed with liberal amounts of compassion. His compassion extended to John Trowbridge, who years before had rescued me and three of my sisters and brothers from sure death in a blinding snowstorm. I never knew if Pa was partial to old John because of that or because he truly liked him.

Old John lived out on the prairie four and one-half miles northeast of Chase Lake in a shack made of tarpaper, cardboard, and old bedsprings. His mongrel dog and beautiful team of White horses were his live-in pets.

I don't know why we called him Old John, other than the fact that we really couldn't tell his age. He was short, thick, and bent, and he didn't walk—he just shuffled along.

His face was mostly hidden by his scraggly red beard. His eyebrows curled around his eyes concealing them, much like prairie brush hides a scared rabbit. When John ate lunch with us once, his handlebar mustache collected nearly half his bowl of soup like a sponge. When he was finished with lunch, he still had some soup left on his mustache. Much to our shock and dismay, he just sucked it off.

John's clothing left much to be desired. He protected his feet by wrapping them in old gunny sacks tied with binding twine which was laced around the sack up to midcalf. My brother, Eugene, once told us that John also had made himself a pair of cast aluminum shoes. John's favorite piece of clothing seemed to a raggedy old wool army coat which appeared too long for him. He wore it winter and summer, no matter how hot it was outdoors.

Pa wasn't critical of Old John or Albin. He had compassion for the two of them, as well as for all others less fortunate. People respected Pa for that quality. Some farmers agreed that Carter was a good judge of horseflesh, too.

Some of our neighbors didn't fare as well as John and Albin with Pa. I recall him making the uncharitable statement about some neighbors to the north of Chase Lake, "Those SOBs are shifty-eyed and can't be trusted any further than a weasel in a henhouse."

Our World From The Back Porch — The signal that dinner was over, came when the last morsel of food was gone from the table and the dinner kettles were cleaned of every scrap. There was no more, we all knew that fact.

After dinner us kids did the dishes, then scampered out to the back porch. With all the chores done for the day, and preparations for the next day finished, my Ma and Pa would join us.

Sometimes Ma would tell us tales starting with "Remember when..." Each of us kids listened intently, trying to picture a different time and place. Ma sure had some good memories.

We oftentimes played *I Spy,* various childish voices ringing out: "I spy the Big Dipper," "Oh! I spy the Little Dipper," or we would yell out the name of the constellations.

We sometimes found ourselves seated around a washtub filled with fresh peas that needed shelling, or a few crates of corn that needed husking. As we removed the husks, we chatted quietly with one another, sang songs, and told jokes. Some varieties of corn needed to be husked then dried for later use, such as popcorn. Usually the popcorn was dried by placing it on an old screen door perched on two sawhorses. When the drying was complete, we rubbed two cobs together to remove the kernels. We enjoyed watching the kernels fly into a tub or basket, and made a game of tossing the nude cobs, like basketballs, into a separate container. The cobs would be used later for starting fires in the stove.

Other varieties of corn were dried and stored, rather than home canned. We reconstituted it much like dried beans. The kernels were soaked overnight in water, then cooked the next day. For cream style corn, the soaked kernels were ground in our old fashioned crank machine.

On occasion, when there weren't any tasks that needed doing we would just pull up a box, a cream can, or a rickety chair, and swap tales about the day's events. Us kids vied for Ma' s and Pa's attention as we shared our own stories. After a bit, when us kids wound down, the sounds of the farm surrounded us, leaving each of us to our own thoughts.

Our porch was in direct line of the cow corral, behind the barn. Since it was after milking time, the cattle rested easy, perhaps glad that their stanchion ordeal was over. Some vocalized their contentment by mooing, snorting, or belching to regurgitate their cud—chewing with gusto, as if they were happy to be creating more milk for the morning milking. Some cows bedded down early, while some remained standing. A few laid close to each other. Some wanted to be even closer, so they would literally fall upon the cows who were already resting, while kneeling to lie down. Still others laid their heads upon the necks of those cows closest to themselves.

Our ornery bull bellowed from the corner of the corral, like a trapped animal in the wild. He stomped and pawed the dry manure on the ground, flailing it over his back. Perhaps, he too, was working out the frustrations of his day. He let us know by swinging his head from side to side that he would butt anyone brave enough to crowd his space.

Simmer nights on the porch, with my family, listening to the crickets chirping and the frogs croaking, were memorable to me. I felt close to Ma, Pa, and my siblings. The contentment that alluded me during the days, graced me with its presence during these evenings. I think the daily distractions of farm chores, the concerns of life during the Depression, and life's disappointments, in general, abandoned us during those brief moments on our back porch.

Around the Farm

Basic Training Country Style — One thing can be said about our life on the farm — basic hands-on education began almost as soon as the babies could walk. We began helping by taking a few pieces of silverware to the table, or by following Ma back from the garden, lugging three or four potatoes or carrots to the kitchen. We washed dishes, rolled the string from empty feed bags into balls, carried stuff to the field or barn for Pa, helped Ma in the garden, and older kids took care of the younger kids. Everybody had chores.

The fun part was when we got to graduate to the stool beside the table, when Ma was making bread. When the bread dough was ready for the pans, she would give each of us young'uns a small piece of dough to make a tiny loaf of bread or rolls. We played with it, "kneading" it until it became a dirty gray color. Then she would show us how to grease our own jar lid with pork drippings, and shape our dough into bread or dinner rolls. The shaped dinner rolls were small enough to fit in Ma's thimble, and were placed in our personal jar lid pans. We got to place our pans in the oven with a little help from Ma. As we expectantly watched for the baking to finish, we sometimes had minor scuffles amongst each other over which pan of the delicacy belonged to who.

Wash Day — One of the few things I remember before the age of five, was Ma bending over a washtub filled with filthy clothes. Absolutely every stitch of clothing on our farm was filthy, sun-faded, and ragged. She scrubbed each piece on a tin washboard, using a bar of her homemade lye soap.

Our laundry day paraphernalia consisted of two size #10 wash tubs, a WashDay brand wood and metal scrubbing or washboard, a bunch of wooden clothespins, and long, sagging clotheslines. In those days, there were no roll action agitators to churn the clothes around, no *gentle cycles* or *heavy duty load* selectors, and no high-speed, multi-temperature clothes dryers—just plain old elbow grease and perseverance. Before the wash was even completed, Ma would be elbow-deep in suds, her swollen hands looking like boiled lobsters. The job, as I look back on it, was dull, monotonous, and completely back-breaking.

"If you wear clothes, you have to help wash them" was a definite reality to us kids. Several of us were recruited to assist with the chore—and believe me, I mean a chore!

First we carried wood, and set the fire. Then water had to be carried from the pump to the kitchen, where Ma heated it in the big old wash boiler. When the water was heated sufficiently, Ma began the drudgery of rubbing the bar of soap on the clothes, then the clothes on the scrubbing board. Once she was satisfied that the clothes were clean, she cranked them through the wringer which was fastened to the edge of the washtub, and down into the tub of rinse water.

From the first rinse, she put the garments through the wringer again, then into the bluing, which was her attempt at recreating the brightness that had long since disappeared. The blouses and aprons had to be dipped in a thick cooked starch. Us kids put the clothes into a bushel basket and hauled them off to the clothesline, where they were hung with wooden clothespins.

The lines were so overloaded that they sagged, allowing the clothes to touch the ground littered with chicken manure. A long pole was placed under the wire to lift the sagging pole. Sometimes on a hot day, the sheer coolness of the flapping wet fabric beckoned us kids to run in and out between the clothes on the lines. I'll always remember the sweet fragrance of clothing dried out doors.

During the winter months, the wet clothing was hung on clotheslines strung throughout the house, stretched crosswise near the ceiling in every room. The lines drooped over the table, the stove, the book case and the couch, and would sag so low that we had to duck our heads to walk. Sitting close to the floor was the only safe place to escape the soggy fabric.

When all the space was used up in the house, we had to hang the clothes outside. The freezing weather had a partial drying effect on the garments. Frozen clothes had to be carefully removed from the lines and transported into the house, because any slight bump could cause them to snap like toothpicks. I recall an incident that seems funny now—but at the time it didn't seem so funny. One of my sisters broke the legs off Pa's brand new longjohns while she was trying to bring an armload of frozen clothes through the kitchen door! That was an unforgivable incident, since the money to buy new longjohns was non-existent in those days. One pair had to last for years! It was considered a luxury to have several pairs.

Later in life, perhaps when I was about 14 years old, Pa could finally afford to buy Ma a second-hand motorized washing machine. The machine jumped, wiggled and gyrated all over the kitchen, but it sure made the job a whole lot easier for my Ma. Eventually the motor wore out, and there was no money to replace or repair it — so it was back to the scrub board for Ma! Which brings me to the question—is it better to have had something nice, and lose it; or to never have had it at all?

Ma's Homemade Soap — Summer days were best for making soap, since the cold temperatures of winter made the matured soap flaky.

Ma would carefully measure the ingredients into the only large mixing vessels we had—which were aluminum. The lye reacted to the aluminum and caused our utensils to turn all black on the inside. Can you imagine cooking food in them? Ma said that lye not only turned the aluminum pots black, but too much lye made the bars too brittle to shave into the wash water. As it was, our knives had so many gouges in their blades that the shavings looked like crinkled French fries!

Because of our large family, and the fact that we used the soap for so many tasks, we didn't always have time to allow it to complete the aging process. Our soap bars were used for toilet soap, shampoo, laundry soap, and for washing lingerie and other so called delicate fabrics—not that we had many.

We used all kinds of fats for soap making. Plain lard did not make the best soap, since it tended to separate. If this happened, we simply reclaimed it. Reclaiming is a process of reheating it, by boiling it in a large amount of water, cooling it, then skimming it. We mostly used mutton tallow blended with small amounts of chicken and pork fat rendered from the skin and scraps of meat, strained through several layers of flour sack fabric, then stored in a cool place until we were ready to make a batch of soap. Ma's recipe for making soap was one can of lye, two and one-half pints of cold water and six pounds of clean tallow, lard or pork fat.

Ma's homemade lye soap was used for bathing, for shampooing our hair and for washing our clothes. It was the "facial care fer a firmer, softer, more radiant look!" Ma exclaimed. Bathing with the soap also got rid of sheep ticks, bedbugs and a bevy of other "creepy crawlies" that attached themselves to us in the outback.

Putting Food By — For some people, late August and early September meant lazy, relaxing days—the dog days. For us, the prairie farmers, it meant scalding sun, lots of dust, dry heat and harvesting. Putting food by, or preserving and canning for our large family took lots of time.

Canning and preserving food went hand-in-hand on the farm, and was not only a necessary, but an expected behavior in the pre-Depression days. Ma canned vegetables, fruits, meats and just about any other edible morsel you could imagine. She made all of our jams and jellies, sauerkraut, sandwich spreads, relishes, gooseberry catsup, and she even made our cream cheese.

Ma was highly aggressive when it came to finding foods to put by for the winter months. She lectured us girls time and again, "If you know what you're looking for and where to go to get it, you can always find food—free for the picking—whether its growing wild along country roads, beside streams or even on the dry open prairie."

She taught us to think of alternative food sources. One such example was wild dandelion greens. Ma and us girls would trudge the untamed countryside for wild dandelion greens and edible roots. She explained to us how roasted dandelion roots, for centuries, were made into coffee, tea, wine and beer. In the summertime, Ma put lettuce and chopped dandelion greens—as tart as they were—in our sandwiches. She used the greens to make salad, which she topped with her famous mustard dressing. Everybody loved Ma's mustard dressing.

Long ago when Ma was busy gathering dandelion greens for us, she had never heard of the television show, *The Waltons*, nor had she ever heard of the actor Bill Greer, who portrayed Grandpa Walton. But Bill Greer knew there was another practical use for the greens. "Just split the stem open and rub the milky sap on any wart you have, two or three times a day—and you won't have warts anymore," he once advised in a television interview.

In the early 1900s, the excavations found under some homes were more than basements or lower living levels. So it was at our farmhouse. Pure and simple, the entire property had all the earmarks of grinding poverty that beset the farmers of that time.

We had a dirt cellar, which had been hewn from hardpan soil and rocks. The cellar was dark, dank, dusty and smelly. The rotting and dust-filled steps had dropped a few splintered pieces along the way. We had to carry a kerosene lantern to be able to see anything, whenever we descended them. The occasional sounds of crickets and scurrying mice scared the bejeebers out of us younger kids. We had the feeling of being in the presence of a great Old World archaeological dig—even though we didn't know exactly what that was like.

Shelves for fruit and vegetable storage, reaching up to the flooring of the house, had been formed with a pickax out of the hardpan dirt. To the left of the stairs, was a huge mound of dirt, beneath which was buried all of our newly harvested root vegetables—potatoes, carrots, turnips, rutabagas and beets.

Toward the end of the winter season, the spuds would rot, and if we accidentally dug into those, the stench that confronted us was unbelievable—it permeated the whole house! It didn't present much of a problem for us kids—we would just wipe our hands on our overalls and keep digging. Ma said we smelled so bad, that we belonged out with the pigs. We knew better, though—our pigs didn't smell that bad, and they surely wouldn't have eaten *those* potatoes unless they were starving to death. Ma would *rag* away on us, "You kids couldn't even catch a cold, you smell so bad!"

The canning ritual usually took at least two full weeks. During that time, with the wood stove going full blast, the kitchen would easily reach 90 degrees. The temperature outdoors was normally 92 to 95 degrees, which made the whole process unbearable for us kids.

We especially didn't like hauling the fruit jars and small crocks up the rickety steps, out to the backyard for scouring. But as with all of our chores, we knew it must be done, so we tried to make it into something fun.

We would select a spot in the yard where we could pry lots of tiny rocks out of the hardpan dirt. I say dirt—and not soil—because it would definitely not support plant life in any form. We dropped the tiny rocks into the bottles and jars, filled them half full of soapy water, then put a lid on them. The best part came next—we would implement the *shake, rattle and roll* agitation process.

If we got tired of sitting on the hot ground around the washtub, we would jump up and dance around it, pretending the jars and bottles were castanets and maracas. The giggling, shaking and bouncing continued until all the jars and bottles were clean. The last step was to rinse them off at the pump. When we finished, we were soaked to the skin. Ma usually took over the task, after she made us each a sorghum sandwich and sent us out in the sun to dry off and eat our lunch.

She would build up the fire with the wood that us kids had carried in from the woodpile and fill the old wash boiler with the water we had hauled in buckets from the pump. When the boiler bubbled up a full head of steam, it gurgled, spewed and rattled on the old stove like a Northern Pacific engine on an unstable track. It was at this stove that Ma must have canned thousands of quarts of food.

She canned chicken the old fashioned way—in the old dented wash boiler. The chicken was fried, usually in rendered pork fat, packed loosely in the jars, then the jars were filled with boiling chicken broth and salt. They were sealed and boiled for several hours.

Out on the farm in those days, we had never heard of the dangers of handling poultry incorrectly. There was no such thing as sanitary cutting boards or disinfectants.

Everything from cutting up chickens to pasting posters and school projects was done on our old round oak kitchen table. The only disinfecting we did was with salt, vinegar or lye soap. And whether the contents of the jars ever reached the required 240 degrees for meat canning is anyone's guess! There weren't any pressure cookers or canners in our county, that I know of. Besides, we were so poor we couldn't have gotten one if they'd been free because town was too far away.

A list of food that Ma canned in 1932 indicated that she had preserved 138 quarts of food, including corn, cherries, rhubarb, gooseberries, plums, blackberries, "chow-chow" and pickles. The year prior to that she had put up 177 quarts of food, part of which were eleven bottles of catsup, twelve pints of sandwich spread, three gallons of pickles and even several jars containing our royal rooster and old setting hens. Us kids knew they had been *canned for misconduct* of one kind or another.

During her life on the farm, it seemed to me that my Ma canned just about anything that didn't talk back. She put up meatballs, lamb and pork cubes, pigs' feet and stewing chickens. She also canned plenty of condiments each fall, like chokecherry syrup, gooseberry jam, gooseberry catsup, citron preserves, ripe tomato jelly, sandwich spread, homemade sauerkraut, homemade cream cheese and wild gooseberry relish. Even the horseradish patch couldn't escape Ma's canning jars.

Ma was proud of the gooseberry bramble patch in the hollow west of the front door. She said gooseberry pie was actor Charles Lawton's favorite. He had stated one time, "It is probably the most delicious confection on the planet for farm folks." Ma practically canonized any creator of an exotic gooseberry pie. Most Americans seldom encounter real gooseberries today. Francis X. Sculley wrote,

"Gooseberry pie is as rare as a satisfied major league baseball player."

The Potato Bug Pickers — When the pig weeds and potato bugs were about to overtake the potato patch, us younger kids were directed to get our kerosene cans ready and go kill the potato bugs. Such an unwelcome demand, I thought! What are we—exterminators, cultivators, honey bucket prevailers? Potato bug picking was one of the most ungodly Sunday afternoon chores, and we had to do it for as long as I can remember.

The process entailed each kid being given a tin can half full of kerosene. Up and down each row we would traipse, lifting all the leaves of the potato plants, checking for the ugly insipid creatures. I believe we picked bugs, much the same as Washingtonians glean berries from the fields—with a couple very obvious differences.

I can remember it being so hot in the field that us kids were sweating, and the blistering sun was sending kerosene fumes up our nostrils until we were near stupefied. To set the can down in the dirt was forbidden, since even one spill cost money. No room for waste at the Carter place! Ma and Pa were very careful about seeing to it that us girls' naked flesh was covered to the knees. When we complained about sweating in the hot sun, Ma would say, "Yer Pa has seen enough 'high-steppers' in his day to know that his girls are going to be trained up proper. You jus' keep covered up!"

Unfortunately, this philosophy didn't apply to shoes. Generally, they were unavailable to us. We would walk barefooted in the scorching black dirt for hours, until the only relief we could get for our hot feet was to wiggle our toes deep into the sandy loam, reaching for a cool spot.

The assassination of bugs continued all summer long until the potatoes were dug for winter. Once the potatoes were dug, we carried them into the root cellar where they were once again buried in a pile of dirt, this time, to keep them from freezing over the winter.

When the undesirable chore was finished, Ma would call to us to "Go wash up, and git the bug juice and kerosene off yer hands." Since there was no running water indoors, we went to the pump to wash up. We were all glad to let the cold water splash onto our hands and face, but most especially onto our feet!

Ma usually rewarded us for sticking it out through the miserable chore with large slabs of freshly fried bread dough, which had been dipped in cinnamon and sugar. No matter how many times we had it, it was always a rare and special treat.

Butchering Day — As I recall, we needed no alarm clock on the farm, especially on such an exciting day as butchering day. At daybreak, Barney the rooster, encroached on the peacefulness of our rest. Soon to follow were our *snooze alarms,* the banty roosters—Hector and Stretch. Stretch got his name because he couldn't make sounds unless his neck was stretched like a giraffe's.

This morning I wasn't outraged to be awakened. This was a day I was looking forward to, because I would get to watch the entire butchering process—from start to finish. I would even be allowed to carry the dishpan filled with the heart and liver to the kitchen, which was a special trust for me.

Excited, I flung the flour sack sheet and soiled WWI army blanket aside, then crawled—not too carefully—over three other sleeping bodies, two at the head of the bed, and one at the foot. I scanned the layout of clothing heaped around the floor like muskrat huts on the icy bog. It pleased me to see my pile intact. Usually, I had to rifle through the stack of dirty clothes, or the clean-dirties, in order find enough clothing to cover my body. I checked for beetles, ants, and other unwanted dwellers and slipped my leg into the dirty overalls. The oversized middy blouse was gigantic. I poked it inside the faded denims, slipped the half-penny nail through one suspender, and let the other one dangle down my back. At times I had more metal on me than the horse harness.

As I left the room, I glanced back toward the bed, and giggled to myself. The sheet with the brand name, *Occidental Flour,* had twisted over my sisters' rumps, making them look like two sacks of flour lying on the bed. I went to the top of the stairs and crouched for my daredevil flying leap over three steps onto the dark landing. The 90-degree angle of the stairs, forced me to brace one shoulder against the wall, so I wouldn't lose contact with the steps, until I reached daylight at the dining room door.

Normally, Pa held butchering day over until cooler weather, but on this fall day, my family really needed meat, so it was definitely time to butcher. It was fairly cool and quiet, and I couldn't wait to get on with it!

Ichabod The Poland China Hog — We had a hog named Ichabod. At one time he had been so tall and scrawny that he wasn't marketable or suitable for our table. Money and grain were in such short supply, that Pa decided to turn Ichabod out to "root hog or die." After a couple weeks, Pa had a change of heart and penned the hog up with a 55 gallon drum of milk, diary residue, water, vegetable scraps, slop, wheat, and barley berries to keep him company. As the sun soured the milk and turned the sprouted grain into ferment, Ichabod gorged on it until he ballooned to an amazing 650 pounds. This, unfortunately, made Ichabod a very marketable hog and suitable for our table. Poor Ichabod—he was Pa's target for sacrifice now!

The end neared for Ichabod. The men were all lined up, ready to stun the porker as he came through the narrow chute, but Ichabod was so mammoth that the swing of the sledge hammer just bounded off him. It would have taken a wrecking ball to stagger Ichabod! Pa believed in the quick method—a bullet to kill him and the subsequent necessary stab to bleed him. These actions, however, didn't seem to phase Ichabod a bit.

He began to run, squealing in agony and fear. We would usually have collected the warm blood for blood sausage, but this time there would be no hope of that. His blood splashed across the cornfield for a half mile before Ichabod finally dropped and died. A stone boat was brought to the scene, and an army of men from nearby farms loaded the heavy hog onto it for the trip back to the barn. On the way back they took the stoneboat through our corn field, crushing and uprooting several stands of corn rows.

At the barn, the hog's hind legs were strapped to a doubletree, which is used to hitch horses to a wagon. It allowed the hind legs to be secured about three to four feet apart. It took several very stout men and a block and tackle installed in the barn door frame, to lift Ichabod from the stoneboat.

He was hoisted up, then lowered into a very large barrel of boiling water. When the skin was sufficiently scalded, the porker was once again hoisted up and tugged over to a slab which was a two wheel trailer converted to a work station. Once there, the hair and a thin top layer of skin was scraped off.

The men again hoisted Ichabod, this time to a vertical position, then began at the tail end to cut open the carcass. As they did so, the entrails slithered down into a washtub placed under Ichabod. Families who made sausage would clean and flush the intestines, or chitterlings, with oceans of water, then soak them in cold water, salt and cinnamon. The salt was used for a bleaching agent and the cinnamon was used to dispel the odor.

Pa split the hog in half with a hand saw and wrapped each side in muslin. Then the pieces were hung from the upstairs window of the house as protection against predators. After the meat was chilled, the sides were cut into smaller portions.

The head was cleaned, baked and preserved for head cheese. The heart, liver, kidneys, stomach, feet, ears and tail were all properly scalded, cleaned and scraped. Eventually, Ma would cook all the parts, except for the heart and liver, with onions and bay leaves and sprinkle cornmeal into the seasoned juice. The stomach was cleaned, dipped in boiling water, turned inside out, and scrapped. All of the pork scraps and juice would be stirred together then packed into the stomach and chilled. This was known as headcheese. It would be sliced up and fried for breakfasts, lunches, dinners and sandwich fillings. I loved headcheese.

Ma cubed the fat of the hog and rendered it in the oven. The strained fat was used for cooking and the cracklings for seasoning scrambled eggs, vegetables and casserole dishes. She made sausage with the pork heart, liver and pieces of lean pork. The ratio of lean pork used was usually three times that of the heart and liver. Salt , pepper, horseradish, allspice and other seasonings were added. By boiling all the meat, including pig knuckles, shanks and feet, the required gelatinous substance, collagen was obtained for congealing.

Even the raw pork rind would be used to slather over the hot stove as a polishing agent for the dingy stove top. Not a single part of the animal would go to waste on our farm. Eventually every part of the animal would be used.

Scrapple was made from pieces of minced or ground up meat which had been cooked with oatmeal or cornmeal. It was then packed in bread pans and chilled Later it would be sliced up and fried. Scrapple was used for sandwiches or meat patties for meals. Each family member was rationed two slices. I knew that when our meat supply ran out, Sunday dinners would once again consist of one slice of ring bologna, potatoes, gravy and bread. If there happened to be a rambunctious rooster or a broody hen available, it meant chicken fricassee time at the Carter household!

Slaughterhouse Maidens — Until my brothers, Bill and Eugene, left to find work and join the CCC, they had always helped Pa with the butchering. When they left, it was up to us girls and Ma to kill the animals when meat was needed. There was one particularly hard time I can recall. I believe I was only 15 or 16 years old. I know it was between the winter and spring because the sheep hadn't been sheared yet.

The plan was to butcher a yearling lamb. I recall that Ma and I had a beastly time trying to catch the animal. Ma was going to hold the lamb down while I cut its throat. For a brief moment, the lamb was down—but only for a brief moment. I knew I had to be fast, but this job required a razor sharp knife, and I was working with a slightly dull blade. The knives around our homestead weren't near sharp enough. Most of the blades were filled with nicks from prying out nails and carpet tacks or from trying to cut wire.

I began to cut the lamb's throat, but the matted wool and dull knife, not to mention my lack of strength, prevented the deep penetration that was needed. Some blood began to flow, but the lamb gained consciousness and began bleating and kicking violently, trying to escape from us. Ma was screaming at me, like a wild woman, "Hur'yup! Press harder! Hur' yup!" I sawed with all my strength, unable to see through the tears that were streaming down my face. My heart was breaking for this little lamb that had to be sacrificed.

Finally the lamb's jugular spurted its life's blood all over us and formed a river of blood between our knees. Ma and I both sat there and cried, knowing we still weren't finished. We had to place the lamb on the doubletree hoist to finish the unsavory task. We struggled through the ordeal, first removing the pelt, then cutting open the carcass and removing the entrails. The remainder of the job was routine, and we went about it as if in a daze. In spite of this tragedy, Ma and I had succeeded in providing enough meat for our family for the next few weeks. Unfortunately, this thought did nothing to reduce my grief for the little animal or to erase the agony we had unintentionally inflicted on it.

Sheep Shearing Mogul of Stutsman County —The younger Carter kids who couldn't do the heavier farm chores were charged with herding and counting the sheep. According to the Carter family's little shepherds, the world's sheep industry was centered in our pasture. There were just too many to count! Even though our flock numbered 100 to 200 head, the number was small compared to those of the true sheep ranchers. Sheep were only an incidental part of our general farming operation.

For many years, Pa had to shear all the sheep with hand powered clippers. Since Pa was the sheep-shearing mogul of Stutsman County, the shears had nearly become an extension of his arm. He had once bobbed my hair with the sheep shears because our scissors were dull.

During lambing and shearing time, Pa was pushed to the limits of his energy. He not only sheared over one hundred of his own sheep each summer, but he also sheared sheep for other farmers in the area, as well. The sheep had to be dipped in large vats of chemicals to kill the ticks and any other little crawling critters that infested their skin and wool. Their entire bodies, including their heads were dipped in the vat until the wool was saturated.

For the shearing process, Pa would snag the sheep by its hind leg, wrestle it to the handmade platform, and sit the animal on its buttocks between his strong knees, securing the animal with pressure.

"Shearin' sheep's like trimmin' grass," he expounded. "Jus' start as close to the base as you can and trim careful like." He would begin by taking the sheep's chin in his left hand and snipping down the throat to the stomach, around the back, down toward the buttocks, finishing up by shearing down the legs. Once the process was complete, the sheep leaped to their feet, and danced around as if they were a bit embarrassed about being *naked as jay birds.*

Pa would gather up the brilliant yellowish white wool, fold it inside out, ball it up, then tie it securely with several wrappings of binding twine. The fleece bundles were placed in tall bags for storage and were hoisted by block and tackle. By my measurement, those bags looked to be about four-kids-high. I can recall Pa holding me by my hands, then dropping me down into the partially filled twelve foot bag, so I could tromp down the individually tied bundles, compressing them as much as possible.

It was dark and spooky down in the those bags. I was terrified to be confined with the sheep ticks and the stench of wool, but I wouldn't have dared tell Pa of my fears. It was times like these when I felt so isolated from everything but myself, that I learned to practice the art of imagination. I pictured myself tromping the wool, just as others had tromped the grapes in wine vats. I imagined myself in many different places, doing many different things—anything to escape the confining spaces and smells of the bag.

To my relief, after much stomping and packing of fleece, my head finally showed above the opening at the top of the bag. By the time I climbed out of the sack I literally flew on my short legs to our immersion site—the horses' water trough—to scrub off any ticks that may have attached themselves to my flesh. Ticks were legion, they got into our hair, our pockets—and if our mouths weren't closed, we were apt to have one for lunch. At least they could be seen, which was more than I could say for bedbugs that sneaked up on us in the middle of the night. I guess I shouldn't have felt too sorry for myself because all the other kids before me had been recruited to do this same job for Pa at sheep-shearing time.

The Two Prairie Surgeons — Ma and Pa often paired me and Marian up to do various chores around the farm. One such chore was skinning dead sheep. We headed out to the west pasture in the blistering sun. The air was so hot it was almost suffocating.

As we ambled toward our destination, Marian decided to take off ahead of me on the path. She was wearing a pair of Eugene's CCC britches, which fit her much tighter across the rear than they had Eugene. It was like watching two bear cubs doing battle in a gunny sack. The temptation was too great for me—strictly on impulse, I swung the razor sharp Bowie knife I was carrying and slashed down, blade first, across Marian's derriere. It sliced completely through two layers of her clothing. The pants and underdrawers burst apart like the first cut of a hung animal at butchering time—but not a prick of the Bowie had touched Marian's flesh.

After the initial shock of what *could* have happened wore off, we giggled all the way out to the pasture. We knew Ma was going to be real mad, not only because of such careless actions, but because we had no patching cloth that would match the pants. Ma and the cut britches were the topic of conversation all the way to the first carcass.

When we finally arrived at the carcass, the stench was abominable. Maggots had already staked their claims on the flesh. There was no turning back for us though. We had to retrieve the pelt for market. The skins were crucial for income.

Beginning at the throat of the downed animal, I made the first cut with the Bowie, and with bare hands we carefully pulled back the wet, slimy pelt and callously pawed through the maggot-infested hide to remove it from the skeleton and flesh that remained. As we came closer to the

83

hindquarters, our hearts raced into a panic. We wanted this job to end in a hurry!

Unfortunately, this wasn't the only dead sheep, there were two more waiting to be operated on by the two young prairie surgeons. With every fiber of our being revolting at the mere thought of it, we knew we had to complete the chore or Ma and Pa would send us all the way back out again.

Some days there weren't many pelts, so we carried them home on the scraper. If there were too many, we would enlist the aid of the stone boat to bring the carcasses back to the farm. We would unload them out behind the barn near the manure pile to be skinned at a later time.

One day, it came to me in a flash exactly why I was giving the manure pile an extra wide berth when I brought the cattle to the barn. It didn't take me long to realize that it wasn't the stench of the manure pile that was so offensive. What registered somewhere below the level of my consciousness was that the silent moan of the non-breathing carcasses buried beneath the shallow surface of the pile burdened my thoughts

This day, we rolled the skins up and toted them home to be scraped and cleaned of excess debris. They would be laid in the hot sun, wool side down, for drying. After the drying process, they were folded, tied, and stored in as cool a place as possible until they could be transported for shipping.

The Anvil, The Two-By-four And Me — I recall a couple of occasions when Pa probably thought having me around was more of a hindrance than a help.

One day as he was trying to sharpen a six foot mower sickle in the granary, I was cavorting in his close proximity, as thoughtless kids will do. I was barely cognizant of him sitting in the seat of the stone grinder, pedaling the wheel, increasing its revolutions—paying little attention as he poured water from a rusty tin can over the wheel to lubricate it. He sat there with the sickle teetered across his lap, guiding the edges of each blade with just the right amount of pressure to its rightful slant.

I was playing near a chest-high wooden block on which an anvil was placed. As all little kids do—I was doing something I shouldn't have been. I was rocking the wooden block back and forth on the uneven hard pan floor when all of a sudden, the block and anvil came crashing down on my ribcage with a great thud. I was flat on my back, dazed, with the breath knocked out of me.

It took just seconds for Pa to toss the can of water aside, hurl the sickle to the ground, and run to lift the block and anvil off me. I could see that Pa was afraid my ribs might be broken. But as soon as he saw that I could stand up and breathe good, he turned away, spat a stream of tobacco juice into the dust, slapped me on the rump, and with all the crustiness he could muster, bellowed, "Now, get the h#$l out of here!" Boy, did I move fast to get out of his sight that day!

That darn granary was sure a jinx for me 'n my Pa—or maybe it was just that I always hung around Pa as much as I could, being kind of a tomboy and all.

Another time, Pa was repairing a mower pole in the yard beside the granary door. He told me, "Go in the granary and git me a long two-by-four, over the rafters above the oat bin." I found the two-by-fours, all right, but they were up too high, so I had to stand in the oat pile. It was like quicksand, each time I jumped up to hit the two-by-four pile in order to knock one down, I'd sink further into the grain.

Pa was outside shoutin' blue clouds of profanity into the air, "Git the h#$l out here with that d$#n two-by-four." I knew better than to dilly dally when I heard his tone. *Just another jump, and I'll have it*, I thought to myself. With one jump, the full stack came down on my head. The last thing I heard was Pa yelling, "Git out here before I have to come in after you!" Next thing I knew, Pa was lifting me out from under the heap of two-by-fours and oats. I was knocked out cold. Pa didn't yell at me any more for at least an hour or so.

Later, to make up to him, I went to the pump and got a pint jar of cold water for him. When I gave it to him he gave me a wink, spat out a wad of Peerless tobacco, and took a long drink. Pa hated to drink water, other liquids satisfied him more. But I knew that he did it just to show me all was well between him n' me.

While I'm explaining about Pa's love of other liquids, let me tell you about his own creation, "countryman's pop": one glass of cold water, two teaspoons of sugar, and one tablespoon of vinegar. After dissolving the sugar, one-fourth teaspoon of baking soda was added and the mixture was whisked to a froth. He said he drank it fast to let the spritz bathe his face, eyeballs and hair.

Goodbye To Drudgery On Our Farm — Wagons and horses were mandatory pieces of equipment on the farm. By 1902 the wagons used by farmers could be purchased from Sears Roebuck and Montgomery Wards for $43.00. A double-box outfit would cost $46.00. They were always painted green with red trim.

Soil management wasn't my Pa's long suit. He had been a trained railroad man. Recall of our tillage machinery hasn't been a top priority for me. I do remember the pieces of equipment that I was personally involved in operating. Our farm crops couldn't have grown without the proper soil preparation. Pa did the best he could with the few pieces of dilapidated machinery for which he had bartered.

Our repertoire of soil management equipment included the all-important manure spreader and the single furrow horse-drawn walking plow. Its true name was the English Walking Plow and its principle parts were the same as the Sulky and Moldboard plows.

Between the '20's and '30's my Pa's attempt to lessen the amount of drudgery on our leased farmland paid off in more ways than one. He had somehow acquired a used lug-wheel John Deere tractor. Pa was able to do his bartering with our sheep, cattle and horses—or perhaps he procured it by some other means. He also obtained a 1929 International flatbed truck with four-on-the-floor—an extra power gear for heavy loads. Pa claimed that the new second-hand truck and tractor put him into the capitalistic class of farmers. Now he could till a larger portion of the wild prairie land, instead of running wild horses and domestic livestock.

With the acquisition of the new equipment, Pa's pride and energy increased greatly. We were taken off the WPA rolls, and I think it did a whole lot for his self-esteem. One day he exclaimed to us, "Now that I got a few jingles in my pockets, we can be more like the uptown folks!"

Farm Tools & Implements — Tools and implements were hard to come by on the farm back in those days. Most of ours were either bolted, welded or wired together, since strap irons were more readily available to us than chewing gum.

Our version of harvesting equipment was a header, which cut the grain and conveyed it into a header box, and a horse driven wagon rack that always had to be kept under the spout of the header. Can you imagine what kind of grammar and tone of voice my Pa used if he turned to see the grain shooting out between the rack and the header spout onto the stubble field? Us kids probably would have found ourselves down on the ground picking up every single piece of grain, even if it took ninety days. Everything that represented cash had to be protected at all times.

An extremely useful implement was the stone boat, pulled by a single horse or a team, depending on the weight of the load. It consisted of two rounded-out fence posts as bottom rails lying about five to six feet apart, with boards or plywood nailed across the top of the posts. A chain or heavy rope was fastened to each of the fence posts. We used the stone boat to haul 50-gallon barrels of water from the slough for watering the garden and washing clothes. It was also used to move heavy loads of rock and to relocate heavy pieces of equipment or furniture. It was an ingenious and back-saving device.

The scoop shovel was a single horse implement called the scraper. It looked like a huge rounded scoop shovel with two handles. A person had to tightly grip the handles, and tip the scoop to its sharp edge, while the horse was ordered to "move out." As the horse began to move, the scraper would dig down into the ground somewhat and scrape the earth. Large mounds of dirt and rock could be moved with this tool.

The drag, the plow, the disk and the spring-tooth harrow were used for breaking up the soil. The row-crop cultivator affixed with pointed polished steel pieces was used astraddle corn rows and garden rows to loosen and weed the soil.

The mower and hay rake were used for making hay in the fall of the year for our livestock. The chisel plow was used to penetrate the subsoil and could be set to the depth of eighteen inches, if needed.

Pa The Plowman — The moldboard plow in its simplest form was a horse-drawn piece of equipment used to turn the soil. The plowman walked behind it, manipulating the blade by using the handles. Solid crucible steel blades were favored for rocky soil. The cast iron blades scoured easily and were used for sandy soil. Large plows with three or four moldboards were pulled by tractors. Ours contained two moldboards, as I recall. It was sometimes drawn by a four horse team with two horses in front and two nearer the operator. Five horse teams were operated with two horses in the fore and three in the aft positions, and there were sets of reins for each team.

The Lister and Middlebuster plows were used when the crops were planted in open furrows such as for potatoes. Since our equipment was scarce, much of the time the huge holes in our potato patch were dug manually while the farm implements were used in the grain field.

My Pa must have tramped a million miles behind a one-piece share plow and later a Moldboard plow, until newer equipment could be procured. The Sulky, a horse-drawn two-wheeled plow with a riding seat, and the Moldboard were forerunners of the Lister plow used in the early 1900s.

I remember a day when I was about seven years old, I got to carry lunch out to Pa while he was working the east field. I sauntered a half-mile to the field, and waited at the end of the row. I sat on a rock beside the wagon track road to wait for Pa. I could hear the distinct sound of steel hitting rocks as the plow shares pulled and ripped at the soil. I could see where the shares bit into the earth, leaving ribbons of black satin. The rooted earth folded away from the steel blade like frosting from a cake decorating tube. At intervals, the blade glinted in the sun much the same as Morse Code signals between the ships at sea.

Pa walked a steady pace with the reins around his neck and his hands guiding the plow. All the way down the row the tug chains jingled, the team snorted unmelodiously and the horses hooves plodded and thumped against the hard stubble. Pa smiled and waved as he caught sight of me. When the team reached the turn-around, Pa shouted "Whoa!" If he hadn't made the command, the spirited horses would have turned and started a new furrow without him. He knew this crazy team of Dan and Pet would run away with the plow if he didn't settle them down before letting go of the reins. The horses, glad for the rest, relaxed every muscle of their tired, sweat-slicked bodies into a sway-backed position.

As Pa approached, I could see that the wind had blown dust in his face, turning his features into a slate mask, accentuating his eyeballs. Dust covered his overalls and converted them into gray marble that looked as if it might crack with the next step he took. A mix of pride, love and empathy overtook me, watching him as he came toward me. He had worked so hard for so long to make a life for Ma and us kids.

He ruffled my hair and said, "Hi, funny face." He had given me this nickname early on in my childhood. It was the closest that Pa ever got to a term of endearment. A wink let me know that he was pleased to see me—and the lunch. His lunch consisted of a potted meat sandwich and water. I had carried it to him in a soiled cloth salt sack which had become more grimy with each use. Two blue Mason jars contained the water. It was a no-frills lunch, as it always was in those days—no fruit, no greens, no vegetables. He spat out his tobacco, took a sip of the water, and spat again before taking a long drink. I had become accustomed to Pa's spitting many years ago. After all, spitting came as natural to farmers as blowing their noses onto the ground. Ma said time and again, "Only the not quite human does that."

Sitting there in the sun with my Pa, smelling the freshly turned earth, listening to the sounds of the horses, and passing the time chatting, I was overwhelmed with contentment. I look back upon that time, and I wonder if my Pa ever experienced hopelessness and futility as he tried to coax crops from the hard pan season after season. If he ever did, he certainly never told any of us.

Hay Stompin' In The Heat — In the '30s, we had recorded temperatures of 114 degrees. Many people died from heat-related causes. It wasn't uncommon to see heatwaves rising and shimmering from the plains for miles around. My bothers, sisters and myself had many times sat in the sweltering sunlight for days at a time, herding sheep and cattle. We had no long sleeve garments and no straw hats to protect us from the sun. The bog and bullrushes in the lowland were our only salvation from the blistering sun.

It was a fact of life on a prairie farm, haying always had to take place on one of the hottest days of the season. This particular day, the temperature had risen to 90 degrees by nine o'clock in the morning, and we were preparing to go out to the south field past the bog. The hay had been previously mowed, raked and placed into windrows by Pa and the older boys. By the time haying season would end, everyone in the Carter family, from the oldest to the youngest, would have participated in one phase or another of the haying process.

My older brothers had already hitched our teams to the hayracks. Pa, Ma and baby Winfred, took the open trailer with rubber tires and the hayrack which was hitched behind the open trailer. Dizzy and Duke, our newly broken western horses, were Ma and Pa's team. Ma had to bring the baby along because he was nursing. Us girls had to ride with John Trowbridge—Dan and Pet would be our team. My older brothers had already gone to a different field to carry out their chores.

Our farmhand, old John Trowbridge, came sauntering down the lane wearing his ankle-length army issued woolen overcoat. None of us had ever established if John had served in the armed forces or not. He worked for food and always seemed to be available to help Pa with the field chores. He looked strange wearing the wool coat on such a hot day. He didn't walk erect, so one side of his soiled coat was hitched up three or four inches off the ground, while the other side dragged in the dirt. As I recall, there was only one useable button on his coat, which was maybe a good thing, it being such a hot day and all. He carried a tin syrup pail that glinted in the sunlight as he approached.

"Pile in, John!" Pa shouted. Our destination that morning was two miles south of the cow path lane toward the bog. When we got to the field, Pa guided the team, circling the full area of windrows which had previously been made by the hayrake. He was surveying for high ground on which to build the stacks and trying to decide how many stacks could be raised. Once he made the determination, Pa shouted out instructions to us.

We reluctantly jumped down off the hayracks to begin our day's work. As the haybucker collected some of the windrows to one spot, we began to form the first of many haystacks. With pitchforks, we distributed the dry field hay into large circles. The bucker continued to travel up and down the windrows, collecting hay for the stacks we would be building.

During the course of the day, most of the hay would be formed into huge stacks to remain in the field and the remainder would be loaded onto the two hayracks by field hands with pitch forks. The hayracks were flatbed, horse-drawn wagons with vertical crossbars which had been built to form *X*s. These crossbars kept the hay securely stacked while it was being hauled to the hayloft or wherever it was going to be stored.

As the haystack began to grow, some of the hay stompers dove in—the hay stompers being us little kids. We stomped and tromped and jumped up and down in the dirty, dusty mass of hay in an effort to compress it. The stackers tossed fork full after fork full in front of us kids, and we continued to tromp, stomp, and compact the hay. As the stack rose, the pitcher found it harder to see us, so most of the hay landed directly on top of our heads. With each rising stack, our sweat rose. The dust collected on our faces until we began to look like miniature Al Jolsons—only the whites of our eyes and the pink of our lips was visible. Such abuse of our young complexions did nothing to promote a softer, prettier, more radiant skin.

It seemed like an eternity before Pa called for a lunch break. He was good at telling the hour by the sun's position in the sky and by the length of his shadow cast on the ground. When the sun was directly overhead and no shadow was cast, that meant it was high noon.

Pa and John unhitched the horses so that they could rest in the shade of the hay-filled rack while we ate. As I recall, there was no water for the horses, even though we were working in the meadow east of the bog where a slough had once been. The only water we had for ourselves was a jug of Pa's favorite fizz water—which by now had lost its fizz and had turned as hot as the noonday sun.

We all gathered in a circle on the grass. Ma set the battered aluminum dishpan down and unwrapped the neatly stacked sandwiches from a tea towel. She had dressed some of the barley bread sandwiches with mashed potatoes, vinegar and onion filling. Some were dressed merely with butter and sorghum. She made no apologies for either the bread or the filling.

Just as us kids were about to take the first bites of our sandwiches, old Trowbridge sprang the lid on his pail and brought forth his donation to lunch. It was burned fried eggs—sealed in the tin pail for six long, hot hours! We all nearly lost our taste even for our own food. The rotten eggs we had often found in our henhouse smelled like perfume in comparison to what John offered us.

When he held out the eggs to Ma, she politely declined, saying, "No thanks, John. I've come with all the food we need." She added, "I'm nursing baby and fried eggs ain't included in my diet." Pa pushed his hat back on his head, mopped his brow with his gritty blue and white handkerchief, and grunted something like, "'Preciate it,

John, maybe later. I can't toss hay on a full belly." John just shrugged, ate the eggs and cleaned up the remainder of our sandwiches. Us kids had to turn our faces to the breeze in order to finish our lunches.

The whole time we were eating, baby Winfred was resting peacefully in the trailer. It usually had a broken hitch, which made it wander from side to side, wobbling its way down the road. The vibration had perhaps created a sort of lulling effect for the baby. He slept through all the noise and the heat of haying time.

After lunch, we continued on for several more hours, building huge stacks. As the time approached to finish up for the day, Pa shouted for us to fill the hayracks for our trip back to the homestead.

Us little hay stompers were once again called into service to compress the hay in the hayracks, much the same as we had done with the haystacks. Some of us climbed up the side of the rack, and others dove into the rack from the wagon box. As the hay was pitched into the rack by the field hands, us stompers did what we did best—jumped, trampled and stomped.

Finally, our day's work was finished. We all boarded the hayracks and the trailer to head for home. We were all hot, sweaty, and tired. Pa and John drove the teams toward the bog, where we stopped to give them a drink for the trip home. The horses waded into the water and drank deeply. Among the sounds of snorting and whinnying, they lifted their heads from time to time, allowing the water to drip from their mouths and whiskers.

While the horses drank, Pa and John went back to top the stacks. They smoothed and compressed the top layer of hay to a peak so that rain water would run off the stack, rather than soaking into it.

About the time they were finishing up, we heard the clank of a cowbell, as our herd ventured across the grassland to the bog. They waded knee-deep into the water, splashing it in all directions in an attempt to cool off. While dallying there, they switched their tails at the flies, and drank the tepid dank water. When they had had enough, the red heifer wearing the cowbell suctioned her feet from the mud and turned to start the journey toward the lane. The rest of the herd followed. After haying for ten hours in the hot sun, we headed home. No rest for the weary, though. We still had to milk the cows and feed the calves before dinner.

Preparing For The Threshing Crew — Most days homesteaders arose about 4:30 a.m. to have farm chores finished in time for a 6:00 a.m. breakfast. It usually consisted of fried eggs, smoked meat, headcheese, fried potatoes and toast. No breakfast would have been complete without boiled coffee, clarified with a beaten egg and a pinch of salt. Although fresh fruit wasn't available, there was always a supply of home canned chokecherries and gooseberries. If it happened to be butchering time, fresh meat was serves, but home canned meat was substituted as needed.

Threshing day was somewhat of a national holiday to those on isolated farms. It was a time when every household was caught up in the hustle and bustle of preparing for the arrival of the threshing crew. The very thought of serving meals to the threshing crews ignited flames of desire to be named the best cook in the county. Every homemaker wanted to be the one to serve the award-winning supper. Ma joked, "It's enough to give any cook a case of the jitters!"

Each farmer's wife, including my Ma, took a long reach into the back of her dusty pantry shelves to bring forth a shoebox of tattered culinary artifacts called recipes. With all the expertise of a test kitchen cook, she would consider and discard mixtures, flavorings and techniques until she found just the right one. Nothing was too good for the threshing crew. The sheer number of men in the threshing crew demanded that Ma make at least five or six pies—with a cake or two tossed in, "For choice," Ma said, as she winked and smiled.

The Threshing Crew — At threshing time, the owner of the threshing rig would travel the countryside with his equipment and crew. They would work hard to assist the entire township in harvesting. They worked until the last farmer's crop was hauled to the grain elevator.

The threshing crew consisted of the engineer, who operated the equipment, separator men, bundle haulers, spike pitchers and grain haulers. The rig owner furnished a water boy to carry water to his thirsty crew if no water was available on the farm they were working.

Each neighbor was expected to furnish at least one farm hand, a wagon and a team of horses during the threshing process. In return, the same would be provided him when the threshing crew came to his fields. Their womenfolk were also expected to come along to help cook for the sweaty, famished crew.

Some areas on the prairie were so remote that the owner of the rig had to bring his own cook and pull a twenty-five foot wide cook shack on wheels. The shack was lighted with kerosene lamps equipped with reflectors. A large wooden table and benches ran the full length of the shack. The benches were converted into packing boxes for dishes when the crew headed for their next job.

The workers would come in from the hot, dusty fields and wash up in an old gray basin sitting on an apple crate outside the cook shack door. Everyone washed in the same water, just as we did on our farm.

The crops were not always abundant, but I remember a farmer from up north saying that a barley crop that he'd worked was so huge the crew had to go in and load up some of the grain shocks so the threshing rig could get into the center of the field.

When the thresher was finally placed, the engine, which was the thresher's power source, was moved to the distance of the length of the wide belt that connected the two. The rig's driver would toot his whistle to announce his readiness for action, and the engine would belch forth pungent wood smoke and soot in readiness of the day's work.

I remember one summer I drove the rack and pitched bundles. I think the pay was $2.50 a week. It was fun for me to be out in the field with six or eight bundle haulers. They would race around the field, whirling, turning and yelling at their teams in order to get into position first. There was no extra pay involved in getting the most loads in, but there was a certain competitive mystique attached to it. That summer I worked two and a half months to buy a second-hand guitar.

Belly Up, Boys — When the threshing crew took a supper break, they would gather outside our kitchen door. "The smell of grub got to 'em!," Ma would grin. Then she stepped to the door and called out, "Time to wash up and eat, gents!" The men would straggle in to the hot kitchen. Take my word for it, the five hours of pitching bundles in the hot sun didn't make the men smell too sweet. Ma muttered, "They smell 'bout as potent as sauerkraut in its final days of fermentation."

The crew lined up single file at the dry sink to take their turns washing off portions of mud caked on their flesh. We recognized some of the crew as hard-working reputable men, but we knew others to be drinkers and carousers from other parts of the territory. Ma whispered to me, "Some of these're ruffians from the next county."

I recall a picture in my mind of Ma, with sweat dripping down her face in torrents, and her arms half in and half out of the huge mashed potato kettle, glancing over her shoulder at me, with a semblance of relief in her eyes that said "The crew seems to be enjoying the meal." Then she turned her attention back to the potatoes, gravy and leaning stacks of odd-sized bowls.

After cooking and serving mountains of mashed potatoes, pounds of meat, gallons of gravy, pots of fresh garden vegetables, loaves of homemade breads and a multitude of biscuits piled high with marmalade, chutneys and jams. Ma appeared happy because the ordeal was over, and because everything had gone so well.

While us girls had served the men, Pa had made darn sure that we didn't speak to any of them. If he had caught us even looking at them, a point of his finger and a stern look would have sent us back to the kitchen in embarrassment.

After the crew had gone back to the fields, Pa said sternly, "Their brains is too shallow for ya to lend yer time to!" There were times when Pa told us more than we cared to know. He could terminate any conversation he didn't wish to share with a mere look. When we complained to Ma, she reiterated what Pa had said and reminded us, "The time will come when you'll thank yer Pa fer stopping things before they happen. It's fer yer own good that Pa tells ya these things."

Hunting—Open season in North Dakota was late summer and fall. In the '20's and '30's, fur-bearing animals abounded in great number and variety. Wild game was hunted, trapped or simply run down. Animals were shot for sport, or sometimes to provide extra income, or simply to provide meat for the table.

My Pa and brothers, Eugene and Bill, were fur trappers, as were most North Dakota residents. The garment industry paid well for the fur of most animals, and the extra income was certainly a God-send to our families. My brothers brought home great numbers of weasels, badgers, foxes, muskrats and rabbits. They were stored in our summer kitchen/winter shed until they could be skinned. Once the animal was skinned, the pelts would be stretched on smoothly whittled boards for drying.

One time a badger froze before they could skin him. He was lying belly-down, directly in line with our door to the outside. His long, tapered, vicious-looking, yellow teeth showed through his partially open, snarling mouth. His extra long half-moon claws were fanned out in front of each side of his head. Us little kids were so scared of him, that we couldn't walk past him to get to the privy. We would near wet our pants before we were willing to scurry by him to get outside. We didn't even like to go past him in the daylight!

Because flickertails—gophers—were devouring the crops, the State of North Dakota was offering one penny per gopher tail. Pa didn't trust us with a BB gun, so us kids had to put forth the greater effort required to trap them. We could be found lying upwind of gopher holes for hours, just waiting to snare them when they poked their heads out of their holes. This was a very important task because it assisted the State of North Dakota and the farmers. Besides—it gave us spending money. We never had any spending money, unless Pa gave us pennies, usually three each. There wasn't usually a place to spend the pennies, anyway, unless it was on a rare trip to town. Our gopher tails helped supplement our meager spending money. But, as the gopher population dwindled, the State reduced the fee to a half cent per tail.

My family also sold the hides of cows that had been butchered or died. The cowhides were neatly wrapped and tied according to strict specifications. Then they were stored over winter until the spring thaw. In the spring, the cowhides would be dried and sold for cash or traded to merchants for food, fuel, and spring seed.

Hunting Buddies—Hunters and trappers from all over the State were drawn to our vicinity because of the abundance of game. Sometime during the course of the hunt, they would saunter to our homestead. They knew Pa to be a good host and a willing storyteller. When they came, conversation took place around a keg of Pa's homemade beer. Stories were swapped among the men, which included hunting, trapping, fishing and politics. We could usually count on hearing a story or two about who had the best hunting dog, and the like. Each hunter took his turn telling a wild unprovable tale of his best hunting victory. A slap of the knee and another sip of homebrew amid loud laughter, was the signal challenging the next storyteller.

Pa felt obligated to relate his story about the time he was out in the field "Jus' this side of the east gate," he said, "I had a double-barreled shot gun, ready to shoot a varmint". I don't remember whether it was a coyote, he was talking about, or one of our own animals that needed to be put out of its misery. Pa went on in a loud voice and a half grin, "I put that gun to my eye for aim, righted my prey and pulled the trigger. The SOB jammed, backfired and near blew my d%$n thumb off!" Everyone laughed uproariously, checked out Pa's thumb, then went on to recite his own gory tale about guns and accidental shootings. When "swacked," as Pa called that state of inebriation, most men spewed out any subconscious opinion they had harbored over the years.

In the winter our house was very cold. There were few rooms, so us kids gathered around the wood fire, eavesdropping on the conversations of our parents and their visitors. There was no family room or television set to occupy us, nor was there a place to send us off to. So there we sat, hearing things not necessarily meant for our ears. Sometimes we learned more from those colorful conversations than we ever learned in biology. "The walls have ears," Pa reiterated every time a conversation came up that we shouldn't hear. This, of course, made us much more eager to wait in the wings within good hearing distance.

We never had any left over food for guests, but Ma did have Pa's favorite—pickled pigs' feet with a few chicken feet thrown in. While the gents gnawed on the bones of the delicacy, they swapped more yarns, whirling the air with tales about what had been, what could have been, and what "just might happen next." When the keg was, of course, empty, they'd announce almost simultaneously, "Well, Carter, winter's howlin' at yer door, so we'll meet up with ya next huntin' season." And they would leave with the promise to return another year.

Considering the aspects of their characters and personalities, the gents may not have been of the best sort, but at least they were company. They provided relief from the monotony of life out on the prairie, where the only things that moved were the clouds and the winter winds.

Winter on the Farm

Winterizing the Farm — There were many more jobs that needed to be done around the farm before winter set in. In the fall, the crew had finished threshing the grain and had hauled it to the town's grain elevator by team and wagon. The silo had been packed to the peak with dry yellow corn fodder and spikey seed heads, and the haymow had been glutted with alfalfa and dry slough hay which had been cured.

Winter was quickly approaching. The roof of the rickety granary had to be patched to protect the newly harvested wheat, rye, oats, and barley from the winter weather. A supplemental feeding operation had to be set up for the animals. They were fed with hay and roughage, but grain was also given to them to fatten them up. Iodized salt licks had to be set out, especially in the sheep pen. The list of tasks went on and on.

Pa and Ma worked so hard, and they expected us kids to do the same. Even with a bunch of us helping out, the amount of work on our farm was phenomenal. There were so many chores that had to be done—not only once a day—but many times a day. The cows had to be milked in the early morning and in the evening. If we didn't milk them on time, they would excrete their precious commodity onto the ground. In those days we sure didn't want the milk to be wasted—or anything else to be wasted—for that matter!

Once the milk was separated, we had to slop the hogs with the skim milk and feed them grain.

The sheep had to be brought in from the pasture, counted and penned in the sheep shed. This chore was left to the little shepherds of the family, who couldn't help with the heavier work. It also provided them with ample opportunity to practice their counting. The horses had to be fed and cared for, and the chickens, geese, ducks and turkeys required a certain amount of attention and sustenance. As if this wasn't enough, the garden had to be harvested, too

Batten Down The Hatches — Pa was a teller of the seasons. When he said, "Batten down the hatches," we knew it was going to be a hard winter. As the colors of fall gave way to the bleakness of winter, the work around our homestead didn't decelerate,—it accelerated because our livelihood depended upon preparedness. The plans for winter started with making our home and property secure.

My brother, Bill, who had learned stone masonry in the Civilian Conservation Corps, spent weeks cutting prairie rocks to build a three and a half foot high planter-type wall around the north side of the house. Bill was an expert stone mason. In the CCCs he had helped to construct miles of rock walls in the Badlands at Medora, North Dakota.

Once the rock wall was constructed, we had to haul raw animal sludge—green manure—from the jointly inhabited cow and horse barn to the other three sides of the house. We submerged the foundation of the house in the green manure to within a few inches of the window frames. This was done to protect the vegetables in the cellar from the harsh cold winter. As we hauled the sludge, the spreader gears kicked out a swath of raw manure all the way from the barn to the house.

When winter would finally hit, the bank would become frozen solid, but until then, its pungent aroma would plague us continually. Banking the *golden insulation* against the house was supposed to insulate us from the cold, but it seemed no matter what precautions were taken, the raw harsh winter still penetrated the house through the broken lath and plaster walls. To make matters worse, the awful stench of our insulation would assault us when the spring thaw commenced.

Though North Dakota suffered through many serious blizzards, the most devastating snow storms occurred in 1906, 1907, 1936, 1950, 1966 and 1984.

I remember the snow storm of 1936. I was thirteen years old at the time. It was a very bad winter. Gales began to blast across the open prairie by late October. The foliage barely had time to turn color before the poplar trees, which we had planted years earlier for a windbreak, began to bend to the tune of the wind and the weight of the ice and snow. Snow scrolls (sculpted drifts) leaped the buildings and filled the low places.

By the time we realized how bad it was becoming, it was almost too late to hustle the dank wool laden sheep from the pasture into the sheep shed. For now, the roof of the shed was well over their heads, but by spring, the manure would be packed so deep that the sheep would have to run uphill into the shed.

Come spring, we would clean the barn and use the dried manure as our fuel supply for the following winter. The foot thick manure would be chopped into 12x16 inch rectangular slabs, loaded on the stoneboat, then hauled to the sunny side hill. There it would be stacked tee-pee style to dry in the sun. During the drying process it would be turned once. Then it would be hauled back to the yard, where it was stacked for use the following winter.

Even after the sheep were penned, the fierce gales sifted snow into the shed through holes where the siding was missing. Doors banged and rattled with each gust until rusty door latches gave way. At this point, we would use a man-sized prairie rock to hold the doors shut until huge drifts took care of the job for us. The barns all had hay hole entries from the loft, and we fed the animals by pushing hay or grain through the available opening.

The biggest problem was in getting to the barn. Every morning and evening, the snow banks in front of the doors had to be shoveled in order to gain access to feed the animals. Shoveling through six to eight-foot snow drifts was a heart attack waiting to happen for most farmers. Pa was glad to have raised two strong boys, Eugene and Bill. It wasn't that Pa didn't pull his share of the work load, but taking care of our big homestead was just too much for one person to handle alone.

I recall the *blizzard from hell* immobilizing the countryside, weighing down tree limbs and making pillars of ice out of people and animals who were unfortunate enough to have been outside. The 60 mph winds pelted many towns, isolating them from the outside world. My family was housebound for weeks. That year, the weather remained severe from January until March.

I remember my brother, Eugene, being forced to ride his horse 12 miles to the nearest town over the tops of telephone poles because the snow had drifted so high. If the frozen snow crust had broken, both Eugene and the horse would have suffocated.

Flue fires were fairly common because of the creosote build up from burning railroad ties, manure, twigs, and scrap wood. If the pipes weren't hammered out each spring, a flue fire was bound to erupt. I recall one instance when our stove pipes overheated. It sounded like a train roaring through the house. We had to use every available liquid to subdue the turbulent blaze.

The snow drifted housetop high, and the cracks in the roof allowed snow to sift lightly onto our quilts and handcrafted feather comforters. Our breaths collected on the quilts next to our faces. Each morning, we awakened to little mounds of frost beside our heads and drifts of snow scattered about on our homemade quilts.

Because the path ended at the snow bank by our back door, we couldn't get to the privy, so we used a chamber pot in the upstairs bedroom. In the morning its contents would be frozen solid to the point of either splitting the metal or mounding the contents to a peak. Snow had drifted so high that the outhouse became a mountain of waffle-woven ice splendor. The splendor ended when we had to take turns trying to dump a frozen pot.

One day, in a panic, Cammie piped-up, "Ya! The privy is frozen over, so now what're we gonna do?" Winfred spouted, "Just hold it!" We usually did. Someone suggested that we stop drinking so much water and eating so much soup, then we wouldn't have to go so often. It seemed logical, but it just didn't work that way at all!

Winter Mornings — Each morning we had to thaw water pails and teakettles. Pa usually got up first and built a fire in the Franklin stove by first stirring up the coals that remained from the overnight banking procedure. Then he would add dried sheep manure blocks, small chunks of coal and kindling. The soft coal ignited rapidly, as did the small bits of dried manure that contained straw.

Ma would be in the kitchen at the cookstove, wrestling with matches, paper and bits of straw and wood chips, trying to fan a spark into a flame. She said it was like a battle zone. It was either get the cookstove going or starve.

Even if I only smelled the smoke from the fire, my thought was, *it'll be warm downstairs.* Pa shouted through the door at the foot of the stairs, bringing me and everybody else to our feet, "Git up and git goin'!" We tossed on just enough clothing to appear decent and made our way down stairs. Pa didn't allow too much flesh to be exposed, only the arms and legs below the knees.

As we gathered around the potbelly stove, the fire finally took off. The blazing flames roared through the holes where the isinglass had once been. The fast burning fuel got so hot it nearly melted the sides of the stove. If anyone had fallen against it, they would've been fried for breakfast.

As I waited for breakfast, I looked out the window, but couldn't see anything. So I stuck my warm tongue to the frosted window pane and made a peek-hole to see what the weather was like. Ma watched me as she stirred the oatmeal in a big pot on the stove. She commented, rather softly, "Yer just like yer Pa. He always has to lop the curtains over the side nail to look at trees that never move, hills that never change, and to watch for company that never comes." I didn't answer—instead I contentedly manufactured more holes while the other kids jockeyed for their space at the window. As I did this, my mind ventured to the time that Bill and Eugene had put a cocoon on the windowsill so it would hatch into a butterfly. Ma told me that I got hold of it, and sucked all the juice from it. She said that was why I was so flighty.

It wasn't until I became chilled that I realized that I was still clad in Pa's made-over long johns with my "barn door" at half-mast. Thank goodness my behind was toward the stove. The other kids giggled, then we began to shove and elbow each other, each of us trying to make a hole in the frost so we could see outside. I slathered my hot, raw tongue over the spiked frost, puncturing the polka dot pattern into an expanded full-moon size. *There*, I thought, *now I kin see more.* It amazed me that the prismatic patterns of the fleece-white snow could glisten even on an overcast day.

Beyond the water pump, great swells of snow had jumped the snow fence over the box elder windbreak. It dropped like wet cotton over the naked branches. Snow swirls had created a blockade between the house and the barn and obliterated the view of the little house at the end of the back path.

Since I held center-stage at the frosted window, I recited a weather report for the kids who couldn't see out. The glistening snow forced me to squint while trying to focus on one area of the yard at a time. The Arctic sculpturing had graced everything in view of my concentrated focus. I could make out the pump behind a razor sharp snow drift. The handle was jutting out, frozen at half mast, midway of its completed cycle. A frozen transparent tomb encased the entire pump, and stalactite icicles tenaciously hugged the water spout.

As the frost began to gain superiority over my binocular type holes, I extended my tongue onto the heavily frosted window pane once again. I pressed it firmly to the frost, until my body heat won out. The ice melted into a pair of frost-rimmed glasses. I scanned the first snowfall of the season. Pa said, "When the snow begins to fly, it's time for Santa Claus to hitch up his reindeer." I was secretly looking for a sign of him, though I pretended to be just looking at the snow-sculptured countryside. With my tongue, I made sloppy slush holes again and again, crafting them to a size that suited me. I pulled my tongue back into my mouth for reheating, just in case more de-icing became necessary. The other kids were doing the same thing. Ma looked at all of us and exclaimed, "At the rate you kids 're going, I might hire ya to wash all the windows in the house next spring, using jus' yer tongues!"

Pancakes And Rommegrot — The sightseeing ended when Pa chanted the call to "belly-up!" *The same tone as for calling the hogs*, I thought. We'd all scamper to the table like soldiers at regimental review, each kid to his or her own place on the bench behind the table. "There had better be no elbowin', pushin' or shovin'. Otherwise, ya won't git to eat at all!" was the threat from both parents.

Pancakes, Norwegian Rommegrot and boiled beans with salt pork were our mainstays for breakfast. We made Rommegrot, a Norwegian style pudding, from milk thickened with white flour, sugar and flavoring. When the chickens had laid well and Pa couldn't take the eggs to town, Ma whipped an egg or two into the mixture. At times, Ma overshot the measure of flour for thickening. The grot then split apart in the saucepan, which made it look like the bed of a dried up lake.

Pancakes were made simply of white flour, milk or buttermilk, eggs and leavening. Ma fried them in rendered fat or fake butter and dressed them up as much as she could for us. She created "panny cakes" by using dollar-size dollops of batter to form a head and body, then streamers jutted from the torso, forming the arms and legs. Fried potatoes were served with every meal. The crowning glory was the leftover hot boiled beans and sorghum or sometimes homemade burnt sugar syrup. If any scraps of meat or salt pork were available, they were tossed into the batter, creating an illusion of having meat for breakfast.

If the wheat crop had come in, Ma would stand out on the north porch fanning wheat. The wheat was poured from pan to pan, letting the gale wind blow the chaff away, while the wind chill factor raised near blisters on her flesh. I had seen Ma stand out on the very same porch in twenty below zero temperatures, like this, stirring a pan of fudge to get it to harden.

After the separation process, the grain was then washed and soaked in warm water overnight. In the morning she would boil it and serve it to us topped with sugar and cream. If there were enough home canned chokecherries or gooseberries, a spoonful would be added to each bowl. It took only one spoonful to each person in our large family to use up a full quart of fruit.

The marred rectangular black walnut table looked like a conference table from King Arthur's Court. It was huge and so wide that we couldn't reach the middle for passing food back and forth. Pa sat at the end of the table in his private captain's chair. No one else ever sat at Pa's place at the table, or in his chair. I imagine that I can still hear Pa stirring his two teaspoons of sugar into the huge captain-sized mug of boiled strong, black coffee, and about a quarter-cup of rich, freshly separated cream. The teaspoon clanked each side of the cup in a noisy rhythmic pattern that resembled the cowbell on Bessy as she journeyed up the lane at milking time. Ma was always seated at the opposite end.

Ma and Pa took turns bouncing the baby on their knees while trying to eat. They fed the newest addition to our family from their own plates at meal time. The babies were always nursed while Ma ate or sometimes, even while she stood at the stove cooking our meals. We had never heard of *Gerbers* out on the prairie. If we had we couldn't have afforded it, anyway. So when the babies reached the age of having solid foods, Ma would chew the food first, then give it to the baby. As the baby grew older, the food was mashed and fed to the toddler from Ma or Pa's plate.

Us kids always had to say "Please pass..." what we wanted, but Pa only had to point and grunt. If we passed the wrong thing, Pa let out a louder unmelodious grunt. Sooner or later each of us became near mind readers about Pa's wishes. Good training!

After breakfast, we reluctantly went back upstairs to retrieve any garments that we had forgotten. Most of the time we needed more layers against the winter chill. We dressed, retrieved the "wrapped rock" foot-warmers from under the covers and took them downstairs where they would be reheated that evening before bedtime. Once we were all back downstairs, we hovered around the frosted window or beside the heating stove in a vain attempt to stay warm.

Milk Deliveries To Uptowners — By the time I reached the fifth and sixth grades, Pa and Ma felt I was responsible enough to deliver milk and cream to the townsfolk.

Me and my brothers and sisters had to make the deliveries on our way to school in our old "school bus" which was nothing more than a rubber-tire trailer with a tall enclosed box on top of it. Hand-hewn benches were built on each side for passengers, and the driver sat in a seat just in back of a sliding window of sorts which allowed the reins to be manipulated from inside the box. Besides us Carter kids and all the milk and cream bottles, we also picked up the Nelson kids, Harold Posie, and kids from the Don Williams family.

The sales of milk and cream brought an extra pittance to the financial resources of our family. The more affluent folks bought our milk and cream for weekend dinner guests. Ma sold the milk for ten cents a quart, later thirteen, and heavy or "spoon-dippin" cream, as Ma called it, was sold for nineteen to twenty two cents a pint. It took a lot of tedious work, but we were used to hard on our prairie spread.

Preparation for milk deliveries was a three fold process: The jars were sterilized and scrubbed in our wash boiler the night before while dinner was cooking and the fire was still hot. Once evening came and the dishes were done, the fire in the range was allowed to die out due to fuel shortages. Then the door to the kitchen, or cold room as we called it, would be closed, and the family would gather around the heating stove to keep warm.

The next day, after milking, we poured the milk from our galvanized pails, straining it through several layers of tea towels into a ten quart aluminum soup kettle while the milk was still warm from the cow. Next, we dipped it by cupfuls from the soup kettle and funneled it into old-fashioned blue glass jars of one or two quart capacity. We placed red rubber jar rings around the mouths of the jars, and topped them with zinc lids containing clear glass inserts. The lids were screwed down tightly, and the jars were wrapped for delivery. In the summertime we wrapped them with wet burlap to keep the milk as cool as possible, and in the wintertime they were wrapped with anything from old army blankets to homemade quilts in an attempt to keep the milk from freezing.

My typical school day consisted of gulping my pancakes and syrup so I could help with preparing and bottling the milk. When that process was complete, we wrapped and loaded the jars onto our handcrafted "school bus". Each of us kids took turns harnessing and hitching the horses and driving the bus. During the 40 below zero weather none of us liked this part of the task, but we were happy to get inside the school bus. Even though it jerked us around all the way to school, it was at least shelter from the elements. We could laugh and enjoy "kid talk" with our friends on the way to school.

I recall one blustery day over at the Derrickson place, I was loading crates of milk for delivery. On my first trip to the bus, the wind caught the door and slammed it against my elbow, embedding a previously unnoticed rusty spike right into the joint—a direct hit on my "crazy bone". The scars serve as my reminder to pay attention to details.

Most mornings were uneventful. We left the yard for the Don Williams place, approximately four miles north of our spread. We back-tracked to the main gravel highway, turned left and proceeded another two and a quarter miles into town. There were times when the snowdrifts would be frozen over, but the horses still broke through belly-deep. All the encouragement us weary little milkmen could muster wasn't enough to urge the ponies, pulling the great weight of the old hack, to lurch out of the snowdrifts. We understood that prairie ponies were expected to do the work of Clydesdales, just as us little kids were expected to do the work of brawny adult males. That's the way it was out on the prairie during the Depression.

After the horses had freed themselves from the drifts, we proceeded on our way to town. By this time, us kids were near frozen to our seats, and icicles had formed around the horses' chin hairs. It was so cold that frost covered their manes, tails, and harness knobs. We lumbered in our embarrassingly ugly wine-red rig that "jack-knifed" its way down icy Main Street. A loose trailer hitch caused our conveyance to jerk from side to side even though the team and wagon pole stayed straight ahead.

We turned left up Schoolhouse Hill. I dropped off the passengers at the school door, then drove the hack back down the hill to Marsten's dilapidated shack of a barn. I tied the horses to the manger filled with hay, where they would remain until school was out.

Once the horses were constrained, it was time for me, the miniature milkman, to set about the delivery of my valuable product. My first delivery would be across the knoll, down by the railroad tracks to the section boss' house. Then across the side street by the drugstore and finally to the Jensen house up the hill by the school. Simon Jensen ran the autobody machine shop in town. Pa had said of Simon and his Pa, Dick, "If they were livestock, I'd judge 'em to be 'prime' stock." Pa's meaning was they were the very best kind of folks.

By the time all the milk and cream was delivered, I was a mess. Jar lids had loosened, and great irregular streams of milk had run down my coat and sleeves onto my overshoes, which had enough metal latches on them to build a Sherman tank. The white rivers of milk down the front of my clothing reminded me of the explosive overflow of foam from Pa's homemade beer. My clothes looked kind of like a frozen backdrop of Niagara Falls. While I was outside in the cold, it wasn't so bad, but once I was inside, and my coat began to thaw out in the cloakroom, it started smelling as bad as the slop pail in our kitchen.

Since I was already tardy, I couldn't go to the gymnasium to wash up. Pa didn't appreciate the tardy marks on my report card, even though he knew that milk deliveries took some time. That's pretty much how my day always started—frustration and aggravation.

I recall one day overhearing a girl whisper to the teacher, "Be sure you don't hang my coat next to hers, or I'll smell as bad as she does!" I told Ma when I got home. She said, "Don't pay her no mind, 'uppercrust' people never had to do a lick in their entire lives. They jus' think they're better'n us." There were many hurtful lessons like that in my life. No one had heard of "peer pressure" then, but us Carter kids certainly experienced it. I remember Ma saying, "Feel bad about it if you want to, or jus' consider that they don't know no better." I think "they" finally got over it, and we all became lifelong friends.

Popcorn And Hollow Legs — We grew our own field corn and popcorn, so every once in a while Ma would make a batch of popcorn for us in the evening. She popped the kernels in rendered pork fat, or sometimes in real butter in a large cast iron skillet over the open flame. If we had cream that we hadn't needed to sell, we made butter out of it and could use some of that on the popcorn along with salt. We'd listen intently for the first sounds of popping, then look at each other and giggle in anticipation of the finished treat. Ma clucked her tongue and said, "You kids seem to be sportin' hollow legs." It was true. We roamed the kitchen most of the time looking into every corner, hoping that some morsel of food might have escaped someone's appetite. It seemed like we never got enough to eat.

Ma's little popcorn shuckers, as she called us kids, had helped to pick the corn in the late summer. We laid it out on an old screen door or stretched wire to dry. When it was thoroughly dried, we rubbed the corn cobs together over a large pan, causing the golden or white kernels—depending on the variety we had planted—to fly into the metal pan in streams.

About the only other food that was available for snacking on was potatoes. When we couldn't have popcorn, our only choices for between meal snacks were either a plate of fried potatoes or a bowl of beans. There was no candy, chips or luscious cakes for the Carter brood.

Joy Rides In The Bobsled — In the winter my family would occasionally venture out across country in the bobsled. Our wagon box was fastened to two sets of divided bobsled runners and pulled by a team of horses. There was a pole between the horses which guided the front set of runners. The second set was fastened to the first for maneuverability. Ma and Pa would load up the foot warmers, mounds of quilts, and bundled kids for a winter journey. It took lots of gear to keep us warm during the trip. Footwarmers, or "hot rocks" as we called them, were rocks which had been heated in the stove then wrapped in old rag rugs. Homemade quilts were draped over our laps to help keep the heat in and our legs from freezing. Our mittens were fastened to a string which slipped through our coat sleeves. The mittens on a string prevented us from becoming the Three Little Kittens who lost their mittens. Our overshoes were made of rubber which covered our feet and legs all the way to the knee. They had metal latches every inch or so. We felt like our overshoes had more metal on them than the hay bailer.

Sometimes we used the bobsled to go to school functions and plays, square dances and other community events. When we reached the schoolhouse, the horses were placed in the barn on the schools grounds. There they would be protected from the elements while we were at the "get together". Inside the schoolhouse, all the trappings of cold weather, coats, hats, mittens and overshoes would be lined up around the room. Almost like at our house—clothes everywhere!

Even though it sounds like we had lots of fun in the bobsled, it was rarely used for entertainment type travel. It was mostly used for hauling winter supplies for the family, feed for the animals and our cream and eggs to neighbors and townsfolk for sale and bartering purposes.

Fantan At Uncle Bert's — Whenever anyone was brave enough to invite our family over for an evening, us kids would be so excited that we could hardly contain ourselves. When the Carters converged on anyone's home, it was similar to inviting the militia to our little town hall. A trip to Uncle Bert's and Aunt Peg's was a treat for us.

As the sled squeaked over the frozen blanket of snow, the harnesses jingled, the horses snorted. The smell of their sweat, as well their other smells assailed our nostrils. We giggled, as kids will, quipping, "The air is so cold, why don't them fumes freeze before we have to smell 'em?" Ma yelled back at us, "Why don't you little hellions straighten up and quiet down before we git to Aunt Peg's and Uncle Bert's? If ya don't, this'll be yer last outin' for the winter!" Knowing how devastatingly boring it would be not to get off the farm for the entire winter, we straightened up immediately. For the rest of the way we were quiet and sat back to enjoy the ride.

Down past the monotonous flatland of the cornfield, out the east gate, and over the winding one track road through the snow-covered hills we bounced. Along the way, a few jackrabbits hopped for cover under icy bushes and weasels scurried along, hunting their holes. The three mile ride was cold but so exciting.

An hour after leaving our homestead we pulled up at Uncle Bert's. Diminutive Aunt Peg was waiting at the door, kerosene lamp in hand. While the men put the horses in the barn the rest of us took off our wraps.

After initial greetings and small talk the adults settled around the large round oak table for a game of cards called Fantan. It was a very popular game back in those days. Since money was virtually non-existent, chips for the anti-up were wooden matches with large red sulfur-filled bulbs on one end. The cards were dealt and the adults settled in for a good game.

As usual, I became bored playing with the rest of the kids and putting jigsaw puzzles together. I decided I'd hang around Pa, hoping to be invited to "set in", as Pa called it. Ma let me know that I was too young to sit in, but she pulled up a captains chair between her and Pa. I was told that if I wanted to watch, I would have to sit still and be quiet.

Just watching soon became tedious, so I began to bunch matches in my small right hand to see how many I could grip at once. I had all the sulfur ends pointing downward. Thoughtlessly I began to rotate the fistful of matches around on the pocked table top. Suddenly, the friction ignited all of them simultaneously. The flames and the cloud of sulfur fumes startled everyone. Pa jumped out of his seat and yelled, "Drop the matches. Drop the matches!"

I was locked in a frozen moment of fright! Ma and Aunt Peg were trying to grab the cards and the remaining unlit matches, while Pa and Uncle Bert tried to make me loosen my grip on the burning bundle. I finally released the cluster of flame—but not until the table was blistered, not to mention the palm of my hand. Pa was concerned about me, but mad as h#$l. He yelled, "Why can't you be a lady like yer cousins?" *Well,* I thought, *I can't be just like anybody else "cuz I'm me*! I knew I had made Ma and Pa angry and had embarrassed them in front of my aunt and uncle. Aunt Peg was irritated about her table. I certainly had ruined the card game and put a damper on Ma and Pa's evening out.

When things finally calmed down, Aunt Peg served us a typical farm buffet of homemade headcheese and liver sausage. There was also deviled eggs, homemade cottage cheese, homebaked white bread, freshly churned butter, coffeecake and pie. She always had two or three kinds of home canned pickles. My favorite ones were a recipe from my Aunt Liza Carter Swanson called chow-chow pickles. The evening ended, and I felt all was forgiven—that is until we were all in the wagon headed for home. I found out then that Ma and Pa's idea of "forgiven" was pretty different than mine!

Thumbing And Wishing — During long winter evenings once the kerosene lamps were lit, we would gather in the sitting room, thumbing through the *Monkey Ward* catalog, wishing for all the nice things we saw. Pa would look through the seed catalog, wishing for an early thaw and enough cash to buy spring seed. While the rest of us thumbed and wished, Ma usually darned socks, patched clothes or crocheted rag rugs. Sometimes she would rip seams in garments that had been handed down to us from relatives. From the hand-me-down clothing, she would tailor clothes for us. From the outgrown clothes of the older kids, she would make wearables for the younger kids cutting around the worn parts.

Some evenings Ma would engage all of us in helping her to card wool for making the following winter's quilts. A hand-held carder resembled today's wire-tooth hair brush. The teeth were shorter and the flat board portion from which the teeth protruded measured about 4x6 inches.

Carders had wooden handles. A bit of wool was placed on one carder, then another carder was dragged across it several times. The result would be sections of soft, fluffy, fleecy wool. We filled baskets full when we carded wool. Since polyfil or batting wasn't available in those days, WWI army blankets and CCC blankets were used for quilt filling.

If she wasn't sewing, crocheting or carding, Ma would be removing buttons, snaps or other fasteners from garments that were beyond repair. My sisters and I remember with fondness, playing with the pretty shapes, colors and sizes of buttons in Ma's button jar.

Christmas At The Carters — It was December, but there was no peal of church bells, no visit from neighbors and no money for necessities, let alone for purchasing gifts. The Montgomery Ward catalog was our Christmas wish book. It came to us country folks long before the first snow fell. Us kids would sit around the fire all evening thumbing through the dirty, ripped, dog-eared, pages. Myself and each of my siblings would tear out a picture of the present we wished for the most. Not that we would have gotten it—but the wishing part was fun. Ma said it was more fun to wish than to actually get, anyway. Us kids kind of wanted to test the theory out for ourselves though.

Sitting around the heating stove on hooked rugs in the circle of light cast from the flickering kerosene lamp, we entertained ourselves telling stories, coloring and singing songs we had learned in school. In among the Christmas songs, we started getting silly, and a few funny ones got into the act. Songs like *Old Man Tucker* that we had learned to sing in "rounds" at school. The words went something like this:

> Old man Tucker's a funny old man,
> Washes his face in a frying pan.
> Combs his hair with a wagon wheel,
> Walks with a toothpick in his heel.

Git down the road with Old Man Tucker.

We stopped singing *Ring Around the Rosie* when Ma told us that it was really a funeral song that was first sung by a street cleaner who collected the bodies of those who had died of the Black Plague. When we stared at Ma in shock and disbelief, she decided she should change the subject to something more pleasant, so she began to count to ten in German. We broke out into uncontrollable giggles and began to mimic our Norwegian neighbor boy's brogue. Instead of "two goes into four", we chanted, "two gazinta four."

Before too long, the pushing and shoving would begin, because someone would snatch the wrong color crayon, or write on someone else's tablet. Sometimes, if one of my older brothers was playing solitaire, one of the little kids would jump up and *accidentally* flip a card out of position. Such antics would lead to a reprimand from Pa. He didn't allow the older boys to hit us little kids. Of course it was another story when Pa wasn't around.

Ma and Pa had been our only Santa Clauses throughout childhood. Ma sat by the heating stove night after night sewing secret things for Christmas. Our Christmases were exciting to us, and they were as good as what all our neighbors had at the time. They were made more perfect because Ma toiled day and night, sewing and fashioning toys and gifts. She created things like sewing boxes made in the shape of overstuffed chairs covered with gingham. The puffy pincushion seats lifted, displaying assortments of embroidery threads, tiny stork scissors, needles, and thimbles.

Ma created monkeys and other animals from mens' tweed-looking work socks, which she had ordered from the catalog. She made Raggedy Ann dolls out of brightly colored fabrics and embroidered unique expressions on each of their faces for us girls. Pa, Bill and Uncle Archie, Ma's brother, usually whittled whistles and flutes or animal statues for the boys. The menfolks always appreciated "long-handle" underwear and work socks.

One Christmas, Ma designed string puppet dolls that had stocking caps with red tassels for us girls. She later showed us how to make our own marionettes for a school program. We made up dialogue for the performance. We practiced throwing our voices and changing our range of voice to represent different characters. We made an apple crate stage complete with draw curtains. Our fabric marionettes had stuffed heads with painted faces and strings attached to the joints. With a tug on a string and a twist of the wrist our marionette would come alive on our little stage. Ma sewed a pebble into each foot to make a loud tapping sound when we maneuvered the puppet into a dance step.

She taught us girls to make dolls from clothespins and hollyhock blossoms, and to fashion a dollhouse from a cardboard box. At times we may even have talked Ma out of some leftover wallpaper for the interior decor. The boys constructed tractors and other vehicles from wooden spoons, rubber bands and matchsticks. Each had an arsenal of handmade slingshots of various sizes.

Sitting around the stove, we played card games—Rook, Whist, Fantan and Bridge, to name a few. Sometimes Ma entertained us by recounting tales of taffy-pulling and counter-hopping at the maple sugar resort in Minnesota.

When it was tree trimming time, Pa would bring in the tree, which had been planted in a washtub filled with dirt. It seemed that our tree was always squashed in the railroad car with a mountainous load of other trees, so its quality usually left a lot to be desired.

While Pa and the boys stabilized the tree, Ma and us girls scurried around collecting red and green construction paper to make paper chain garlands. Ma helped us make paste out of flour and water to glue our paper pieces together.

Some of the kids were allowed to pop popcorn in a covered skillet on the front of the stove, with a reminder to shake the pan vigorously to prevent the kernels from burning and sticking to the bottom. When it cooled, it would be used for our cranberry and popcorn garlands. Heavy thread was treated with beeswax in preparation of stringing the colorful objects.

We cut foil stars from Pa's empty Peerless packages which would be used with the construction paper on our garlands. When everything was ready, we stationed ourselves around the big table. Some of us strung popcorn and cranberries, while others made paper chains—first a red link, then a green, then a link of silver Peerless foil.

When all the decorations were finished, we carefully draped chains over every available nail, curtain rod and doorway. The spindly Christmas tree was laden with the cranberry and popcorn garlands, candles in tin clip-on holders, a few garlands of red, green, and silver crepe paper and foil and an assortment of Grandma Walters' old tree ornaments. The candles would get hot enough to melt the frost on the window, but never did God allow the tree to catch fire. Whittled wooden jumping jacks and whistles were a big part of our Christmas ornament collection.

Our stockings were hung several days before Christmas—not *by the chimney with care*—but from ten-penny nails pounded into the window sill in the sittin' room. Our names were scribbled on tablet paper and pinned on the toes.

Our big celebration always took place on Christmas day in the sitting room. We would gather around the potbelly stove to watch the blazing fire, tracing the occasional sparks that escaped through the vents where the isinglass had been.

Later in the evening, we would pop another batch of popcorn over the open stove lid in the cast-iron frying pan. A corncob was placed through the ring on the tin lid for easy lifting, and a tea towel was draped around the cast-iron handle. The skillet clattered, metal against metal, when we shook it back and forth across the stove lids. The sound of the popping corn and the smell of the melting butter was warm and comforting.

Although we didn't have much money, Christmas was a joyous time for my family. Ma and Pa did their best to provide the excitement and wonder of Christmas for us. Aunt Cora Carter, one of our more affluent relatives, always sent a box containing candy, apples, oranges and nuts. The goodies were a rare treat for us. Since life had offered us no opportunity to be spoiled, we were always overjoyed and appreciative of anything we received.

The Great Depression
And Family Tragedy

The Great Depression — Many of us are well acquainted with Friday the 13th and all of the mysterious tales that accompany the date. But how many of us have witnessed first-hand a Friday as dark as the Black Friday of October 1929?

When I was nearing six years of age, we moved to Medina so Ma could go to work at the Buckwalter Hotel as a cook. Shirley reminded us about how we had to take the baby, Winfred, I believe, across the alley to the hotel where Ma would nurse him, then we would take him home and care for him. Pa and the oldest three kids worked the Huggarude place. There were no jobs, no money and not many goods.

How bad were the days of the great Depression? Bad enough that even the rich were poor. Ma had told us that "Unscrupulous bankers mishandled and hoarded funds." Many financiers committed suicide. Farmers were forced off their property by Federal Land Offices. One could measure the seriousness of the times by sighting many examples Men stole other men's horses, cattle and sheep. Some cut the hay from another man's property. Some stole food, eggs and chickens. Some even fought over free manure.

Hard to believe, I know. But I recall grown adult males fighting over a barn full of sheep manure that a farmer named Kincaid was giving away, free for the taking. The sheep manure was packed three to four feet deep and had been trampled rock-solid for several winters. News about the "free for the cutting" manure took the community by storm.

By the time my Pa and brothers got to Kincaid's place, a long procession had already formed. Dozens of wagons and wagon masters with hired hands came from all over to get the free fuel. A fisticuffs free-for-all ensued. Unmusical snorts, grunts, groans and bloody noses followed. Mens' shirts were ripped and suspenders slashed. Obviously, the treasure wouldn't be won by shouting obscenities, nor by gentleman's agreement. Pa and the boys hung back, because they didn't want to fight. Pa said, "Fighting makes men look like they carry their brains in the seats of their pants." *Pa ought'a know,* I thought.

The shouting and fighting spooked teams of horses, causing them to run away. Their owners started to chase them and just kept on going. I don't recall if anyone truly won the fight. Ma had her own theory about the ruffians, "Bunch of damn morons." I thought, *Ma can be pretty verbal at times.*

The Great Depression is said to have begun with the catastrophic collapse of the stock market prices on the New York Stock Exchange in October 1929. Besides ruining many thousand individual investors, the decline in the value of assets greatly strained the banks and other financial institutions.

The failure of so many banks, combined with a general nationwide lack of confidence in the economy led to much-reduced levels of spending, demand and production. The result was drastically rising unemployment. Many broken-spirited men rode the rails in packs in search of employment in the larger cities. My Pa rode the rails West to work on the railroad in Montana.

In the late '20s and early '30s field harvest took a dive along with farming prices. Even our old hog, Ichabod was worth only $2.00 on the hoof. Since it was going to cost that much to ship him, Pa decided to fatten him up for sustenance for the family. Food riots were common throughout the United States. Despair missed no one, but the midwestern United States was hardest hit.

President Franklin Delano Roosevelt implemented a massive number of programs to promote recovery from the depressed conditions. His projects were known as the ABC Programs. The TVA (Tennessee Valley Authority), the WPA (Work Projects Administration), the CCC (Civilian Conservation Corps), the AAA (Agricultural Adjustment Administration), and the FERA (Federal Emergency Relief Act), were just a few.

The CCC program was designed to put jobless unmarried men to work, and was credited with helping 2.5 million men survive the Depression. It taught them job skills, and they accomplished thousands of construction and other projects across the nation, from forestry and park restoration to flood control and disaster relief. Regulars got $30 a month, with $25 being sent home to help support families. The financial help was sorely needed by most families.

Clothing During Depression Days — Our dress code on the farm was geared to the livestock and potato patch functions. We wore ragged and faded hand-me-down overalls to grub in like full-fledged hired hands—only without the pay. I remember how Ma patched, darned and stitched to keep our clothes functional—not pretty or beautiful, mind you—just functional. That meant the clothes covered the main parts of our bodies. I believe she probably had a thimble for every finger. I look back and wonder where she got the time to care for the kids, the farm, the house and the animals, and still do all the sewing, patching, darning and cooking.

It's clear that clothing selections were no problem at our house. Each of us had one dark outfit, sponged once a week, whether it needed it or not. To dry them we threw them over the wire that held the upstairs rooms' curtain partitions. If my clothing was ever laundered, the fact has completely slipped my mind.

As the middle child, clothing for me was like everything else—hand-me-down. The time had passed for being pampered like the younger kids. If I was ever pampered, I forgot that part, too. I hadn't yet reached the time when I needed decent clothes for town school like the older kids, so I reaped the full benefit of make-do or do without.

In a different time and place as the proverbial middle child, I would have been psychoanalyzed to death. But Pa counseled me, "All you have to do is think about somethin' else." He maintained that what you set your mind to, good or bad, you always get. *Nonetheless, Pa,* I thought, *you don't know my secret thoughts. You don't know how I feel 'bout my made-over clothes.* I perceived those who Pa called "our betters" to be "know-it-alls" because they had fancy clothes and big houses. Pa's precepts gave us courage, but they didn't create self esteem.

Ma made me my first dress when I was thirteen, for eighth grade graduation. With it I wore my very own brand new shoes. On dressmaking day Ma got out an old piece of wrapping paper, smoothed out the wrinkles and pinned it to the garments I was wearing. She then snipped out a pattern, using my own measurements. While she busied herself oiling and threading the treadle machine, she sent me upstairs to look in the dirty clothes pile for a chocolate brown dress that had previously been made over twice and worn by two of my sisters.

The clothes were in a mountainous pile of the very dirty, the "clean" dirties—these could be worn a second time if need be—and the carelessly tossed "duds for make-over." I began sorting at the edge of the pile and finally dragged the rumpled brown dress to the surface. The right side was like crepe, but Ma was going to turn it shiny-side-out for me. Ma said, "The brown satin sheen of the inside will go good with yer taffy colored hair."

She doused the dress in warm water, rinsed it and hung it out to dry on our clothesline that sagged between the corner of the house and the chicken coop roof. When the dress was dry, Ma ironed it with a glad iron heated on the range top. Then I ripped the seams open. When that was finished, she patiently restructured the dress, reversing the fabric. When the dress was completed, Ma said, "It looks real rich." I felt proud when I smoothed the new dress over my gangly body. Ma accused me of "sashaying around in front of the tarnished old mirror," like I was "queen of the lumber wagon set." Although I would have liked new fabric, this was pretty good, sturdy material—even with the shiny side out.

Ma made some of our clothing out of old printed gristmill flour sacks. Cow feed, chicken feed, flour and many other items came in these multi-colored bags. Ma removed the string from the truly pretty bags and rolled it into big balls for future use. The flour sacks were washed and pressed. On our next trip to town, Ma would try to match the material of the flour sacks with some new cloth, so she would have enough yardage to sew up some much needed clothing for us girls. Sometimes she got lucky and found a good match. The flour sacks that weren't so pretty got boiled in lye water for hours, then hung out on the clothesline for days to be bleached in the blazing sun.

We used flour sacks to make underslips, bloomers, kitchen curtains, tea towels, tablecloths, pillowcases, hand

128

towels and pot holders. Torn bits of sacking made handkerchiefs—both large and small. Ma saved all small scraps—nothing was wasted. When she had collected enough bits of cloth, she sewed them all together in long strips, and crocheted them into rag rugs.

Most women used flour sacks to make utility aprons. The aprons served as alternatives for a clean dress if company showed up. Ma's apron provided a good place for a shy kid to coyly hide from strangers, or as cloth to wipe the tears and runny noses of her brood. Ma also used her aprons to wrap around her arms to keep the chill off, and to carry baby chicks from the nest, eggs from the henhouse, and corn and vegetables from the garden. Aprons served as banners to country women, identifying them as farm wives. I don't know about anyone else, but my own apron—not made from flour sacks—now hangs on a nail in the kitchen just like Ma's used to.

The Family Cobbler — The '30s were hard times for 13 to 15 million Americans. The hardest hit was the middle rural area of the United States, where we lived. The motto of the day was, "Use it up, wear it out, make do or do without." We were an imaginative lot who followed the example set by our parents in our "make do or do without" notions. We patched holes in our shoes with everything from cardboard to inner tubing—when it was available. Now and then we found an unpatchable inner tube from an old junk car and cut portions of the tube for garters, rubber bands and shoe sole patches. When the sole broke loose, we used a wide cutting of an inner tube to stretch around the foot and the shoe. This would temporarily hold the sole in place until Pa could afford leather and nails to make decent soles.

Out of necessity, Pa practiced the art of cobbling. With only the bare collection of tools, he repaired shoes for his brood: a cast iron shoe-last, an awl, shoe nails, beeswax, a large curved needle, extra heavy thread, a carpenter style claw hammer and a sharp jackknife. Several evenings during the year he settled himself and his equipment into a corner by the kitchen range. He would tear off old sole portions and trace around them on thick leather or a thinned down tire tread, then soak the leather in water to make it more pliable. With the shoe-last held between his knees, a hammer in hand, and a mouthful of small shoe tacks, a tap, tap, tap began. If it was wintertime, Ma kept the range stuffed with wood and scraps of old tires to keep the cobbler comfortable while he worked away on those fiercely cold nights.

Fancy Footwear — Have you ever walked an eight foot circle a dozen times in new shoes that pinch your feet? Well, that's what we did. "Don't step off the rug," Ma would say, "or Montgomery Ward won't take them back." Sometimes we would lie and say they didn't pinch, because we knew that if the shoes were sent back we wouldn't have shoes for two or three more weeks. Ma ordered the shoes in a surprisingly simple way: she applied the "trace around the foot" method, and the foot-print paper became the order blank! When the soles wore out, Ma traced around the foot again, this time on inner tubing. The inner tubing trace was inserted into the shoe—and Voila!—The life of the shoe was extended. Once again inner tubing saved the day!

Shoes For Elves And Giants — Care-package shoes which we sometimes got from relatives, were the old fashioned high-button shoes with the pointed toes and hour glass-shaped wooden heels. Ma just took the hatchet and chopped the heels down. If they didn't come out even, which was often the case, she just kept whacking away until only nubs were left. The results—always uneven in height. When we walked in them, the toes of the shoes pointed skyward. The ornery kids at school called them "elf shoes." I was painfully aware that my shoes never met the expectations of my peers.

Once when we received a package containing shoes, Ma doled out a pair of sturdy nursing shoes to me that were two sizes too large and they were white. To my way of thinking this was totally unacceptable. To fix the problem I painted them with black enamel. When I finished they looked so new and shiny. I took my first proud steps in them, but to my dismay, the enamel cracked in a bunch of places. The shoes looked like a pair of zebras! I ended up wearing those little zebras to school for two years. It was during my most impressionable and sensitive years as a child. I was devastated—ashamed and embarrassed.

The Union Suit — In the winter we all had to wear the pesky union suit—also called long johns. I wondered what age I would have to be before I could discard the irritating things. They were acceptable while I was in primary school, but during the upper grades, I always resented the creases at the ankles, the bulging knees and the constantly wrinkled ribbed stockings. My folks said colorful bloomers were out of the question—they were just too impractical.

I knew I couldn't win this battle, so I pursued another avenue: half way to school, I would stop, roll the underwear legs up under my skirt, then secure them with a garter of half-inch inner tubing high on my legs. I sat in class for eight hours each day feeling the tight tubing. It was like wearing a blood pressure cuff all day long. Be assured, I let the underwear legs down to their full length before I got home!

The Crazy House — As a kid I was constantly plagued by horrible things that I had overheard while eavesdropping on the older folks. Back in those days, the axiom, "Kids should be seen and not heard"—at least not until they were asked to sing or dance—was taken quite literally. I remember Ma, Pa, and the neighbors bantering about incidents that had occurred at the "crazy house" in

Jamestown, and about the kid down south who couldn't be stopped from beating his head against the walls.

They discussed the leper colony at Crystal Springs, about ten miles across the prairie. They went on about the sorrowful, diseased people who were hidden away in the colony well off the one-track road. Though bothered by the conversations, I knew I wasn't allowed to ask questions—questions that may have helped ease my mind. I had heard that they were so sick and it scared me. Ma said, "I s'pose they were caught by the grappling hook of God, and are in bondage to decay."

Now it is known that leprosy is a chronic, mildly communicable disease. Old wives' tales had once made it out to be a highly communicable disease. The efforts to control leprosy have hardly been brilliant. According to *The Home Doctor*, R. Scott Stevenson, Prentice Hall Press, and E*ncyclopedia Britannica*, "Hansen's Disease is the medical term used for this acid fast microorganism. During the 19th century, the Scandinavian Peninsula experienced a fairly extensive outbreak, especially in Norway."

Death in Small Doses — When I was a child, so many things unnerved me by day and literally haunted me by night. Out on the plains life gave us much opportunity to witness the death of tiny animals. The demise of varmints like weasels, mice and rats caught in our traps, or gophers that we snared for a penny per tail, didn't particularly bother me because they were nonverbal creatures.

In spite of my feelings that the varmints' deaths were of little account, I found myself always rationalizing that it was okay because we needed the pelts and tails for our livelihood. It was simple! We slaughtered animals for food and skins so that we could survive!

The newborn lambs, calves and chicks that were unable to survive on their own did disturb my emotional empathy. Perhaps in some way I felt that I could communicate with them. My indirect participation in their deaths may have served as an introductory training in how to overcome human emotions.

Ma said, "When you git things on a small scale, they're more manageable." In the early days, country folks repeated old wives' tales so often that I believed them to be forebodings.

Stark Reality On The Farm — Tragedies involving farm animals were difficult for me to surmount. An episode that set my emotions into a tailspin was the time when Uncle Bert's cow fell into the well. Cows are nosey creatures by nature. For some reason the cow had ventured into the well house. The platform over the well was only strong enough to hold a single person. The ample weight of the animal broke the platform, and the cow went plunging into the well head first, breaking her neck and all four legs.

Neighbors assisted in hoisting the animal out of the well using a winch, a team of horses and a sling. The well was siphoned, but it had been contaminated. For many months after the event the family had to haul their drinking water from the neighbors' well. As I recall, the contaminated water was boiled and used strictly for washing clothes. Haunting thoughts of the dead cow lingered, and caused me much stress for years after the incident.

When I was seven years old, a neighbor, George Halverson, had penned his mule in the barn with the horses. Apparently a horse had bitten the mule. When the other horses smelled the blood, they began kicking and biting the mule. The horses had reverted to their innate characteristics, as their animalistic behavior raged on. In the morning the mule was found dead. This was a disturbing scenario for a seven year old girl. Understanding was difficult at that age, or perhaps at any age.

The wild country in which I lived proved to be my training ground for overcoming great fears and sorrowful emotions, and hopefully, for building courage and brotherly love.

The Dust Bowl Days —The Dust Bowl was the name given to the Great Plains region devastated by drought in the '30s depression-ridden America. Most early settlers used the land for livestock grazing until agricultural mechanization combined with high grain prices during World War I enticed farmers to plow up millions of acres of natural grass cover to plant wheat. When drought struck from 1934 to 1937, the soil lacked the stronger root system of grass as an anchor, so the winds easily picked up the loose topsoil and swirled it into dense dust clouds called "black blizzards". The dust storms wreaked havoc, choking cattle and pasture lands. The wind literally picked up the rich top soil and whisked it from one state to the next. North Dakota dirt and dust landed in central Wisconsin. Animals suffered, and many farmers had to vacate their farms, which had been buried under the dirt and dust.

People everywhere hired men to "witch" for new water for their livestock. Often they placed a winch over the well-site to pull up buckets of dirt. Much of the time they had to dig down 60 feet before they found water. They installed wooden curbing against the outer side walls. Most farmers used hand pumps, but installed 52-foot windmills if they could afford them.

In the summer of 1937, there were few crops and very little hay. Because of resulting poor economic times, farmers had to sell off their animals at give-away prices. Most of them were forced to go to work for the WPA.

Our Family's Greatest Tragedy — When I was nearing twelve years of age, a tragic day, which shall live in my mind forever, began when our mongrel dog, Carlos, again howled skyward. He wouldn't be quieted. Ma leaped into a state of panic, perceiving something bad was about to happen. "Every time a dog howls, it means someone's gonna die."

In mid-March of 1935, at our Chase Lake homestead, a numbing catastrophe tore through the midst of my family. My brother and constant companion, Cameron Earl, age nine, began having convulsions.

We had just finished a meal of commercially canned meat and tomatoes. Ten cans of the food had been issued to my family a week prior to the incident. The food was part of a state program called FERA (Federal Emergency Relief Act). My family, as well as many of our neighbors, received commodities as part of a program to feed the poor. FERA was often referred to as "Poor Relief".

Never had I known a time when Ma's home remedies had failed, but this time, all the mustard water and sweet cream given to promote vomiting didn't work at all. It was after supper, as I recall, that Ma and Pa were hovering around their bed just off the sittin' room. We knew this had to be a seriously grievous time, because never, after the age of two years, were any of us kids allowed in their room. Now our Cammie was in there, lying on their bed, very sick and in a convulsive state. Us kids sat motionless on the ebony leather settee in the sitting room, fearing the worst. Not a word was spoken. I thought pleadingly, *God, don't you know that Short and me are not only brother and sister, but best friends? Please make him well.*

The convulsions worsened then they finally ceased. A deadly silence blanketed the room. Pa came into the sittin' room. He wasn't a church-going man. He didn't cry, he just hung his head and slapped his overall-clad thighs in agony. Ma wept sorrowfully. She couldn't bring herself to leave Cammie's side. Us kids remained silent and transfixed, where we sat lined up like wooden soldiers on the settee.

One of my brothers went to fetch Rachel Sand, a neighbor who lived beyond the Jenkins's farm, over by

Cobblestone Hill. I had often thought of her as the "stone woman." When she came in answer to our sad news, she looked old, more feeble and heartsick—yet not so much as a gesture escaped her that could have been construed as pain or sympathy. She just walked in, crossed the room in front of us, and stopped at Ma's old upright piano near the front door. Her large black piercing eyes had turned sorrowful and compassionate. She sat warrior-straight on the rickety piano stool, her gnarled brown weather-beaten fingers on the stained piano keys. She uttered not a word, but began to play the most melancholy music we had ever heard. Rachel played on and on, *Star of the East*, *The Old Rugged Cross*, and *When The Roll Is Called Up Yonder*. I became convinced, there in the dim flicker of light from the kerosene lamp, that Rachel's leathery skin aglow like foxfire had illuminated her into a true angel. Her taut black pompadour, in my young eyes, became a gold crown. I was hearing the music of the spheres reverberating through this lady.

Defenseless and beaten, we all sat watching the fire flickering its images on the walls and ceiling, listening to this heavenly music, and wondering how we would go on without our beloved Cammie. Ma said later, "That's what death and trauma does—it forces us into new beginnings." Little did we know the horror had only begun.

It was very late that night. The flames of the fire had died out, just like the flame of life within little Cammie. We hadn't yet been able to retire for the night because other family members were beginning to take ill. Three more children, my sister Gladyce and brother Winfred and baby Duane had to be hospitalized. Before the ordeal was over, my Pa had also broken out with infectious boils. The attending physician suspected food poisoning. Pa groaned, "Can't understand it, everything has gone haywire." Ma whispered to us later, "we kept looking at all you kids and wonderin' which one of you would be next."

The Funerals — We all walked around like zombies. The very feet of my entire family had been knocked out from under them. It was as if we had collectively slipped into another dimension, preventing us from our own individual thoughts. We moved through the day and evening as through a veil of mist, waiting for the curtain to be lifted. No doubt about it, my family was caught in the jaws of nature, and nobody knew who had set the trap.

Cammie's funeral drew much attention in the county, perhaps for two reasons. The first reason was probably because of a true feeling of compassion for our loss, and the second was that many of our neighbors were also receiving the government-issued food.

I can recall that day without effort. We were all dazed, and our hearts were doing strange things that we couldn't understand. We seemed thrust into a different world.

Blanche was ironing clothes for the family to wear. I charged up the stairs and sorted through the pile of clean-dirty clothing. I found a flowery dress. I put it on and hopped down the stairs. I was glad to be going to town, but detesting the reason for going. My life had been a hum-drum existence thus far. Now I was aggrieved to the point of incoherent thoughts and actions.

Blanche caught sight of me, and chastised me for my choice of dress. She wouldn't allow me to wear the dress. She said, "Yer gonna wear black to the funeral. Now go back up and put on yer sponged school dress and yer black stockings." I was already sad about Cammie, but now it was even worse. They weren't going to let me dress up pretty to see him for the last time. My lower lip quivered, and there was a lump in my throat as I headed back upstairs to change.

Ma and Pa were at the hospital with Gladyce, Winfred and Duane. The hospital staff wouldn't allow Ma to nurse Duane for fear she may also be contaminated with food poisoning. Ma agonized later, "I think the baby cried himself

137

to death. I could hear him crying from way down the hall. He cried day and night for a week." She was tormented, as we all were. It was certainly an experience of medical mayhem that none of us wished to experience ever again.

The church was cold and unfamiliar to me. The sound of the late comers' booted heels on the plank flooring made me feel there was a lack of respect for our bereavement. Once everyone was seated, I could hear only the sounds of our grief and the minister's voice. I watched the coffin intently, hoping it wasn't too late for Cammie to change his mind and come home with me. I knew all too well what it was like when an animal died, but I wasn't too sure whether people could come back if they wanted to. I was frightful when I heard the minister say that God never allows a man to die unless he has fulfilled his mission here. As any little girl would, I wondered, *what was Cammie's mission?*

The preacher painted a word-picture of a better land beyond. *Lot you know*, I thought to myself. I silently questioned why this had to happen. What did we do? Why did our lives have to change so drastically? Hadn't Pa helped our neighbors all he could? After all, I thought, we're not a cold spirited lot. We were trained by Pa, who often repeated, "You just got to learn to tough things out, but ya gotta help yer neighbor, too."

I looked at the bouquets of yellow snapdragons and pink prairie roses on top of the casket. *Cammie would like those. I bet he would have liked some of the blue, pink and red bachelor buttons I helped plant by the front door, too.*

The funeral service lasted long enough for us to drench our torn napkin-size flour sack handkerchiefs. When it ended everyone stood waiting for us to go forward. I was strongly urged to walk to the front and view Cammie, but I balked. It took only a tap my the shoulder from Pa to encourage me decide to go and peek in the casket. After the funeral, Pa made us kids go over to Mrs. Westman's house. I didn't want to leave Cammie. Tears streamed down my face.

A few hours after Cammie's funeral, my sister, Blanche Mae, lapsed into a diabetic coma from shock. She succumbed March 17, 1935, at the Jamestown Hospital. My eighteen month old brother, Duane, had also lost his battle to live that same day. The funeral for Blanche and Duane was held at the Medina School Auditorium, where crowds came to pay their respects to a Carter family member for the second time in a week. They were buried in a common grave. The devastation showed on Ma and Pa's faces as they left the grave site.

Before Cameron was buried, doctors at Bismarck, North Dakota had performed a postmortem autopsy for a bacteriological analysis. These doctors refuted the verdict of the childrens' two doctors at the Jamestown Hospital. Their claim was that Cameron had passed from septicemia (blood poisoning), Blanche from a diabetic coma and baby Duane from pneumonia.

The survivors of the ordeal were my six year old brother, Winfred Leal, my three year old sister Gladyce Lucille and my Pa. Gladyce and Winfred were believed to have had the same infection. Gladyce's eyes were affected, and Winfred's illness brought about rheumatic fever and a leaky heart valve, but by the Grace of God they lived.

We learned then, by watching Pa and Ma that "grief is unprofitable." We learned that we were too ignorant to argue with God intelligently. Long after the fact, I learned from the greatest lady one could ever meet, Dr. Edna Lister, that we must conquer our minds and emotions, before they conquer us. Had I known this at my young and impressionable age, I wouldn't have spent so much time letting my mind work over the "pity and fear" of life's lessons.

Life Following the Funerals — Our home, for a time, became a diabolical wasteland. Ma said later, "A shock like that's enough to explode the brain cells into orbit, and make the blind see." Nature's "cloak and dagger" messenger had come and gone. It took with it three of our family members We were plagued with an insatiable desire to reminisce, painful as it was. We were simply unable to put the pain behind us and surge ahead. As Pa put it, "The mind's darker side switches to full bore."

Although it was said later, Andy Warhol's statement fit our 1935 situation: "Everyone can be briefly famous." In our case, we became famous for all the wrong reasons. Because of our tragedy, my family had become newsworthy. Every reporter from coast to coast wanted the byline. News hounds hid behind the knoll lying on their bellies with cameras aimed toward our farmhouse ready to snap photos of our poverty and my grief-stricken family. One day Pa spied them. In grief and anger, he aimed a 12-gauge shotgun at them, and told them to "Git off my property". My entire tragedy-stricken family watched as Pa drove the media from our land. Papa said they would spread our names all over the news "Like we're poor white trash." It was yet another dimension of tragedy, and we were staggered by his proclamation. I often recall Pa's words on that terrible day, "All we got is ourselves, kids."

Over the course of the tragedy the dogs kept howling. I know that our cumulative thoughts about the old wives' tale held us captive. Perhaps we gave it too much credence.

Sometime later, while lying belly-up on the scorched grassy slope, I watched our red heifer suck water from the bog. I wondered if I could forget about what was lost and start building on what was left. I thought about Carlos and his howlin'. It was eerie. How could a dog be more intuitive than humans, anyway? Dust and ashes would have adequately describe my personal feelings. I felt as Sodom and

Gomorrah had probably looked—wasted. Had anyone asked me how many points there were in a compass, my answer would have been, "North, south, east, west and where I'm at."

I missed the matchless opportunity of prayer because I didn't know how to pray. I'm sure my conscious mind didn't know there really was a God. For this reason, the ingredient for healing remained veiled from me.

Because of the deaths and the media attraction, our lives, our hearts and our minds became like a book with its pages blown open and fluttering in a strong wind. This was "iron-country". It took courage and fortitude to endure and to overcome catastrophic happenings. Pa set a fine example of such courage and fortitude. Two days after the funeral he moved the entire family. We left the old homestead on horse and wagon and we went across the county to the old Challman place. A few years later we moved into the next county onto the Derrickson place.

It seemed like the end of the road for death, but it turned out to be only a curve in the road. My Ma and Pa are gone now. Just as my mate of forty years, and my brother Bill and sister Maridelle. "They simply turned off the lights of their minds and left us."

During these events, I learned that grief can be a killer, that death is really a graduation, and that we decide the end of our days, in a vow, before we sojourn on earth. I learned that happiness is an attitude and not a feeling. That man changes to the degree that he chooses to trust God. That to be of greater value to Him, we must be the ambassadors of hope for the world. "Love is forever", declared Jesus. In Shakespeare's play, it is said of Joan of Arc that after they burned her at the stake she returned to say, "When will the world recognize its saints? When?"

School Daze

The Early School System — Prior to the beginning of the 20th Century traditional curriculum was accepted in the United States without question. During the colonial period British practices and traditions dominated our curricula. Even when the United States began to print its own textbooks following the American Revolution, the content was not materially changed until the 20th Century. After 1890, drawing, civics, history, language, grammar, reading, spelling, writing, arithmetic, nature study, geography, music and physical education was taught.

The first organized school district in our region was located in Paris Township in 1886. Early public school buildings were nonexistent, so classes were held in church basements where several women assisted the teachers. The organization of the mother and teacher club was perhaps the forerunner of the Parent Teacher Association.

With the inception of Townships, after the Homestead Act of 1862, schools were usually built in the corners of the Townships. Our school was built in the corner of Chase Lake Township. Many immigrant families were living in and around Chase Lake. A review of "Who's Who" of the first Chase Lake school teachers reveals a rich ethnic mix: Jay Joyce, (1923-1925), Sadie Whorley, (1924-1925), Marian Pratt, (1925-1926), Mary Halverson, Martha Peterson, Rachel Thorsness, and Jessie Dunsmore.

Role of the Country Teacher — During the 1930s our rural schoolhouse had become the center of community social events and ceremonies. Central to all activities was the country school teacher, who was forced to take on the roles of janitor, cook, nursemaid, babysitter, confidant and social activities coordinator.

The school marm, as we affectionately referred to her, found herself doing much more than teaching children the three *R*s. She had to build the fire to keep the schoolhouse warm, clean the floors with chemically treated sawdust, patch worn books, heat our soup at lunchtime, and provide us with the necessary education. The teacher was also the director of all school programs and community events.

In our Township, the teacher's contract encompassed what we would refer to today as a minimum wage with volumes of rigid rules. The regulations forbade the wearing of cosmetics, facial paint, short dresses, and gaudy colors. The contract strictly warned against being in the company of men, especially in carriages; being in ice cream parlors; and dating and marriage during the contract period. She was directed to wear double petticoats at all times. The rules and regulations alone, not counting the number of jobs she was required to perform, would have put most people in a body bag long before their time.

The educational system in the Chase Lake District didn't present us with a culture shock. It did, however, teach us to read and write which paid off on my first trip to the big city. There were very few traffic regulation signs to read, but there were many advertising signs posted on barns and buildings along the way. The most interesting, were the Burma Shave signs which began to appear in the mid '30s. It is said that over the years, 7,000 sets of the signs entertained travelers across the United States promoting the product. The signs were spaced a few hundred yards apart, and were designed to be read one line after the other, as the car proceeded down the road. They were both humorous and safety-oriented.

The signs said things like: When you drive--If caution ceases--You are apt--To rest in pieces; Listen, birds--These signs cost money--So roost a while--But don't get funny (as if birds could read!); Famous last words--Of lights that shine--If he won't dim his--I won't dim mine; Hands on wheel--Eyes on road--That's the skillful-Driver's code; and Twinkle, Twinkle--One eyed car--How I wonder-Where you are! These signs were easy to read and very entertaining.

Exceptions To The School Rules — The idea of kindergarten classes was a new form of tiny tot education in our territory even though it had began in 1856 in Wisconsin. My brother Bill got to start school at four years of age because Ma and Pa didn't want my sister, Blanche, to walk the two miles alone because of her poor health. Or perhaps they didn't want her to feel lonely in school. The rest of the clan started school at six years of age.

Journey To School — The school we attended, Chase Lake School, was built on a knoll northeast of the lake. It was situated beyond a marshy spring which was blanketed with a field of cattails in the fall. The tops of the tall spindles looked as brown and rich as fresh Havana cigars—the kind all smokers dream about. In due season, the cattails with their rich ripe beauty would burst into cream-colored weightless puffs that would blow away and propagate in the wetlands.

Us kids walked two and a half miles to school. When the school bell pealed, we were oftentimes still slopping around in the marsh gathering a few late cattails. We'd run as fast as we could clutching the cattails, our syrup pail lunch buckets, our half-cent pencils and two cent newsprint paper tablets. The cattails would be taken home and transformed into beautiful backgrounds for our dried floral pictures.

In winter the trip to school was very different. The snow was sometimes too deep for us to walk the usual route over Chokecherry Patch Hill. The lake was usually frozen so deep that it would have supported a team and sleigh, so we walked across it.

My sister, Shirley, reminded me of an incident in which our teacher dismissed school early, forcing us to leave the safety of the school house. We walked across the frozen lake in a blinding snowstorm in 42 degrees below zero weather. Unable to distinguish landmarks us kids drifted off course. If old John Trowbridge hadn't been crossing the lake, the four younger Carter kids, myself included, might have been frozen to death. By the time John happened on us some of our toes, fingers and a few noses were already frozen.

John helped us into the sleigh with some effort. The intensity of the gale winds shifted the sleigh on the slick ice, making it difficult for us to board. When we were seated in the sleigh he covered us with a well worn tarp of sheepskin. We began our journey to the homestead with the frozen snow squeaking and crunching under the weight of the moving sleigh runners. The sound was loud enough to be heard above the roar of the gale winds.

When we arrived at home, Ma and Pa were pacing frantically trying to decide where to begin the search for us. Over Chokecherry Patch Hill? Down by the Cottonwood? Or did the *teacher*, Pa thought, *have brains enough to keep the kids at the schoolhouse?*

As we climbed from the rig, "Our brains churned so hard worry'n they near turned to mush." She packed our frozen parts with icy snow crystals. "So you thaw out nice and easy," Pa said.

When it was determined that we had suffered no permanent damage, Ma aided our recovery with fresh hot fried bread dredged in cinnamon sugar. John celebrated his moment of glory over a bowl of Ma's homemade soup. He had appeared at the *well appointed time* in his bobsleigh, drawn by two of the country's finest matched teams of snow white geldings. Had he not come along when he did, the four of us would have become nothing more than statistics. Pa said he was beholden to John for saving us kids. After that day, we never made fun of John Trowbridge again, except maybe once. But that's a whole other story!

Our teacher didn't fare so well with Pa, though. He instructed her to never send *his* kids out in a blinding snow storm again. He declared angrily, "It's too d$#n easy to lose yer bearings!"

Our One-Room Country School — As we puffed our way into the schoolhouse each morning the pungent aroma of freshly oiled floors assailed our nostrils. The teacher's desk sat in the front of the room. Her seat assignment called for first graders to sit at the smaller desks directly in front of her desk. The older kids got to sit in the larger desks toward the back of the room. The left side of the room next to the windows was the enviable position enjoyed by the eighth graders.

The old black-jacketed coal stove sat at the back right side of the room in front of the coal shoot. Coal dust, wood chips and sawdust was tracked around the room all day, everyday. A huge blackboard and the stage stretched across the front wall, behind the teacher's desk. Pictures of George Washington and Abraham Lincoln adorned the walls. There was a map of the World that pulled up and down like a roller-style window shade.

The "grand ole" school clock sat in the corner droning its incessant tick-tock, tick-tock. When we were supposed to be studying in the warm quiet room, the hypnotic ticking would near put us to sleep. Our lighting system was kerosene lamps and later gas lamps. Bookshelves were pushed into every vacant spot on the wall. They held blackboard erasers, boxes of chalk, colored construction paper and pens and tablets for penmanship class.

Martha Peterson, our penmanship teacher taught us to put long tails on our letters, using our whole arm, not just our "squinched up" fingers from the wrist forward. Ma said Martha had the most beautiful handwriting she had ever seen. She said Martha's *Qs, Ys* and *Zs* had the most wide open graceful look with long tails, even more so than Ma's own penmanship teacher had.

At the beginning of the year, the teacher had all the students print our names and addresses for her records. Since there were no rural mail boxes on the prairie we indicated our addresses using land descriptions.

In spite of there being many immigrant families around the lake the Carter family and our relatives comprised the major portion of the student body. Us Carter kids maintained that the school should be named the William H. Carter School, since most of the students were children of Earl and Lillian. Almost all the remaining students were our first cousins: children of Edgar and Libby Mell, Albert and Evelyn Carter, Ernest and Emma Campbell, and our second cousins, the Bill Jenkins' family. My brother, Eugene, remembers a crowded classroom of twenty six ranging in ages from five to sixteen.

Each day when the nine o'clock bell was rung by an appointed eighth grader, we would stand facing the flag at the front of the room, and recite the *Pledge of Allegiance.*

Back in those days lots of kids worked hard on the farms, and it was common knowledge that very little time was dedicated to school work. Because of this many teachers gave merits or points for household and farm chores. Merits were disseminated based on the age of the student. Some chores that one might get credit for were: gathering the eggs from the henhouse, currying the horses and ponies, milking the cows, trimming lamp wicks, washing the globes, or learning to put a recipe together.

Pranksters In The Schoolhouse — By the time I started school, the teacher had lost control and the bullies of the school had taken over. The Halverson and the Sand boys, were cousins from a large Norwegian family. They were the school bullies that carried out one dangerous and crazy prank after another. They hung us smaller kids by our suspenders on coat rack hooks in the cold hallway and left us there kicking and screaming. Our teacher wasn't tall enough or strong enough to lift her tiny overall-clad charges off the hooks, so there we stayed until the hoodlums felt like taking us down.

They bored holes in the wall between the boys' and girls' outhouse, so they could get a "birds eye view". Most of the girls suffered from ballooning bladders ninety-nine percent of the time simply because we knew they were spying on us. None of us dared venture a trip to the outhouse even while class was in session for fear one of the rowdies would follow us. It didn't do any good for our teacher to go with us, because she couldn't control them either. We didn't dare tattle to Pa about them, or he probably would have beaten the heck out of the entire bunch—maybe even their fathers, too!

The pranksters pulled many dirty tricks. One episode involved them tossing the schoolhouse door key into a snow bank, locking us out in the morning cold. We stood there shivering until they decided to break down the door to the coal chute to let us inside. When Ma heard about this she exclaimed angrily, "Trouble with those kids is they don't have anything occupy their minds, so they jus' cause trouble for everybody else."

The rowdies walked to school in the middle of winter without a coat. They worked the rock piles and fields without gloves and shirts. They were "macho" before "macho" was "in". Most of the time they played pranks on each other, too. Their favorite prank was to get their little brother, Stanley, to drink homebrew then insist he walk a straight line. When he couldn't they figured maybe a little more homebrew would help. They would pour more of the stuff into Stanley's mouth, then go off and leave him to his own devices.

Ma thought that the Halverson and Sand bunch were born to parents that were too old to supervise their brood. Maybe our thoughts were only imagined about their age, like with Old John. The school teacher disagreed with Ma. She said, "We're just dealing with heathens!"

Me and My Country Education — I *must* have learned *something* constructive at school, but for the life of me I don't recall what it was. My parents seemed to do a better job of training than the school system did.

I learned a lot by listening to the other grades recite in class, but I think Pa and Ma taught me the most valuable knowledge for use later in life. Pa taught me to offer a firm handshake, and "Look a man straight in the eye when yer talkin' to him. It shows courage and good character." His mottos and admonitions to us kids were: "Children should be seen and not heard." "Speak only when yer spoken to." "Don't ask for second helpins when you're eatin' at someone else's house." "Sit still at the table." "Jus' answer yes or no when yer asked a question." "If anybody pries into our business, Mum's the word. I Don't want no family news leakin' out to the uptowners."

The three *R*s were never really important to me. If anyone asked me, "What do you take at school?" My answer was, "The schoolbus and lunch." Curriculum never entered my mind. I always prided myself on being a serious baseball player, though. I was second pitcher and a fair batter and outfielder. I loved sports of any kind, including relay races. Any wins I had, had to be considered miraculous, I guess.

When I was fourteen, Doc Melzer told my parents that my heart was in trouble, and warned that I shouldn't play any kind of sports.

I recall an incident when Doc drove by the schoolyard at lunchtime and saw me running the bases. He stopped his old car, walked out onto the playing field and literally dragged me out of the game toward his vehicle. All the way back to his car, he was sternly explaining the consequences of overexertion to me. He drove me out to our farm and informed Ma of my actions. Boy, was Ma angry with me! She told the Doc, "The little b@%# won't listen to a thing we say!" I guess my thought was *if I believed everything anyone had to say about me, there could never be a me. I would become their opinion or prejudice of me, or if I stopped to look back on my mistakes, I could go nowhere.* So I kept on running relay races and playing baseball.

Since I took second place in the All-County Day Declamation Contest, I felt pretty confident in that subject. I memorized two or three pages of recitation, then let my voice, gestures, and body language, illustrate the story to the audience. Mr. Peterson, the school principal, helped me bring out my strong points and improve the weak ones.

I knew, also, that I was great in Glee Club, particularly since we took first place in the All-County Day contest. I was the soprano in our quartet. Like Ma's, my soprano voice had to be tempered with a little softening and lots of breath. Our music "department" excelled. We took first place in best vocal group, best soloist, best quartet, and best band.

Ma always chided that I wasn't a serious student of "things that counted—like school-housin'." "But you can make a silk purse out of a sow's ear, but that's jus' so much *skyfodder* out in the world, stupid kid," she muttered under her breath. Ma was *sorry* about me. She told me it wasn't my fault that I was behind the barn door when the brains were passed out.

My rationalization was, with eleven other kids to tend Ma couldn't afford to hand out bouquets of compliments. Pa often said, "It's like breakin' a horse—first the discipline, then the treats." Little did I know that Ma and I would eventually find our common ground.

Animal Antics

The Newborn — While working in the woods one day, my brother Bill's softer side poked through loud and clear when he came across a baby deer, not more than one or two days old. The mother had been killed, and there was no hope of survival for the fawn. Bill wrapped the little guy in his coat to keep it warm until he could bring it home. It lived in Ma's kitchen for a couple weeks and was fed with the infamous nippled bottle. As the deer grew older, it followed the cow around the barnyard and became a pet to all who walked by on the road.

The Teetering Billy — My brother, Bill, had his own tactics when it came to taming farm animals. He just tormented them until they became so mean that us young'uns couldn't get near them. Such was the case with old Billy, the goat. Brother Bill, and perhaps Eugene, would take the goat by one horn and its tail, swing him 'round and round' then let go of him. Billy got so dizzy he staggered and bumped into anything that was in his vicinity with each successive twirling, the goat became angrier and more agitated. One day after such an episode, he got so angry that he began to ram a large wooden crate that was standing near the barn. He backed up as far as he could to get up enough speed to do the intended damage, then gave a great starting leap. With head and horns in the butting position he sped forward at breakneck speed. Over and over again the goat slammed into the crate. He kept this up until he shredded the crate into virtual tooth picks. From that day on, anything that was in his path became a target for Billy's battering.

Another time, Billy jumped up onto a two-wheeled trailer that Pa kept out by the barn. As Billy walked up one end of it, everything appeared normal, but when he stepped slightly forward of center point the thing became a teeter-totter and catapulted him headlong into the side of the barn. This outraged him so, that he turned around and repeated the process, only to be launched once again into the wall of the barn. The more he was hurled, the more enraged he became. After some time, I think he might have begun to enjoy his little escapade. It seemed as if all of Billy's attention was focused on the teeter-totter, and all of us kids became the spectators.

Sheepish Tales — We had to bring the sheep flock in at night to protect them from the coyotes and packs of wild dogs. At the mere scent of a coyote these dingy balls of fluff also known as sheep, would bolt and outrun the sheepdog. I believe they could have outstripped the wind if given the opportunity! Some had a tendency to leave the flock for reasons of their own. Because of this and the fact that there were so many coyotes—we had to count the sheep in the morning *and* at night.

One morning Pa was counting the sheep while my sister Marian held the gate open, allowing only one sheep to leave at a time. The sheep shed gate consisted of two old cast iron bedsteads wired together in the center and secured to the side frames of the doorway. The counting ended on a sad note. Somehow Pa spooked the sheep, and they rushed the gate, mashing Marian's fingertips between the iron frames. Her hand was struck and every time one of the sheep hit the metal, the gate mashed her fingers again and again until they all turned black and blue. She eventually lost the nails on her injured fingers.

Another time, our old buck sheep, Jiggs, pinned Marian down for hours. She threw her shoes, books, rocks, and anything else she could reach from her sitting position—to no avail. Ma finally heard her screams and came to the rescue, shooing old Jiggs away with flapping arms and apron. I think it was the expletives that came from Ma's mouth that scared Jiggs away.

Countin' Sheep — No, I'm not talking about counting sheep to go to sleep! Every day ended in the same monotonous way on the farm. Everybody had chores of some kind or another that had to be done before supper. Counting the sheep was one of them. The sheep, cattle and lambs had to be rounded up from the countryside, counted, and brought back to the barn. If one was missing, Pa sent us back out on the prairie to find it—even if it was the dead of night!

Such was the case one summer night sometime after midnight when Pa had been in town for an extended period of time. His cronies had been entertaining him at the local bar where it was fashionable for Pa to be filled with hilarity and merriment. By the time he returned home, everyone was sound asleep. Not only was he tipsy—he had left both his cash and his frivolity at the bar. *Now Pa's mind was on the sheep.*

Pa roused Marian and me from a sound sleep and asked us what the sheep count was for the night. When it appeared that our count didn't match the one he anticipated, we were not only called to task, but told to get out of bed and get dressed. He took the soot-blackened lantern and set out to count the sheep himself—Marian and I scampering behind him. If you've ever seen a sheep herd, you're well aware that they scatter and run at the slightest provocation. Pa spat tobacco juice, waved the lantern skyward, mumbled a few obscenities, and firmly resolved that one was indeed missing. With that he commanded that we saddle up a pony and go look for the alleged lost sheep. He told us, "Get on the pony and head out to the prairie right now!"

It was eerie. The night was extremely dark, and the coyotes were howling. Marian and me were carryin' on in a state of panic. As Ma put it, we were "crying bloody murder." Our conversation as you can well imagine, was that we would leave home as soon as possible to get away from Pa's meanness. We were riding a horse named June, though in reality she should have been named *Disaster*. She was the same wild and skittish horse that had dumped Shirley and me into the dugout several weeks prior to this night.

Coyotes howled all around us—we were scared! What if a coyote attacked June? Our dilemma was how to stay on the horse in case of an attack and where to find the lost sheep, if there truly was a lost sheep. The sheepdog, Blue, our constant companion, followed along. At times he would weave in and out between the horse's legs attempting to get under her in case of an attack. The horse pranced, sidestepped, and tried to break into a gallop. Marian reined her in, thinking that we would have a better chance of survival at a slower pace. Coyotes who had cubs hidden nearby were known to attack large animals with a vengeance. Horses would strike with their hind feet in killer fashion. If that happened, we would be bucked off to become coyote bait.

While riding through the darkness of the night, Marian recounted to me a similar experience she had while riding out to the pasture to bring in the horses. Evidently, Marian had ridden the saddle pony too close to a coyote den in which a mother had just given birth to pups. The prairie warrior took out in vicious pursuit of Marian, the pony, and the sheep dog. The frightened dog kept dodging in and out between the legs of the horse for protection, and the horse kept swerving to miss the dog. Marian was hysterical and attempted to shriek louder than her company of dog, pony and coyote while galloping home hell-bent-for-election. Pa said, "By the time Marian got back to the barn and we went back out to kill the coyote, it had disappeared, moving her young pups to a safe place."

That night Marian and me roamed the prairie together, crying and feeling sorry for ourselves. After an hour of searching, we failed to find any lost sheep, and we reluctantly returned to the farm. Thank heavens Pa was asleep when we got home. I was pretty sure that I saw a look of regret on his face the next morning. I could tell when he was sorry for his actions—his tone became gentler, and he made rash promises that he knew full well he couldn't keep.

What did I think of Pa's correctional procedures then? Not much. What do I think of his correctional procedures now? I can say without a moment's hesitation that it was the best training I ever could have received to prepare me to overcome hardships, to be brave in the face of adversity, and to move along to better days grudge-free.

Ma's Guide To Raisin' Chicks — My Ma could have written her own book about raising chickens. Practically every farmer in the country raised poultry for the purpose of producing meat and eggs for table use, for sale or for bartering. We raised 100 to 200 chicks at a time. All flocks were tested for disease before they were shipped.

We received the baby chicks in large boxes. We unloaded them, and placed them under a "brooder," an inverted metal umbrella with a heat lamp in its dome and tiny screened watering trays and feeding troughs in the center. Until the chicks could fend for themselves, the older kids had to hold each one in their hands and dip its beak into the water. Occasionally us younger kids got to help, if we promised not to squeeze the chicks too tightly. Some chicks were so dumb that they didn't know enough to drink. I remember becoming so frustrated and impatient with them that I was tempted to drown the little buggers. Sometimes tiny chicks had to be taken inside the house and placed in a warm oven, which was occasionally shared by weak spring lambs, home-baked bread, biscuits and pasties. Once the chicks had grown to a certain size, we fed them rations of a balanced mash mixture.

The Old Biddies — Mediterranean breeds frequently became broody. When they did we called them biddies, they had an endless mothering instinct. They not only set on their own eggs, but would set on every other hen's eggs, too. Biddies in the henhouse presented a real problem for us kids. When I was sent to gather eggs I made sure that the biddies' nest was last. No matter what tactic I used to sneak the eggs out from under them, they managed to peck me hard enough to draw blood. I'd wear long sleeves—even if it was only Pa's old underwear shirt—and for extra protection I added a pair of gloves. Don't you suppose the darn biddy would peck the one place not protected by the sleeve and the glove?

My folks wanted the hens to set, but if they weren't watched closely and the eggs weren't removed daily, a baby chick might be found forming in an egg that was intended for scrambling, that Pa intended to sell. Sometimes Ma had to go out to the henhouse and do her own style of coaxing As she put it, "make those feathers fly." Sure enough, Ma went in swinging and the hens went airborne. Feathers flew and so did the manure from the roosts, as the flock let go of the boards. It looked like a snow storm in the henhouse, but Ma won out—she got the eggs from the biddy.

A most notable biddy wouldn't surrender the nest. She was on the verge of ruining the eggs by incubating them too long, so Ma once again came to the rescue—the biddy had to go! She was taken to the chopping block, where Ma grasped her legs tightly with one hand the hatchet raised in the other and the biddy's head on the chopping block—the woeful biddy fought for her life—and lost. She ended up on the Carter dinner table that night!

Singein' the Hen — A Sunday dinner or a special occasion dinner was the one where you might have found the Carter family eating an old stewing hen—otherwise, a ring of bologna split fourteen ways was more likely to have been dinner. Us kids were inducted in the service of assisting Ma with the capture of the hen. We would throw feed out into the yard and while the chickens were preoccupied with eating, Ma would snare the leg of an old stewing hen with a hooked staff. She would take it to the chopping block and cut off its head. Then we began the chore of plucking its feathers.

Back in the kitchen, Ma would chuck a huge wad of paper into the firebox, then grab the dead hen by its feet and neck and rotate its nude torso over the blazing flames to remove all the surface hair. Old hens, we were told, like many older women, have to contend with the hair problem. "Thank God," Ma shared, "us gals don't have to be laid belly-down over an open flame to remove 'em." I thought for as little as Ma ever got to church, she sure thanked God a lot.

Once the chicken was singed, salt was rubbed into the skin, then it was rinsed. Ma said the Chinese women used this method to draw out bacteria. The chicken was put in the cooking pot, then Ma added salt again during the cooking process, along with vinegar to draw the calcium out of the bones and into the broth. I hesitate to say this, but us kids were usually glad to see a biddy go into the cooking pot for two reasons—first was we were always hungry and second was biddies were mean-minded.

A Weasel In The Henhouse — If you've never witnessed a weasel in a henhouse, you've missed knowing how desperately everything in nature will fight for its individual preservation. Weasels are arch enemies of the chicken flock. Whenever we heard a commotion in the henhouse, whether we were in the barn, on a horse, or on the porch, everybody bolted to the henhouse. We would all yell and screech like a bunch of lunatics as we flung the door open.

The hens would go airborne in terror and hover in the rafters of the chicken coop. Feathers would blast the air in swirling puffs, while bits of chicken litter and straw would hit our faces like hailstones on a stormy day. It was always the same—the weasel was outnumbered! Sometimes he was the victor, but more often than not, he lost out on his prospective meal.

Tails Of Milking — During bug and fly season, the cows would get to switching their tails so hard they would nearly knock us kids off our three-legged milking stools. Whether or not a tail hit you in the face depended on how tall you sat on the stool. The smaller ones of us kids were the true victims!

Once when the cattle were swatting flies especially viciously, us kids—I can't recall who all was with me—tied all their tails to the support posts of the barn. When the milking was done, we turned all the cattle out, yelling and flapping our arms to startle them into moving quickly out of the barn. We heard a big commotion at the back of the barn, and turned around to see that we had forgotten to untie one cow's tail. She had tried to charge out with the others, and had jerked her own tail right in half. Us kids were horrified! We knew Ma would come to the rescue—and sure enough, she did—with Bag Balm. It came in handy on the farm. We used it as an all-purpose salve to treat anything from cuts, scrapes and punctures to dry skin. I'm sure it had a multitude of uses we never even thought of.

Us young'uns were always the ones that had to teach the newborn calves how to drink from a pail in order to wean them from their mothers. Our method was to grab the calf by the snout, and force its mouth along with our fingers, into a pail of fresh milk. The calf was supposed to suckle our fingers, at the same time sucking in some of the milk. We usually had to almost wrestle the calf to the ground to get its nose into the pail.

One time a particularly ignorant and impatient calf kept biting my fingers and rooting me around with its friskiness. After several minutes of this, it nudged me so hard that I lost my balance and fell into a pile of manure, spilling all the milk. I got so mad, that I picked up a two-by-four and cracked the calf right between the eyes! It slumped to the straw in a pathetic unmoving heap. I screamed bloody murder for Pa, who came running "heck bent for election". He leaned down to check the calf, but it was impossible to tell if it was dead or alive. Pa ran for the "toadstabber"—a name that us kids had given the extra long butcher knife that was frequently used on our farm. With it, he quickly severed the calf's jugular vein. It was necessary to bleed out an animal quickly, if it was going to be used as food. If you didn't, the meat would become tainted and unfit for human consumption.

As awful as it sounds, the memory of this incident remained bittersweet in my mind for a very long time. I guess bitter—because I felt tremendous sorrow for what I had done, but sweet—because it was the first time I had ever tasted veal. Up until that day, old roosters, setting hens, and hogs were the only meat I had ever eaten.

The Days Of The Horse — Running horses on the farm was mandatory when living on the skirts of the raw range. The horse was a towering giant among farm animals. All the Carter kids were good horsemen. My older brothers broke fierce, wild, western horses, and rode in rodeos. Us girls, true to our English heritage, could ride sidesaddle like royal ladies or we could ride standing up on a pair of horses, one foot on the back of each horse. Sometimes we were forced to farm with only partially trained western horses. They were skittish and spooked the other horses.

Very early one summer morning, Eugene had to go out and drag the west field with a four horse team and a double drag. A farm drag is an implement constructed of an iron frame with protruding railroad-type spikes, used to tear up the soil, and remove weeds, much like the rototillers of today. Ma and me were at the house when we heard Pa yelling and a horse squealing and groaning in agony. We near ran a city block to the field where Gene was working. When we saw what had caused the commotion, Ma nearly had a heart attack. The drag was flipped upside down with the horse on top of it and Eugene under both. How something like that could happen, I never knew. Maybe too sharp a turn had tipped a section of the drag, or maybe the "spicy" horse was acting up. Thank God, it turned out that Gene wasn't hurt seriously. He was pretty bruised and sore, though. Fortunately, the horse recovered, too.

Dizzy And The Magic Potion — We had a bald-faced bay gelding named Dizzy. My brother, Bill, was trying to tame him and was thrown several times. That was enough to give Bill an attitude. From that point on, Bill stuck with Dizzy until he came out the winner. After Dizzy was broken he became a tame work horse except for his habit of unpredictable biting. We could never trust him. He was cantankerous and bit anyone who came near his head. He would swing his neck around at lightning speed and snap like a snake.

One day Pa said, "I've had jus' 'bout enough of that bay geldin'. He needs a lesson!" And out to the corral Pa went. One of Pa's favorite habits was chewing wads of homemade snuff or Peerless tobacco. On this day he had chewed an extra large wad, saving as much spit as his mouth could possibly hold. He cautiously walked toward Dizzy's head. "I had to be careful," he said, "'cuz I didn't wanna swallow the spit if he swung 'round first." As expected Dizzy did swing, and Pa was right there to spit tobacco juice directly in the gelding's eye. Dizzy pulled back, stomped his foot, shook his head a couple times, and gave a loud snort. That seemed to be the magic potion because Dizzy never did bite anyone again. Bill had also tamed Dizzy's partner, Duke. But in spite of them being broken, we never could trust these two unpredictable horses for riding.

June, The Red Flag And Me — June was another bay horse that we had on the farm. She was skittish and shied at every unfamiliar thing she saw or heard. If something appeared suddenly she shied, which means that she jumped sideways on all four feet simultaneously. This is fine for the rodeo horses on their approach to calf roping or some other stunt, but its unacceptable on a farm because its a quick and easy way for a horse to dump its rider.

Shirley and me oftentimes used an old duck blind dugout for shelter from the wind and heat while herding cattle and sheep. I think the hollow had been created by the Indians for cover, or by buffalo for a wallow. The last time we were out that way, we inadvertently left a red coat in the dugout. This day as we rode by the dugout at Kentucky Derby pace, June caught sight of the bright red coat and jumped sideways on all fours, dumping us into the hole, still in our sitting positions. She galloped away, and we were left to walk all the way home carrying the red coat.

Another mishap involving June was the time that Ma and me were preparing hills for planting cucumbers. Ma was manning the scoop-shovel. It was a device shaped like a big flat scoop with handles and was pulled along in an upright position behind a horse—kind of like a modern day earth grader. A person held on to the handles, controlling the shovel so that it dug into the earth at an angle when the horse pulled forward. We used it a lot on the farm for moving medium amounts of soil and rocks.

This particular time I was riding June. We had finished moving the load of dirt to where we needed it for the cucumber hills and had returned the scoop to its proper flat position on the ground. Ma said, "Take June over to the barn." I started toward the barn at a slow pace. All of a sudden the scoop hit gravel, grating stones against the metal, and the resounding noise spooked June. She set out at a dead gallop for the barn with me hanging on for dear life. Ma was screaming at the top of her lungs, "Duck! Duck yer head!" I saw the frame of the barn door coming straight at me. I took Ma's advise and ducked just in time to avoid becoming a "headless horseman". June and me hit the entrance to the barn at a full gallop nearly busting through the other side of the barn.

Living on the raw edge of the prairie seemed to stimulate my overactive nature to the point of lunacy. I jumped off rooftops, down hay holes, off haystacks, and danced and hopped around on the weak dilapidated pig house roof without ever once considering my own mortality! As Ma often pronounced, "Yer always into too much tomfoolery!" *Tomfoolery* being Ma's favorite expression for foolishness.

Incident At The Quicksand Bog — To the northeast of our farm, the soggy splendor of lush green meadow fed by underground springs, stretched one mile to the foot of the venerable cottonwood tree at the edge of the alkali lake. The grass became very coarse as you neared the tree. Pa once scrutinized the top of the tree and said, "She grows twelve foot each year, 'gainst all odds, even alkali." The tree was a landmark and beacon for many a weary pioneer who had searched for suitable land.

The tree should have functioned as a danger signal, warning travelers of the quicksand bog. I can't recall anyone ever posting a sign. The danger was immediate for man and beast. Ma said that many unsuspecting animals and weary travelers had no need for funeral arrangements if they so much as stepped one foot in the bog. A quicksand bog works the opposite of an underground spring. It's an area where the convulsing, sucking sand, like Attila the Hun, captures its prey and leaves no survivors.

At times I dismissed Ma's yarns as partly imagined, or perhaps as another of her methods of escaping boredom. But the day came when her rantings became a reality. Late one afternoon, the loud excited shouts of several men jarred us from our complacency. Hooves pounded, harness tugs jangled, and all were running in a charge similar to that of the Light Brigade. The men were barking out commands like frustrated army sergeants to their new recruits. They all carried shovels, ropes, pulleys, and other rescue paraphernalia.

The terror in the mens' voices signaled us kids to run close behind the mob, which was moving toward the danger zone. Sure enough—they were headed for the quicksand bog. We got there and saw one of our ponies sinking rapidly into the mire. Only her head was visible by the time we got to her.

Pa and a neighbor rigged a nonslip knot on the rope and lassoed the pony's head. They hitched a team of horses to the other end of the sturdy homemade rope. "This part is very tricky," I heard Pa yell out. The men could spur the team on only when the pony lurched. Everyone knew that the pony's neck would snap like a twig without synchronization by all concerned parties. Us kids watched in agony, realizing the pony was almost too tired to go on.

Pa anxiously watched, like the captain of a schooner caught in swirling ocean waves. With his uncannily keen sense of timing, Pa yelled, "Giddy-up!" just as the pony lurched again. The neighbor men shouted advice to Pa,

"Slack off, Carter!", "Tighten up the rope, Earl!", and "Earl, you started the team too quick!". If Pa minded the free advice, he sure didn't show it. That was a first for Pa.

The entire episode lasted for two harrowing hours. The team seemed to realize that they, too, played an important part in saving their prairie companion. Us kids were gathered in a huddle off to the side. We were tormented at such a sight. *The poor pony!* I thought. All the girls were rolling the hems of their dresses into unsightly knots, while the boys sidestepped, checking the tilt of the pony and the slack of the pulley.

Eventually, with Pa's words of encouragement and us kids coaxing, "Come on girl, you kin make it," the pony gave one last heave, springing herself to freedom. We all cheered and jumped up and down. The slime's evil grip had lost this round! The men looked relieved. Pa unhitched the team as the pony shook herself like our sheepdog when he was dunked in the lake. I knew the pony would never venture into the quicksand bog again.

Entertainment on the Farm

Childhood Entertainment Sans Microchip — It didn't take a battery, a microchip or any other expensive electronic gadget to entertain us kids. We used our ingenuity and resourcefulness to entertain ourselves, because we knew there was no money for toys, books, and games.

My favorite summertime activities included building things, like scooters that could give a small child enjoyment. Half the fun was searching for small wheels and old pieces of rusted equipment in the junk heap behind the clothesline. It made no difference to us whether the wheel was geared or smooth, or if one wheel measured six-inches and the other eight. Because when combined with an old hay rake seat—voila! a new apparatus was born that scooted along just fine for us.

We would drag it up hill and down dale until we came to the highest and longest hill we could find then we would *let her go.* We yelled with glee, not only over our new invention, but with the wind hitting our faces we knew we had found something wonderful and joyous about living in the open country.

We made yo-yos from wood and string, hunted round pebbles to use as marbles, and made darts by filing the ends of nails to a point then sticking a cork on the opposite end. Our dart board was a picture cut from the Montgomery Wards catalog, tacked on the side of the outhouse.

We made slingshots from sturdy crotches of tree limbs. The fork portion was cut to about four or five inches long, and notched to accommodate a cutting of rubber inner tubing. Then a piece of leather was fastened to the ends of the inner tubing to form a pocket for the projectile. Our choices in stones for ammunition was directly proportionate to the size of our victims. If we took a bead on a pigeon or a gopher with our forked weapon, they were *goners.* The little birds and prairie animals met the same plight with our snares.

Infrequently though it was, we were sometimes allowed to go roller skating at the town hall. The rules on the floor were that skate wheels had to be pre-oiled, wheel axles adjusted, and ankle and instep straps tightened. A small fee was collected from those wishing to skate. I can't recall what the fee was but I know it took most of the pennies I had earned selling my gopher tails.

The talking machine was hooked up to a loud speaker, and when the music started, couples of all ages would glide out onto the chalk-spread floor. At intervals the announcer would call out "couples only," "beginners only", or "artistic skaters only." If you didn't qualify for the particular category you were required to leave the floor.

At the skating hall, as well as at all the barn dances and square dances, the event ended with the Grand March. Everyone would scamper to choose a partner: sweethearts went hand in hand, some experienced skaters chose to help beginners, and some of us little kids grabbed each other, to keep from falling down. Around and around we would glide to the sounds of the Grand March. Another week had ended at the skating hall.

The Playhouse — In those days some kids were lucky enough to have tree houses, and some dug caves into the hillside, not only for play but to seek refuge from their peers and parents. Us Carter kids and the Ochsner kids, our neighbors, used old rusted-out hulks of cars for our playhouses. The old cars were usually dumped out by the bog after having been used for parts by folks from a neighboring town. Sometimes the car had simply been cast aside by someone rich, who had replaced it with something much better. To us Carter kids, rich meant any financial condition better than our own—which didn't take much!

We located the perfect relic for use as a playhouse on the hillside near the bog. The exterior of the old car body was the same color as our homestead—wind-blistered blue. The driftwood look was definitely *in* on the prairie. The elements had scoured everything around us, the buckboards, the buildings and the cobblestones. Even the alkali lake and the dirt on the ground were wind-blistered. We used Daisy, our pony to haul the relic on a stone boat from the side hill back to our playing area closer to home.

The car's wheels were missing and rust had corroded the doors with grit and nearly devoured the hinges, making the doors squeak and groan from being sprung out of line. Being resourceful, we slathered the hinges with rendered mutton tallow we got from Ma's kitchen crock, marked *"save for cookin' and throat poultice."* It stunk in the heat of the day—but then—so did the pig yard, the privy, and the dank culvert surrounding our main house. The seat cushions were abused by the elements and had fractured like thirsty clay during a heavy drought. Giant puffs of dingy stuffing projected from the larger splits each time a pair of tiny buttocks plopped on them.

We used the rusted, pock-marked dashboard as a window sill, decorating it with a broken green glass bottle we had unearthed in one of our treasure hunts. In the bottle—considered our precious vase—was a freshly picked bouquet of fragrant wild flowers, including white honeysuckle, pink wild roses, royal blue buffaloberries, milkweed pods, rushes, and cattails.

View From The Balcony — Though the playhouse was lots of fun for us kids it wasn't nearly as much fun as playing in the upstairs windows of our farm house. The view was always was better from the balcony. We could look over at the Jenkins' place beyond the west gate, and even flash mirror signals, pretending that marauders were hiding in the gooseberry patch.

From the balcony vantage point we could get a better shot at sparrows, pigeons and gophers with our hand carved slingshots. We discovered that the farm boys east of us used their upstairs window in the dead of winter for yet *another kind* of target practice. The frozen yellow streams in the snow were evidence of their behavior. Every time we passed their house with the team and wagon it triggered Ma's mutterings, "That jus' jars me," she would shriek. "Them big boys are too lazy to carry out a slop jar."

Field Of Dreams Ala Carter — We invented many other ways to pass the time as we lollygaged in the field of dandelions and tawny yellow flowers. Small voices rang out, "Les'see if you like butter?" Our litmus test consisted of holding a yellow flower under another kid's chin. If it reflected yellow on their skin—"Yup!" we would squeal, "You like butter!"

Sometimes we would cut dandelions as close to the ground as possible then braid the stems. We tied each group of braids onto the next group until we had enough to make beautiful belts, bracelets and crowns. Ankle and arm bracelets abounded but we made only one *crown*. It was special, and we drew straws—really stems—to determine who would be crowned queen for a day.

We sat in our flowery field of dreams for hours, sometimes chatting with one another, sometimes just watching the cloud formations float across the North Dakota sky. Oftentimes, we would wander through the meadow, picking dandelions, wild onion tops with white flowers, blue buffalo flowers, and pink wild roses for the dining room table.

By the end of the month, our beautiful yellow carpet of flowers would be transformed into a field of white cotton-like puff balls. Each ball would contain hundreds of porcupine spikes with miniature white stars projecting from them. Once the star lifted off, it would land in a new place. It is in this place that a new dandelion would appear the very next summer.

The Cottonwood Therapist at Chase Lake — For reasons unknown, *contrast* encompasses my most prominent recollections of life on the homestead—the happy times and the catastrophic times. Almost daily, problems that modern language calls "the general adaptation syndrome" confronted me. I was afraid I'd become a defenseless pawn upon society's new breed, even though I was trained to be a responsible worker at a very young age.

Adults paid little attention to the feelings and emotions of kids in those days and met any "adaptation syndrome"—wallowing or complaining—with a whack alongside the head. Ma said, "Yer head is like the sediment bulb in the jalopy—sometimes we gotta knock the sediment out to git a spark."

My analyst was the venerable old Fremont cottonwood tree. She stood like a sentinel on the southwest hook of the lake, her roots secure and deep under the quicksand bog. It was there on the moist grassy knoll that I would fling myself down, casting my eyes upward to her branches of shiny, rustling leaves, looking for answers to my burdensome quest for a better life.

With the broken end of a honeysuckle stem clenched between my teeth, I staked my claim on the land of plenty as did Abraham. My claim encompassed all that I could see on every foot of prairie and field that I walked. I yearned to travel far and wide, see as many people as I could see, and perform as many different lines of endeavor as seemed fitting. Between draws on the honeysuckle stems, I hummed *Whispering Hope* which I had learned from a record on the old talking machine.

Lil' Archaeologists — About 40 rods west of the house at our front gate was the culvert. To me it seemed like one of the most exciting places on the homestead. The culvert and the things I could glean from it held such a fascination for me. Every chance I got, I tried to encourage my sisters or brothers to go there with me to excavate *important stuff.*

In the course of one of our big digs, we found mute expressions of prairie life clogging the damp channel. With sharp sticks we excavated the pile of debris. When the sticks proved limiting we would get down on the ground and reach inside the culvert as far as our short arms would allow. If conditions felt right, we would crawl in as far as we dared without getting stuck. I recall a time when my brother, Cameron—we called him Short—got stuck, but we were able to yank him out by his feet. The water seepage from the hillside, along with the rotted matter in the culvert, made it not altogether odorless. So when Short was pulled free, he smelled like the rotting potatoes in our cellar. Needless to say, we did our best to avoid him the rest of the day.

One time during such a dig, we unearthed a collection of precious things like broken colored glass bottles, rusty potted meat cans, a well rotted Montgomery Ward catalog, a few caption sheets from a Rangeland Romance magazine, a rusty rotted harness tug, and a few rusty bent Copenhagen box lids.

This particular day we gathered our broken pieces of glass—mud and all—then ran barefoot down the dirt road past the gooseberry briar, the horseradish and rhubarb patch, and past the house and barn to the well. At the watering trough we washed and polished our treasures. We sorted them according to color, and dried them in the blistering sun. If a piece of glass was too big to meet our needs we smashed it between two rocks. Having obtained the perfect sizes and colors, we set out to create our own designs.

Amongst fits of giggling and excited chatter, we pasted the colored bits of glass onto windows of our old car body playhouse. We would step back and admire each others' creativity—oohing and aahing over it as we did. This type of fun was commonplace, but we never tired of it. If the windows of our current playhouse happened to have been previously broken out, it didn't bother us—we just pasted the bits of glass to an old chicken coop window first, then propped it in the window space of the car. We were always quite proud of our handiwork.

The Mounds — Miles beyond the west gate of our homestead, as if in memorial to the winds, and enshrouded in ancient mystery, the remains of the handiwork of Native American Indian mound builders stood sentinel over the prairie. The array of serpentine earthwork contours meandered across state lines for miles.

It was thought that the mounds may have been used for fortification as buffalo wallows or sacred memorials. Some of the wallows in our area near bodies of water, were used by hunters for duck blinds.

Archaeologists speculated that the peaceable Mandan tribe might have built the mounds, and their ancestors, they believe, built the Great Serpent and other mounds extending down to Southern Ohio.

While herding sheep and cattle out on the plains quite some distance from the mounds, us kids found many arrowheads, teepee rings, and other Indian artifacts. The dust storms of the 1930s had swept the topsoil down several inches, carrying it from state to state. This process had unearthed these objects, making them easy to find.

I would examine each artifact, trying to imagine the history that went with it. As each piece was found, it was thoroughly inspected and appropriately admired by all the siblings, then tossed in a bucket for safekeeping at the house. It wasn't until after our Grandpa Walters left our farm to go back east that we lost track of our treasured collection. We found out later that Native American artifacts were a very desirable commodity to collectors in the East who were willing to pay good money for them. This seemed to us like a very big coincidence.

In Search Of Treasure — Us little kids didn't have too many chores to do when school was out for the summer. This gave us plenty of time to roam the open prairie looking for treasure. What kind of treasure? Only the finder could tell you that! Yet, like fish attracted to bait, we would bite on anything that glistened or glowed in the sun—bits of broken glass, old bottles, pretty rocks, and wild flowers.

We would walk barefoot for miles, stepping on thistles and jagged rocks, sometimes nearly tromping on snakes that were slinking into the bushes. We combed the shores of the bog, the buffalo wallows, and the duck blinds looking for old shotgun shell casings.

Sometimes we wended our way deep into the rushes where it was cool, to pick luscious green ones for braiding. Contentedly we would sit for hours braiding first a three-strand rope, then a five-strand, then six, and so on until we had enough for a mat. At times we fell asleep in the hot sun with the sounds and smell of the water cooling us.

The faint clang of a distant cowbell would awaken us. The red heifer, who wore the bell, was leading the herd home for milking. We knew we had better get back to the farm for the milking—besides, we were getting hungry. Ma's hard barley bread and sorghum sandwich didn't have holding power for us growing kids. We sucked wild honeysuckle stems and ate wild onions to fill in the gaps. Ma said, "Jus' to keep yer mouths goin', I 'spect."

After a long day of treasure hunting, chores, and milking us kids could eat. All food—any food—tasted good to us. Ma regularly bragged to visitors, "Our kids don't turn their noses up at any food. They like anythin' that's put on their plates." Maybe we were all nearly starved to death and didn't even realize it. When the call, "Belly up", left Pa's lips it didn't take any of us long to get to the benches behind the table. Of course, we did it in an orderly single file fashion, because if we answered his call by running, pushing, and shoving, we received that steely-eyed look that could stop an eight day clock along with a harsh reprimand that wasn't soon forgotten.

Ma And The Carter Chemical Gardens — In addition to Ma's duties in the field and in the house, she somehow managed to become a real craftsman. She would gather up all the old records that were too scratchy to listen to, and put them one by one in boiling water for a few minutes. When she took them out of the water, she would flute the warm edges up and out. As they cooled they returned to their firm state. And *voila!*—the old record became a fancy trinket tray. She sculpted and molded them into items of beauty and gave them as gifts. A virtual flower garden of flat dishes, fluted bowls and frilly trinket holders covered every flat surface in our house.

Ma made chemical gardens of special beauty by placing two or three pieces of coal in a dish and sprinkling it with two tablespoons of water, wash-day bluing, and canning salt. Then she would measure out two to three drops of Mercurochrome on each piece of coal. Given time, the chemicals would interact and the creation would magically sculpt itself into a an unusual and colorful shape. I thought her dish gardens were the most beautiful pieces of art that human hands had ever created. They adorned our table, the piano, and other spaces of our house.

Community Events

Country School Christmas Program — When school started in the Fall we were excited because it meant that the Thanksgiving and Christmas seasons were close. Early in the term we were all given slips of paper which had our parts for the school Christmas play on them. Rehearsals were held during school hours, but many a student could be heard reciting their scripts on the way to and from school and while doing household and farm chores. Us kids worked for weeks getting ready for the school Christmas program. If we finished our lessons quickly, the teacher allowed us to use the last hour of the day to decorate the school room. Construction paper stars, paper chain garlands and Christmas tree cutouts abounded. All decorations were proudly displayed around the room with the name of their creator scrawled across the bottom right sides.

I remember a school play in which we needed a fireplace. We made it out of a huge cardboard box. Bricks were drawn out on the sides and front, and each student got to color a brick. During the years when we were fortunate enough to have a "rich" school teacher from the city, we were given colorful crepe paper to decorate with. Red and orange flame-shaped cutouts were placed in the fireplace opening.

Christmas programs were usually held on Friday or Saturday nights at approximately eight o'clock p.m... This gave the teacher time to "shake down" the coals in the heating stove and have the students carry out the ashes, so that the stove would work well the night of the program. It also allowed time for the farmers and school kids to complete their household and farming chores and get dressed before returning to school.

When the big evening finally came, the teacher stood on the stage and announced the program and the midnight lunch which had been donated by the parents of the students. After the program the teacher presented bags of sticky candy and an apple to all the students. Parents and kids alike, all left the old country schoolhouse happy, and looking forward to their own home celebrations of the joyous season.

Community Picnics at the Grove — The grove was always our favorite community picnic grounds. It was as if Johnny Appleseed had dropped his pack—only the seeds turned out to be chokecherry trees and cottonwoods, instead of apple trees. Pa snorted about the few no-account volunteer trees. He said the volunteers were caused by the wind scattering seeds from the surrounding countryside. Because of this the grove amounted to a thicket of scrub brush trees, cattails, dandelions, and chokecherries on a small island that jutted out parallel to Chase Lake. It was located to the west and across the emerald green marsh, behind our one-room schoolhouse. The community picnic was usually held in May following the end of the school year.

The route to the picnic was the same road that we took to Chase Lake School. We sometimes drove—but usually walked—out the east gate and over Chokecherry Patch Hill which descended to a creek near the school. This time of year the creek was gushing, bubbling and foaming with tiny white caps. Pa said it was spring runoff. The green marsh caused by the underground springs ran perhaps a mile or so along the lake and behind the school house.

We couldn't take the horses across the marsh to the grove, so we tethered them at the school barn. Us kids helped carry the wash boiler full of food, dishes and some tin plates. Our dishes at home were hotel stock—too heavy to carry around. I would have gladly dined from tin cans if necessary. I was deliriously happy just to be going to the picnic.

For us Carter kids—it was a day to remember! We got to be wild and free, to play games with kids from neighboring farms, to climb trees and eat lots of food that wasn't from our own kitchen. Somehow food always tasted better if it came from somewhere else. Ma, weary of the excitement of all us little kids said, "At the grove, you kin roughhouse all ya want. You can't hurt those trees! Jus' git rid of some of that energy!"

Brooks and streams doglegged the entire lowland making it a veritable sea of ooze. It was here that I could *show off* my spindly-legged prowess and agility by jumping over the stream with one giant leap. For me, hamming it up always added to the adventure of the festivities. In his enthusiasm of the event, one of the kids from a neighboring farm pushed me. So—what did I care that I sank to my ankles in the muck? And that the piece of inner tubing which secured the oversized shoe to my foot had snapped, leaving the shoe lodged in the mire? I vented my anger on the kid who pushed me. I had achieved my wicked swing by practicing to be the best snowball heaver in the county. After I showed the kid why he shouldn't have pushed me, I retrieved my lost shoe. The coordination required to perform my heroic leap came from being a good hopscotcher and a pretend circus performer.

Most of us kids busied ourselves with playing out by the edge of the grove, watching for all newcomers, and announcing them as they neared the area. We could hear the ladies talking about the coffee preparations. Each lady at the picnic had her own method of coffee making. We knew that Ma's way was the very best—she thought so too! But Mrs.

Guerney Sand won out! Rachel said she made her coffee by using an old Scandinavian method. Hearing this, the other ladies asked Rachel to brew the coffee for the picnic. She responded with, "Ya, ye betcha! I vil do dat. Norvegians got ta have it strong und black."

She set about filling a 30-cup percolator with water from a five-gallon cream can. "Da can vas vashed," she interjected as she dipped and poured. She added two full coffee mugs of fresh ground coffee and one-half teaspoon of salt. The pot was covered and placed on the grate to boil. She stepped back and said proudly, "Vait til ya sip dis Norsky mud."

After the coffee boiled ten minutes, Rachel whipped two eggs—shell and all. She moved the huge pot away from the flames, then stirred in the whipped egg mixed with one cup of cold water. She instructed, "Dat soothes da grounds." My Pa said Rachel definitely took the coffee brewing prize.

The instant us kids smelled the brewing coffee and the smoke from the fire, we ran toward the fire pit. Gathering around, our eyes eagerly searched every dish, trying to decide which we might tackle first. At our house we had plenty of food to fill our bellies, but nothing that was really good. Bleached white flour made up fifty percent of our daily food supply so we were starved for tasty food.

Mrs. Halverson always brought yams. The John Ochsner family brought a gunny sack full of muskmelons, and the Emanuel Ochsners brought a baked bean and rice dish. Ma and Mrs. Sand brought freshly dressed pullet stew with dumplings.

Ma also brought a big bowl of fresh young garden lettuce to serve with sweet cream, sugar and vinegar dressing. She had mashed beans with chopped onion and added vinegar, to make her famous delicious sandwich spread. Sometimes she would bake an angel cake or make barley and wheat bread, and for some reason it would fail to rise. If this happened she would bring them to the picnic anyway. Her motto was, "Don't throw it away, make it into somethin' else." In the '30's, they hadn't created package mixes, yet. Even if they had, our checks from the sale of cream wouldn't have covered such extravagances. Bread pudding was our usual dessert because it could be made from the bread that got hard and dry.

There were huge baskets of home-baked breads, crocks of freshly churned butter, and bowls of potato salad. Someone had just butchered, so there was slivers of fried meat in onion and sour cream sauce. The men, of course, brought their homemade beer which they packed in cold water from the spring because ice wasn't available.

We had no hamburgers no hot dogs or potato chips in those days. Sharing the more expensive food stuffs was impossible—these were, after all—the Depression days. The potato salads varied: some contained sour cream dressing and sweet pickles and others contained dill pickles and vegetables. If it happened to be laying time for the chickens there were lots of hard-boiled eggs and plenty of two-quart jars of home canned fruits.

Most of the ladies brought their newest and most attractive flour sack napkins and tablecloths. They brought along their handiwork, the family patching, or a piece of embroidery to keep themselves busy after the meal. Country women never left home without their hand-sewing.

The Carter kids were getting antsy. Ma shooed her brood away from the fire with a sharp retort, "If ya don't git away from the fire, y'll get nothing to eat!" We lowered our eyes, scuffed the dirt with our feet, and grudgingly moved away from the cooking area.

It wasn't long before we forgot the reprimand and joined the other kids running into the scraggy wooded area to climb trees. Soon we were all hanging upside down by our legs from the sturdy limbs. We had to see who could stay hanging the longest. We got so dizzy that we were barely able to walk. Watching each other stagger around caused us to go into giggling fits. We passed the time playing tag and hunting for caterpillars. We went in search of branch crotches that our Pas could cut later to make into slingshot shanks. Us Carter kids could usually be found out on the prairie with our slingshots, using any moving object for target practice. Nothing was safe from our *shooting eye*! Wild birds, gophers, snakes—you name it! Even the farm animals who wouldn't respond to our shouts of "move along" or "turn around" suddenly found reason to do so.

As usual at the picnic or at any other gathering—for that matter—the men joined each other around the beer barrel to *shoot the breeze.* They leaned against the trees sipping home brew and discussing planting season and most every other farming problem that existed in the territory. The women tended the kids, prepared to serve the food, and pretended not to hear the colorful language drifting across the breeze-way of trees toward them. In direct proportion to the diminishing beer in the keg, the volume of the *unholy alliance* crescendoed. Us kids had learned early on to steer clear of their vicinity at times like these.

The smell of smoke and boiling coffee grew stronger, letting us kids know that it was almost time to eat. Finally, the magic moment arrived! The sights, sounds, and smells of the grove picnic excited us all. We joined our neighbors and friends around the tables and on blankets on the grass to participate in the camaraderie and eat our meals. The men exchanged interesting stories, and the women compared recipes and handiwork during the delicious meal. Us kids talked excitedly about anything and everything. It was a veritable buffet of the best cooking we could ever imagine.

As I think back on the picnic, I find myself wondering how many people can say they have breathed the fresh clean air that we did, not only at the picnic but everyday on the open prairie. And how many can say they have enjoyed the taste of homemade foods from fresh farm ingredients: homemade breads baked with homegrown yeast and jams and jellies made from fresh garden vegetables and orchard fruits. I think of the deviled eggs Ma made from honest-to-goodness fresh-from-the-nest, North Dakota eggs. Her favorite recipe for Prepared Mustard, which she used in her deviled egg mixture came from a 1926 issue of *Dakota Farmer's Magazine.* These deviled eggs were a big hit at our grove picnics and other functions, as well.

After the meal organized relay races, baseball games, sack races, and apple bobbing contests were available to us kids, and to any adults that were brave enough, or tipsy enough, to participate.

I had so much fun that day, and I know my sisters and brothers did, too. I hated to see the fun come to an end. When our parents summoned us to head to the wagon for the trip home I was so disappointed. I wished the picnic could have lasted forever. Here we could all forget the monotony and drudgery of farm life. We hadn't even left the area yet, but were already planning and scheming looking forward with anticipation to next year's picnic at the grove.

Winning Creation For The Basket Social — There weren't too many organized community activities that excited me and my sisters and brothers as much as the Basket Social. It was the main event of the year, other than the Christmas program at our rural schoolhouse.

The word was spread by threshers, hayriggers, rodeo riders, and the McNess and Watkins salesmen, traveling through our community. Months in advance of the function, we would get the exciting news. Out here on the prairie lots of warning was necessary for assuring the attendance of a large crowd. Farmers who went to town as infrequently as two times a month, needed time to buy or trade for the miles of multicolored crepe paper and other items necessary to produce award winning baskets for the social. The town merchants were always pleased with the business that the Basket Social generated. People would come from afar to buy the brightly colored paper, ribbons, potted meats and other things for the gala affair.

I thought *getting ready* for the occasion was as much fun as the social itself. Dreaming up and creating the winning basket took many hours of conspiring, practicing, and processing. Each evening, after we had completed our chores, the dinner dishes, and our lessons, us kids gathered on the slivery wooden benches around the huge table to help Ma make her basket for the upcoming social.

She let us each make a basket of our own, too. Ours wouldn't be entered for the bidding, but merely used for our own enjoyment and entertainment. Our little hands would fidget restlessly, waiting to get on with the task. We would nudge each other and giggle with anticipation, not only of the event itself but of the fun yet to be had designing and constructing our own works of art.

Ma doled out short lengths of colored crepe paper to each of us, creating a collage of gaily colored streamers across the tabletop. Several pairs of snub nose kindergarten-style scissors and coffee mugs filled with homemade paste also graced the table. In preparing for this evening of fun Ma had previously cooked flour, salt, and water together to form a paste which we used for all purposes. We even made beads for necklaces out of the putty type substance.

It was here at our old round oak table, by the light of the kerosene lamps, that us kids worked on our baskets. The heating stove crackled its song to remove the chill from the air, and the smoke from the untrimmed wicks of the lamps whirled up the sides of the chimneys, creating eerie shadows on our faces and the jumbled mass of streamers.

We didn't notice the simple beauty of the flickering glow or the comforting sound of the fire—these things were routine in our lives. It was the seldom occurring moment of fun that we were enjoying most. I was content to be with Ma, listening to her comments about each of our baskets and hearing her rare melodious laughter.

It wasn't long before the snickering, giggling, nudging and punching began. With so many of us acting up at the same time Ma lost patience and warned, "You ruffians will go upstairs to bed, if you don't calm down, now!" Nobody wanted to mount the spooky dark stairs alone so we soon complied with Ma's orders.

We were finally able to get down to business. We began brainstorming ideas. My idea was to make a basket incorporating stocks of grain. One of my brothers suggested a gingerbread boy and my older sister decided hers should be a drum made from the Quaker Oats box. Ma said us kids had the God-given talent to make a silk purse out of a sow's ear. I laughed at the thought, but was secretly happy with the compliment and recognition from Ma.

We busied ourselves pasting and creating ruffles, rose buds, spirals, and curls in our personal choices of streamer colors. Ruching, pressing, folding, and ruffling, we each tried to come up with unique ideas for a winning basket. Soon we got the idea to spit on the red crepe paper and dab it to our faces for rouge and lipstick. Ma told us we looked like a bunch of flappers.

Ready to begin her creation, Ma came up with the very best idea! Ma's resolve was to make her basket a replica of a renaissance hat, popular at the time of her coming out debut when she was 23 years old. We were spellbound, as we watched Ma's face come alive with a soft look as the mental image of yesteryear burst forth. She said proudly, "If we can't afford a real hat like the one I had, I'll jus' create one!"

She started her project by cutting a pattern from some

old brown paper. Then she cut a cardboard rim from the bottom of a large Quaker Oats box. This was to be the crown of the hat, she explained. She stitched the crown and brim together with Grandma Walter's curved darning needle and flour sack string stiffened with Grandpa Walter's lump of beeswax. The entire project was then covered with burnt cream colored crepe paper. Upon completion of the hat shell, Ma lined the inside with a bleached sugar sack. "The top of the sack will be cinched tightly so it will have a finished look," she told us.

She had dyed yards of cheesecloth a soft orange by boiling it in old fashioned Rit dye. This would be used for the hat covering and veil. After the final rinse, she plunged the cheesecloth into a thick boiled sugar water and draped the sticky mass over the indoor clothesline that was strung throughout the dining room.

While the cheesecloth dried, she continued on with her project making crepe paper tea roses. Earlier in the season us kids had picked milkweed pods down in the marsh by the school. We filled the pods with dried red and green cherries, colorful beads of the cooked flour paste which had hardened, and beads that we had made from thin tightly rolled pieces of colorful magazine pictures. Ma arranged the dried milkweed pods with just the right amount of dried wild roses, blue bells, and honeysuckle, and added crepe paper leaves to make a beautiful floral piece to go on her hat. "Just enough to make it rich lookin'", she explained, "not cheap or overdone."

The next night we gathered around the table once again, each armed with our own individual design, needle, string, paper, and cup of cooked flour paste. We took turns culling our string over the beeswax lump. While we worked away on our projects, we watched Ma as she perfected her creation by stretching the stiff luscious looking soft orange cheesecloth over the simulated hat.

The most amazing surprise was the finishing touch that Ma had produced for her project. She had riffled through Grandma Walter's worn trunk and uncovered an old tintype photo taken of herself at her coming out party during the spring of her 23rd year. The patina of its filigreed frame was nearly rusted through around the outer edges. We thought it might be her wedding brooch—Ma had been beautiful in her younger years—not that she was so old now! She was only 37, but her life on the farm, together with having so many of us, had aged her beyond her years.

She proudly and gently nestled the tarnished cameo-type pin into the center front of her beautiful basket hat, and gave a light tap on the frame to be certain that it was properly secured. The multi-colored beads that us kids had fashioned dangled in a set of three on one side of the brim.

Ma stood back and gazed lovingly at the basket. We could see that she was not only proud of the basket, but perhaps was longing for the comfort and joy of the easy life of her younger days. "I wore a hat that looked a lot like this for my debut, the spring I turned 23," she recounted. It wasn't surprising that Ma wanted to relive her comfortable and carefree debutante days. Now she was a prairie farmer's wife with eight kids—we had no way of knowing that she would have four more kids by the time she turned 45—and a never-ending workload of cooking, cleaning, scrubbing clothes on a washboard, working in the fields, making clothes, canning food, and planting what seemed like an entire city block of garden. Ma picked up the hat, paused for a moment, then gently placed it on top of the cluttered 1800s bookcase.

After a short time of surreptitious pokes with the needles, snickering, muttered words, and elbow pokes to each others ribs needless to say, Ma sent us all to bed. The mountainous profusion of paper would have to wait yet

185

another day, or for "However long it takes fer you young'uns to decide to behave!", Ma declared harshly.

By the next evening we were anxious to once again try our hands at creating our baskets. Our assembly line piecework continued on. We soon became proficient bead molders and crepe paper tea rose makers. We gained expertise in making bows, pencil spirals, ruffles and streamers. Our gingerbread boys wore bright green collars and suits of brown with white buttons. We hustled to finish our baskets which we had decided to make from two quart syrup pails. We could only decorate the lids and put crepe paper bows on the handles because the paste wouldn't stick to the tin.

As the big day approached, our excitement mounted. Each day we would come up with another idea for our basket. We pestered Ma so much, that she finally declared, "If you kids don't stop botherin' me, and do yer chores, yer not goin' to the social at all!" We knew better than to press the issue.

Feast For The Basket Social — The time came to pack the baskets for the social. Deciding on what food to put in them was a bigger challenge than creating the pretty containers.

The consensus was to fill the baskets with Ma's sour cream fried chicken. Everyone said she made the best fried chicken this side of the county line. Hard-boiled pullet eggs dressed with Ma's famous egg mustard dressing made the tastiest deviled eggs in the territory. The dessert of choice would be a coffee cake, mainly because our commodity flour was too coarse for making fine textured dessert cakes.

I went out to the chicken house with Ma to help her pick a biddy that would be going to the Basket Social. As she laid the biddy's neck across the chopping block, she muttered, "Carter always finds money enough for his wants, while we go without!" I knew this was her way of justifying the killing of the biddy. But what she had said was true—to a point. We weren't starving, but us kids were hungry for the kind of food that we had heard about. As she raised the hatchet over the biddy's neck, Ma concluded, "This biddy refused to give up her infernal settin'. She was ruinin' every egg in the henhouse."

Back in the kitchen Ma scalded the biddy, plucked the pin-feathers and singed it over lighted pacers on the open lids atop the firebox. It was cut up and put in a pot to simmer. Later it was smothered in sour cream and flour then fried. Ma saved the prime cuts for the basket finger food. She ground the remaining parts to mix with potted meat for sandwiches. The chicken morsels and sandwiches were supplemented with home canned currant sauce then placed in the basket. It was tied securely with a dyed green string. I smiled with pride at the basket. Yup! Biddy would be going to the Basket Social, alright!

Us kids were ecstatic when Ma said we could cut each sandwich into triangles and wrap them ourselves in the wrinkled waxed bread wrappers from a loaf we had eaten on our trip to Dunseth to see Bill and Gene at the CCC camp.

Laughing and giggling, we discussed what the other ladies might be bringing to the Basket Social. Each one had her own specialty. We expected Mrs. Halverson's basket to contain Lefse, and Mrs. Ochsner's to contain bean and potato sandwiches. We just knew that no one's basket would compare to our Ma's.

The Big Day Arrives — After what seemed like a lifetime to me the long awaited day finally arrived. As my excitement mounted, nothing seemed to bother me. Even my brothers and sisters didn't seem as obnoxious as they usually were. Our disgusting chore of cleaning the gutters behind the milk cows went smoothly, and—wonder of wonders!—there was no complaining. After our chores, we carried water from the well to fill the wash boilers for our baths. Once the fire was built for dinner, Ma would heat it on the stove.

After dinner we dipped a small amount of hot water from the boiler to wash the dishes. We were very careful not to use too much of our bathing water, lest we would have to carry more from the well. In those days, if we thought about sanitation at all, it would have been our last thought—the very word itself sounded foreign to us! The most we ever thought about it was when we heard Ma say, "Go wash yer face and hands," But bathing wouldn't bother any of us this time—this time it was for a special occasion! Baths all done, kids all dressed, and baskets all packed, we headed out to the yard for our transportation.

"There won't be room for all the teams of horses in the lean-to on the school grounds. We'll take the Model T," Pa declared. We all piled into the jitney. The big kids sat in the back seat with the small ones on their laps. Tiny toddlers sat between Ma and Pa, with the baby always on Ma's lap. Any leftover kids stood on the floor behind the front seat. Pa tied a chicken crate on the rear bumper to hold all our precious baskets. We were so excited!

Starting the Model T was a major chore. Pa fitted the crank and spun it a time or two. The engine coughed and choked, then silence. Pa yelled, "Push the spark up." By the time Ma could reach over her basket creation and around all the kids, Pa had spun the crank another round. "Now shove the gas lever," he shouted. While he cranked himself to a sweat, Ma mumbled to no one in particular, "I told him cranks can snap a man's arm when they kick." Finally the jalopy sputtered to a purr. Pa, with a look of relief on his face, jumped behind the wheel and we were off to the Basket Social!

Pa was all dressed up in his Sunday best. He sat ramrod straight behind the wheel. He yelled back, "Always keep two hands on the wheel when going breakneck speed!" We were going all of 30 mph, for Heavens Sake! Out the gate to the east we chugged, and turned left up over Chokecherry Patch Hill. With each irregularity of the prairie road, the non-absorption tires hit the rut and bounded out with a teeth-jarring thud. Each thud put cracks a little deeper in the paste on our baskets. Darn it, I thought, I wanted to make an impression at the social.

We complained intermittently about the bumps, then giggled over who we hoped would *not* get Ma's basket. I said, "Boy, I hope John Trowbridge don't git it." My sister Shirley said, "Albin Roselle, either." We tittered and nudged one another. Pa finally got tired of the commotion and yelled over the noise of the Model T, "Quiet down, or ya won't be eatin' with yer friends, y'll be eatin' with me!" Ma chimed in, scolding us in her strained voice, "How many times do I have to tell ya? It ain't right to be funnin' over those with slack minds."

Anticipation mounted as we chugged up the last steep hill near the school house. It was the very same hill on which our brother, Bill—wanting so much to impress the new school marm—drove over the hill so fast that the teacher, who was bundled in a quilt to protect herself from the chill factor, was run over. She scrambled from beneath her pile of wraps unhurt. We joked about the incident and badgered Bill for years after that.

"Big crowd." Pa said, as he throttled down to park. As we all piled out of the car Pa warned, "Walk like ladies and gents." As we crossed the school yard we heard him add, "I don't wanna hear nothin' but compliments 'bout my kids," his tone reflecting the unspoken words, *Or you know what y'll git!*

Inside, school desks were lined up around the room and a few tiny babies were snuggled in mounds of wraps thrown over desk tops. Women kept their places by their children, while the men formed a stag line around the huge jacketed stove near the door. Chewin' snuff, spittin' and smokin' was the craze at the time for young males, and a few no-account women—Ma's term. Flaked wax was sprinkled over the oil soaked rough wooden floor. Sometimes a product like Lux Flakes doubled for shaved paraffin wax. The wax made it easier to glide while dancing.

The Hillbilly band for the evening—Billy and Lois Holmes' band from up the spur—squeaked out country favorites. (Billy later became my sister Marian's husband). Older folks honored the young by dancing with them. Young children danced all evening long to fox trots, waltzes, polkas, schottisches, two-steps and square dances. The hand clappin', foot stompin' music ceased by 11:00 p.m. to allow for a short bit of entertainment by the locals.

It was a proud moment for Ma and Pa when Marian and I sang duets of *Home on the Range, She's Got Rings on Her Fingers* and danced the Charleston. We also danced a jig for a minute or two, then I burst forth in a yodel that my brother, Bill, taught me. Bill could have been on radio, he was so good at yodeling. Ma said, "He does better 'n Gene Autry. Only difference is, Bill didn't bone up on the guitar." Stage fright finally got the best of us, so Marian and I hurriedly performed an *Allemande, left and right,* and quickly ended our act with a reasonable facsimile of *Two Gents Do-Si-Do*, and then exited the stage.

I remember another time, Ma and Pa tried to get Marian to entertain a group—she must have been only two or three years old. They had her perform wearing nothing more than an imitation toy drum around her chubby pink body. The planned performance ended up consisting of Marian standing ramrod straight and still. She seemed to have forgotten everything she was supposed to do and just stood there showing off her cute little body. Pa finally had to carry her off the stage. As for *our* performance, Marian and I didn't mind that we were being upstaged by the heap of decorated baskets stacked beneath the American flag.

The fidgety gents had been waiting somewhat impatiently to bid on the baskets. One basket in particular captured great interest—Freda's, the school teacher. Since Freda boarded with us, every male for miles around over the age of twenty had for weeks begged us Carter kids for a hint as to the shape, size, and color of her basket.

Back in those days, money was so hard to come by. The men had all earned their monthly salary through labor intensive jobs like: fencing, rigging, roping, plowing and milking. They all hoped that their money would be spent courting the favor of the teacher.

I think the teacher probably could have cared less about who would bid on her basket, since it was about time for her rigid contract to end at the Chase Lake School District. Ma said Freda had a mind of her own. "She breaks every rule." Ma often said, "If she wears her dresses any *shorter*, she'll have two more cheeks to powder!"

The Bidding Begins — The auctioneer and his helper stepped onto the stage. It was finally time to auction the beautiful baskets. Most males took deep breaths, hoping for some divine guidance to steer them wisely toward Freda's basket.

"Who'll gimme 25 cents for this fancy basket?" the auctioneer bellowed. "Gimme 25, gimme 25!" The gent over by the coal bin thrust a burly haymaker skyward. "I got 25, 25, who'll gimme 30 cents, who'll gimme 30, gimme 30?" The bidding went on until the whole table was emptied of all the baskets except for my Ma's. Then the auctioneer shouted: "How much ya gimme for this beautiful Sunday go-to-meetin' hat?" Young men pushed their way to the front of the stage line. This—to be sure—*was* the teacher's basket. Frenzied bidding commenced. Wranglers bid higher and higher, attempting to outbid each other for the fabulous basket. Very soon the bidding topped out at the unbelievable price of $1.75. The highest bid came from a gent named Dude. Ma was ecstatic, and us kids were thrilled with the idea of her basket taking the Grand Prize! Flushed with excitement, Dude sauntered to the front of the room to collect his prize. As he accepted his winnings, other men were nudging him and teasing him, because the whole motley crew of party crashers thought for sure the basket belonged to the *teacher.*

The auctioneer called for the attention of the boisterous crowd. On the count of three, the bidders were to open all the boxes and baskets to identify the donors. I remember the moment being so quiet and intense. I knew that when I was old enough to have a basket up for bid, I wanted it to be enjoyed by someone nice. The time had come, now all the baskets were opened. Almost everyone was looking toward Dude to see his reaction. When Dude opened his beautiful hat basket, much to his dismay, he found that Ma was the creator of the basket, not Freda. Naturally Dude was crushed when he discovered it wasn't the teacher's basket, but that of a married woman with twelve kids. I remember that day, even in his disappointment, Dude was more gentlemanly than Pa gave him credit for. Ma admired Dude for that. He told Ma, "That was the best chicken I ever ate."

Ma told me that the quilt she won for first prize was secondary to the privilege of having lunch with a handsome cowpoke from beyond the lake. Ma was a looker in her day, and she had come from a family with money. I imagine it was good for her ego to have the attention that her beautiful hat basket brought her that day. Dude went back to being a rowdy cowpoke with hurt pride, but Ma stayed happy forever after.

The Gentry always kept a possessive eye out for Ma, and it was no different at the basket social. I didn't believe Pa to be a jealous sort, but he always had to be in charge lest his popularity be diminished. When the rowdies from the neighboring town had arrived and moved in doors, as if they had become the new keepers of the cloakroom, Pa kept an eye on them. He knew all about the guy named Dude from up the spur. Dude was a heller for good times, like Pa himself, especially when he imbibed beyond his limits. You can be sure Pa really eyed Dude after he won the bid for Ma's basket.

Fracas at the Social — After supper, the music started, and Dude moved back toward the stage line. After a few dances, Dude asked Ma to dance, "In thanks for the dinner 'n all," he said to Pa. They danced, then Dude moved off to be with the men over in the coal chute area. A moment later the noises of a scuffle came to us from behind the jacketed stove. A group of men were shouting, pushing, shoving, and hurling expletives at one another—the likes of which some of us kids had never heard before.

By this time the music had come to an abrupt halt. Mothers were screaming for their children, and scurrying around to collect them. Most of the ladies hurried to the front stage, away form the main floor, each yelling threats to their husbands, "If you don't stop...!" Threats rang forth accompanied by more expletives and more yelling. At 2:00 a.m. the so-called *social* had come to an abrupt and unhappy end.

Pa survived the brawl with one black eye, a bloody nose and disheveled, soot-covered clothes. "Damn fool prob'ly broke my nose," Pa swore. "The ba#$%*d will git what's comin' to him later." On the way out to the car, Pa recanted the story, "The hooligans joined Dude in trying' to teach yer Pa, and the whole of Chase Lake District, just who's King of the Territory." During the fracas, one of the thugs had sneaked into the coal room, got an axe, and raised it up over Pa's head, about to bludgeon Pa from behind. Just then

Divine Providence, in the form of our good neighbor, landed a fist to the jaw of the would-be assailant.

Us kids were filled with terror, humiliation and disgust. How could Pa have acted that way? How could he have made such a fool of himself, and us too? Was he alright, or was he hurt bad? Pa was prone to imbibe a bit beyond good judgement at barn dances, country socials, or any place there was an audience. "Well, at least yer Pa isn't as bad off as he was at the Peterson Township dance," Ma mumbled to us.

She told us that one time, early in their marriage, they had gone to a barn dance in Peterson Township and "ruffians had *ruffled* yer Pa's feathers once too many times during the evenin'." It seems a fisticuff had began, ending with Pa singlehandedly throwing seven of the hoodlums down a hayhole in the barn where the dance was being held. She choked out breathlessly, "He came out of that brawl wearin' only one cuff of his silk weddin' shirt, and a bunch a cuts and bruises."

As we all climbed into the old Model T, Pa was outside the car cranking feverishly, botching the job even more than he had at home. I knew it was because he had *too much under his belt*. Ma told Pa he couldn't drive—but then neither could any of the rest of us—so Pa ended up climbing in behind the wheel, and some kind soul passing through the school yard cranked the engine to life.

Topsey-Turvey On Chokecherry Patch Hill — You would think there's no possible way to have an accident on a cowpath road—even if the driver *is* inebriated. *That is, unless* a ditch or sharp incline runs parallel to the road. Well, let me tell you we made it just fine down the first steep incline that night, the car *jack-knifing* only once. We could hardly breath for fright as we chugged across the marsh and up Chokecherry Patch Hill, where the road ran only two feet from the ridge drop-off for three-quarters of a mile. One washout brought the ridge to within a foot of the ruts where Pa was driving!

Sober, Pa could make a Model T do marvelous things like jump ditches, ford creeks, and outrun fast-stepping buggy horses. But inebriated, it would be an exercise in ingenuity between the driver and the drop into the chokeberry patch.

Sure enough—the washout won! We bolted off the ridge toward the lake at 25 mph in a death-defying plunge, and the Model T cut a 35 foot swath through trees and brush! The bushes shook, gears squealed, the motor roared, coughed then sputtered, and the car came to a crushing halt, lodged on a pile of brambles and a substantial group of downed trees. None of us paid any regard to the possibility of the gasoline blowing up.

In a panic Ma yelled, "Anybody hurt?" Pa shook his head then slurred, "Plunging headlong into the chokecherry patch was simply a navigational error!" Pa was a true "Gentry," a man of extreme confidence. Ma croaked, "It's a good thing the brambles stopped us. We would have headed right into Chase Lake!" Pa barked back at her, "Well, we didn't, woman!" Pa was irate. In his usual bout with ego, he would have liked to blame one of us for the incident, but since none of us drove he knew the ploy was useless.

To Pa, the only way to make the Model T walk across mud was to place both the spark and the gas levers to maximum and shoot full speed ahead. When this didn't work, Pa's glance told us kids, "Time to get out and push." We quite often were called upon to push when the car wouldn't start. The gleam in Pa's eyes told us he was thankful for lots of strong kids.

As it turned out, we didn't have to push. After several attempts to free the car from the mud, Pa resorted to extreme profanity. He spewed his outbursts with such fervor that we expected the car to levitate from the shockwaves created by Pa's language.

Pa told us that we had better start walking, because this car wasn't going anywhere tonight. We all got out of the old Model T and started climbing up to the ridge. We were dirty, tired, and winded as we trudged the mile and a half back to the homestead.

Passing through the meadow just beyond the rise, a madrigal of meadow sounds captured my attention. Haplessness subsided as I enjoyed the rhapsody of peeps, chirps and resonances that filled the air. Bleating lambs, chirping killdeer, singing crickets, and squawking sandpipers seemed to sing a kind of harmony along with the croaking frogs and the calls of the whooping cranes. I imagined the beautiful chorus was a message to me to "Cheer up! Cheer up! Cheer up!"

As we tramped toward home, I thought our lifestyle surely provided us experiences, like this, that made us feel somehow Pa was in partnership with God in training us kids "the hard way." I knew Pa figured the Lord would take care of him and his body, even if he didn't know how to take care of himself.

The Pied Piper — I remember my first trip to the circus, the shrill sounds of the circus calliope beckoned us, from just over the hill, beyond the Crazy House. It was blasting out a brisk version of *The Sidewalks of New York*, which seemed to reverberate throughout the open prairie for miles. As we approached the circus grounds in our rig, we saw many other people in cars and wagons journeying toward the sound—as if the Calliope were a Pied Piper and we his faithful subjects. At first us kids thought that we were hearing whistles of some type. Then we saw it! It was a huge white wagon with wheels, an old truck really, much like our red school bus. It was vividly painted with pictures of circus attractions and the like. The strangest thing about the wagon was its whistle-like music. We had never seen a calliope before, and were amazed at the way it played music, seemingly by itself. We learned later that the calliope was played like Ma's piano, on a keyboard which controlled thirty-two steam whistles, each belching out their own tone.

The calliope motored throughout the main streets of town, throttling down just long enough for the driver to announce that the circus would have two showings today—one at 1:00 o'clock p.m. and one at 4:00 o'clock p.m. I stared as the announcer talked through the funnel-shaped megaphone. Gee, one of those things might come in handy for calling the hogs or my brothers and sisters. Instead of a having gadget like that, I had to achieve the same result, by cupping my hands to my mouth and yelling loudly, most times straining my vocal cords.

The crowd followed the calliope to the circus grounds. We had to park quite a distance from the "Big Top". Further out in the grassy pasture, the teams and horses were tethered in the blazing sun. They munched grass patiently while waiting for their owners. Us kids were fidgety and impatient with the anticipation of seeing our very first circus. It seemed to us, like it would take forever to get to the tent which housed the three-ring arena!

As we maneuvered closer to the entrance of the tent, we could hear the roaring of the caged lions and Bengal tigers, the snarling of the bobcats, the shouted commands of the trainer, and the fierce cracking of his long black snake-like whip. The excited townsfolk, and farmers alike, jostled and shoved each other through the entryway. Dirt and dust filtered into our shoes, between our toes, and up our nostrils. It created little *mudpies* in the corners of our eyes, but we were used to it because of working in the fields. The clouds of silt along with the odor of sweat and animal debris, created a crude atmosphere. It reminded me of our barn and the animal pens at home.

Before we could climb the bleachers to our near top perch toward the end ring, the elephant trumpeted a few wild and eerie calls. I didn't know if it was scolding its calf, or if it was just generally complaining about having to entertain the audience. It took nearly half an hour for the crowd to get settled, and the ringmaster to take his place on the platform.

Finally, the ringmaster picked up his megaphone and shouted a welcome to the audience—to "the most exciting show on earth!". The spectators clapped their hands and roared with delight. To the music of the lively circus band, he began introducing the performers by name, announcing the ring number in which they would be performing. As each name was called, the performer came bounding into the appropriate ring.

All performers, including the men, were dressed in brilliantly colored costumes embellished with sequins, beads, tassels, and rhinestones. Some of the ladies wore headdresses that were at least two feet tall. There were costumes with plumes of ostrich feathers, sequined bustiers, tutus, and long dresses with flowing, filmy trains—the likes of which I had never seen!

This was all new to me! I know my mouth must have been hanging open a mile. I was so amazed by the sights, sounds, smells, and excitement of it all—not to mention the indecent clothing of the ladies! Ma said, "It's *risqué*. All performers dress risqué to git the attention of the menfolk. Kinda like the burlesque dancers of the 1800s." Pa always referred to the burlesque dancers as the *burleyque* dancers. I sneaked a peek at him to see if he was looking at the ladies, but Pa seemed to be enjoying everything in general, and nothing in particular.

One of the ladies wore a hula type skirt made of shimmery cellophane-like strips. During her act, she shook her hips and gyrated around the stage. As she did, the skirt started to shed strips of the flimsy material. We giggled and poked one another. One of my sisters said, "She better stop before we see something that's not a part of the show." We all near split with laughter at the remark.

The ringmaster continued to introduce the various performers of the circus. The trapeze artists, who would perform aerial gymnastics; the female English side-saddle riders; the male and female team of bareback riders who would entertain us with acrobatic feats on loping horses; and the star of the show, the lady who would whirl around a pole, high up off the ground, doing acrobatics, while hanging only from a leather strap. The next group of folks he introduced was the clowns, the jugglers, the fat lady of the circus, and the midgets. As you can imagine, us kids had much to say about the fat lady of the circus and the midgets. We had never before seen such little people! When the introductions were complete, the show began.

In the center ring was the tightwire act. We held our breaths as the performer pretended to slip off the wire. The misstep on the highwire seemed to elicit greater distress from the audience than from the performer himself.

The Shetland ponies intrigued us the most, being as how we were farm-animal-oriented. These dinky snow white ponies created such excitement in us kids. They were so cute and whimsical looking. "They came from the Shetland Islands," Ma explained, "they've curried them down real nice." The ponies were only about forty inches high with extra long manes and tails that were fancied up with bright pink *doodads*. Each of their heads were fitted with pink feathery plumes that bounced with every step they took. We were so enthralled with all of the animal acts. The animals seemed so well trained. They were nothing like our animals at home.

With each act, the crowd clapped, cheered, groaned or roared with laughter in all the appropriate places. Pa bought us each a small bag of peanuts in a red and white striped bag for a penny a piece. There was cotton candy—but unfortunately, none for us. It was three cents for the billowy pink bundle, but Pa said we couldn't afford it. I asked Ma if we should save the peanut shells for the pigs, but she said no. I thought the shells would have made good bedding for our animals—of course, we would need *a truckload* for the pigpen. I was willing to eat a truckload of peanuts to help out the farm! But then—that's the way us kids thought.

One of the final circus acts was the beautiful lady who did acrobatics while whirling around from a leather strap on an extremely tall pole. She first grabbed the leather strap in her teeth and twirled herself around very fast. It was enough to make me dizzy! Then she changed positions, fitting her ankle into the strap, and performed more gymnastic feats while hanging by one ankle.

She finished her performance with gyrations and maneuvers which, to me, seemed humanly impossible. It was very scary! Ma leaned over and threatened me and Cammie, "Don't you two try this at home!" Cammie punched me and challenged, "I dare you!" My retort was, "I double dare you." "I double dare you ten times!" he stated, matter-of factly. Ma chose to shut us up by giving each of us a knuckle bounce to the head, and in near megaphone intensity shouted, "The two of ya, shut-up!"

As the performances came to an end, the circus band played some lively tunes, signaling the performers to come out and take their final bows. The finale was an indication that my first circus was over—too soon to suit me—I might add! It had been one of the most exciting times of my young life.

During the entire trek to the parking area and all the way home, us kids relived every shred of fun we had had at the circus. We discussed each detail over and over. Once we got home we couldn't wait to emulate the highwire acts we had seen. We knew just where we could go for the best highwire imitation! Our barn had two-by-four partitions on which we could do our balance beam performances. For some weeks to come, we entertained ourselves with the highwire barn beams, and practiced our bareback riding techniques on our farm ponies.

The clowning around came naturally—we didn't need any more practice for that. Like everything else, the novelty of our circus trip wore off and we drifted to another of the great challenges of childhood—that which suited our fancy at the given moment. I did, however, accomplish the one great feat of stand-up riding. My memory of that day at the circus sustained me for a very long time.

Head, Heart, Hands And Health — Back in the 1930s, the 4-H Club brought a welcome diversity to the monotony of prairie life for many kids. The clubs originated among rural youth and was sponsored by the U. S. Department of Agriculture. Its name was suggested in the pledge, "I pledge my head to clearer thinking, my heart to greater loyalty, my hands to larger service, and my health to better living, for my Club, my Community, and my Country." It afforded scientific instruction in farming and agriculture—as scientific as we could get in the 1930s—and home economics. 4-H taught us everything from the proper way to curry our ponies to the best feeding materials for our sheep. Agricultural activities consisted of raising a garden or learning to grow a field crop.

I'd look forward with great anticipation to each monthly meeting at Cora Mae Amick's farmhouse. She was our 4-H leader, and I really liked her. She had been a school teacher and had all the qualities I thought fine ladies should possess. She was friendly, fair-minded, spoke well and treated us kindly.

I recall Mrs. Amick teaching us girls the basic ingredient lists for making pies, cakes, and pastries. She lectured on the elements of a well-balanced diet, which was very different then than it is now.

My favorite 4-H project was learning how to make my own dress. Mrs. Amick taught us to create our own dress patterns from pictures we saw in catalogs or periodicals. I learned all about measuring circumferences, shoulder lengths, neck and skirt lengths to fit my body measurements. For demonstration purposes, Mrs. Amick took the measurements of one girl so that we could see what to do. Then we measured each other. As we measured and recorded the numbers on our paper tablets, we laughed and giggled. The assignment was to decide what style of dress we wanted to make, draw out the pattern, then sew the dress. Mrs. Amick announced that the prettiest and best constructed garment would be entered in the Stutsman County Fair. We were all very excited.

I decided my dress would be a canary yellow organdy with pink, yellow, and orangish-red tea roses. I chose a pattern for the top which was fitted to my no-chest skinny body. During those days I was nearly twenty pounds underweight. For me, "thin was definitely in." I planned that the dress would have ties at the waist which would meet in a bow at the back, a fairly large collar that would hug my shoulders, plain short sleeves, and a three-tiered gathered skirt.

Little did I know that I had bitten off more than I could possibly chew. All went well until I got to the skirt pieces. Each section gave me more fits than the one before. I was forced to gather each tier separately, taking care to keep the length even. I sewed them, first by hand, then with Ma's old treadle machine. Oil spills were not uncommon when attempting to learn machine care. As I chewed my lips and gritted my teeth in concentration, the dress took form. As I stitched and ripped, I cried and re-stitched. Crying and ripping and re-stitching went on and on until the fabric was nearly worn out. The perfectionist in me wanted each tier to have a perfectly ruffled, perfectly hemmed appearance. I attached the tiers with French seams in order for the delicate fabric to hold during my playing, rough-housing, and all purpose sitting.

After many laborious hours, my dress was finished. I breathed a sigh of relief as I tried it on. In my estimation, it was the most beautiful piece of work I had ever seen, and it was all mine. I couldn't wait to show Mrs. Amick. She loved it and determined that it should be entered in the fair.

The big day arrived all too soon! Cora, Ma, and me went to the fairgrounds and put my dress on display in the proper section of the show. Cora said, "Be sure you write down every step you took, and the cost of your dry goods, and notions, otherwise points will be subtracted from your score. You'll have to be on the platform, too, and tell all about it." That was the scary part, because I had a real hard time admitting that I had made a mistake—more like several, during the course of the dressmaking project. Pa told me, "You better be strictly above board, girl, or folks won't have respect for you, and you won't respect yerself."

Pa was a stickler for "honorableness", but like many of us, he often fell short between the "tellin' and the livin". I recall one time I was at Hanson's Hardware with a school friend I'll call Pearl. She stole candy from a half-penny candy jar. I panicked and snuck out of the store. When I got home, I made the mistake of telling about the incident. Pa yelled and forbade me from every playing with Pearl again. He repeated to us kids time and again, "Yer judged by the company you keep."

The Stutsman County Fair — The long awaited County Fair was buzzing with homemakers carrying their homemade breads, pies, pastries, cookies, jams and jellies to the appropriate booths for the judging. Ribbons would be presented to first, second and third place winners. The

Grand Champion Rosette would be announced and awarded sometime during the fair.

Ma didn't enter her canned goods in the home-canning division. She said that her family-style canning just wouldn't fit in and "besides, food is for eatin' not for showin' off." Ma recoiled at the thought of competition of any kind. Her favorite saying was "We're as good as the best, but no better'n the rest."

Fair day was fun for us kids. There was no money, so we could only ride on the free merry-go-round, but we could "scuff around" the grounds and watch everyone else having fun. There was livestock judging for the Future Farmers. I'm not sure if the Future Farmers title had been used back then, or not. There were games, rides, food, arts and crafts, and the latest in farm machinery displays. There were no high-end home decor items, no saunas and hot-tubs. Everything was basically country crafts. Back in the '30's, if you couldn't make it with your own hands—it wasn't worth much to farm folks. The women gravitated to the handmade quilts, baby clothes, and the hooked and braided rugs, while the men gathered around the farm equipment displays, the agricultural booths, and of course—the booth for making home-brew.

During most of the day, I was breathless with anticipation. Would my dress win a prize? Would the judges like it? Was it the prettiest in the county? I remember Cora Mae's surprising words, "Ferne, now aren't you glad you did your sewing project well, you won second prize for this beautifully made garment." I was ecstatic. I not only had a beautiful new dress, I had a ribbon, as well.

Fireworks ended the celebration, and we all went home happy. Each taking with us, a little piece of a big memory. As for me and my dress, just two weeks after the fair, on a Sunday afternoon, while playing tag and roughhousing with neighborhood company, one of the boys yanked at the belt of my new dress, and ripped a part of the skirt right out. I was crushed. Ma patched it later, but it never meant the same to me after that day.

The Day of the Twister

The Day the Twister Hit — The day began like any other day, devoid of new things and interesting challenges. I threw my arms skyward in a long stretch, partly because it was an involuntary movement, and perhaps subconsciously because Pa said, "You could take a lesson by watching the animals. They stretch the first thing when they wake up in order to energize their overly relaxed muscles."

The barnyard rooster's unsolicited early morning wake-up call had set the young cocks of the flock into motion. They came to attention, stretched their scrawny necks, raised their hackles and croaked forth a reasonable facsimile of a rooster's crow. The hens ducked, squawked and scratched the hardpan for bits of food. It was a henhouse hallelujah chorus!

Submerged in sleep, brought on by exhaustion from harvesting in the heat the day before, I still managed to hear the fowl choir. I turned over, face down on my straw-ticking mattress. My feather pillow felt so cozy. I popped one eye open to see if the day was acceptable. It was—but little did I realize that on this gorgeous late summer day in the '30's our homestead would become a target of nature's fury. I wiggled from under the hand-carded wool comforter.

Pa's call from the foot of the stairs seemed to harmonize with the creature chorus going on in the barnyard. "Git outta bed! Another big day ahead." It was my turn to start the chores, gather kindling and round up the cattle for milking. I slipped over the lumpy mattress ticking and peered at the heap of scattered clothing on the floor. My clothes were near the top of the pile. I retrieved the pair of stiff-legged overalls, stiffened not by newness, but by weeks of accumulated grime. I hopped and teetered on one leg in an attempt to thrust the other leg into the rigid wrinkled overalls. The denim shirt I wore was my brother's, so naturally it was well ventilated with rips and three-cornered tears made from crawling under the barbed wire fences. I didn't have to worry about shoes—I had none.

Sleepy-eyed, I made my way through the boys' room and descended the dark landing of the stairs. As I touched the unsecured door knob, the door sprang open and startled me. Ma said, "Either the house is on tilt, or you kids've been swingin' on that door again!" *Lots of things around here were on tilt,* I thought. In those days of hardship and strife, I wasn't always optimistic.

Making my exit through the conglomeration of furniture in the dining room and kitchen, I glanced about to see if a scrap of food might have been left from the night before. Foodstuff was never visible or in sight at our house—and for good reason—what with all the hungry mouths to feed. Doing the next best thing for my empty stomach, I stopped by the water pail, plunged the long-handled dipper into it and scooped out a drink. After swishing it around in my mouth, like I had seen Pa do, I spat into the swill pail. I was thinking another dipper or two should last me until breakfast was ready.

I walked out onto the high old wooden porch. Cupping my hand over my brow to tolerate the brilliant rising sun over the east knoll, I did a quick overview of the dooryard. Neither grass nor weed grew in the soil that had been packed hard from the travels of heavy farm machinery. Ma said, "Even the soil has the breath knocked out of it in this Godforsaken country. The worms and parasites can't survive, let alone us human folks." There were times when I had to agreed with Ma.

I bounded down the steps in my bare feet. The dirt was littered with pebbles of all sizes, rusty bent nails, metal washers, and chicken leavings. At this point, I thought it would have been nice to wear old John Trowbridge's tire tread flats strapped on with gunnysack leggings. I stooped to pick up a dried twig, wondering where it had come from, then lofted it toward the granary. Obnoxious roosters raised their combs and flapped their wings, as if to say, "I'm the boss here!" The flock of chickens scattered briefly then began to follow me, hoping I would toss them some grain as I passed the granary.

At first I walked past the granary, but they were obviously going to follow me out of the yard, so I came back and tossed them some chicken scratch. It consisted of millet, flax seed, wheat, rye, barley, oat kernels and sunflower seeds—the food that we should have been eating all along. As I roamed among the flock, I sensed the peace and grace of God's dew-laden, mystical morning. The pigeons perched on top of the pigeon house ceased preening and fluffing. They swooped down into the midst of the chicken flock for their breakfast. Ducks, geese, and turkeys joined them and the pecking order began in earnest. Some chickens were quietly eating and scratching as only hens can. Ma said, "The hens are like mothers, they'll scratch for every bite of food available, no matter what."

The hogs were confined in the pen surrounding the original old rock-and-mortar one-room homestead house. I was oblivious to the stench because of my daily contact with it. *Hogs don't know the difference,* I reasoned. From a wallowing crouch, they grunted, sloshed through the mire and began hugging the feeding trough. They pushed, squealed, and bit at one another, crowding the runts to the periphery. They nearly decked me by banging against the fronts and backs of my knees as I poured the slop of milk, mash, and vegetable peelings into the trough. I climbed the fence to leave. My thoughts were, *no wonder they call them hogs, they really are!*

Creating a diversion for myself, I gave my pitching arm practice by pegging a stone at a target, carefully avoiding the few remaining windows in the granary. I strolled to the knoll behind the sheep shed, and squatted to pick a few wild honeysuckles. I pressed them to my lips like a taster in a confection factory. It was sweet to my tongue. I felt like my tummy was so empty that it touched my backbone.

I was a bit leery about opening the sheep gate. A few days before, the frightened sheep had rushed the gate, crushing my sister Marian's hand and she had lost all her beautiful half-mooned fingernails. Today the sheep were at rest. A few fluttering ears repelled the swarm of tiny gnats that hovered over their warm fleeces. Happily for me, the chain was on the gate.

I looked at the derelict old rusty machinery parked on the parched side hill as I strolled through the lane to the south. The cowbell clanged in the distance, and I saw that the cows were belly-deep in the bog, drinking, stomping about, and switching flies with their wet sloppy tails. Each time the red heifer dipped her head toward the water, the bell's piercing peel changed to a hollow muted clang. *Splashing in water apparently affects cattle like it does humans,* I thought. They all gravitated to the water before heading in for milking. They only needed a little encouragement from their herdsman—me.

I drove them back up the lane and rounded the hill to the barn where Pa was waiting impatiently, a milk pail in one hand and a three-legged stool in the other. Instead of speaking, he spat tobacco juice, cleared his throat, and pointed toward the barn door. Pa wasn't so good at talking, but he was sure proficient at pointing and grunting orders. If we failed to guess correctly about where his finger was pointing, Pa showed his darker side.

We milked the cows, ate breakfast, packed our lunch box and drinks, harnessed the teams, then traveled back through the south lane, again to the lowlands, to make hay. We had already mowed the slough hay, dried, windrowed and bunched it into stacks called haycocks. Using a team hitched to a hay bucker, we scooped the bunched hay up and took it to a specified spot to begin a stack. Later we would use the hayrack to bring the hay to the loft.

I was the hay stomper of the day. Everyone in the field pitched hay over the high boards of the rack, I climbed up over the side of the rack and began to stomp the forks full of hay. As the perspiration dripped from my brow and my body, the men pitched up bundles of flying spears, and I jumped to and fro, up to the sides of the rack and across the middle. Whenever someone tossed a fork full, I rushed to the rescue.

I was exhausted and sweaty, but at least this time my brothers hadn't tossed a horse skull on the rack yelling, "Here, stomp this!" like they had done once before. The skull had caught me alongside the head, just above the eye. Divulging the name of the brother who impulsively tossed the bleached white horse head wouldn't be honorable of me. It sure did hurt like the devil, though. I sported a half-closed eye for the rest of the school year. One of my schoolmates taunted me, "Ya look like a pirate. Where's yer eye patch?"

After a few hours, Pa stopped pitching hay, shielded his eyes against the sun with his old battered brown hat, and said, "It's high noon—time to break out the grub." We were all glad to stop.

We tethered the horses to the side of the hayrack where they munched continuously while we hunkered down in the shade of the load. As we sat there eating, over the course of time, the gently roving fleecy clouds and the bright sunlight began to mutate into angry restless black clouds that began twisting and churning. The air became heavy and breathing was difficult. Clapping of thunder burst forth, then turned into a low groaning rumble. After a few moments of silence—too much silence—we noticed the birds and animals hunting for cover.

As the clouds fumed into bunches of twisting, black, spikey mounds, Pa said, "They're real angry." In a nervous voice he continued, "Dutch (his nickname for Ma) was right. The horses have been stepping 'round for a coupl'a hours and the Blue's jumpy." Our sheepdog, Blue, had been intermittently crouching, prowling and flopping on our laps.

When the first seriously brisk wind blistered into our nostrils, *The Gentry* stood up and faced west. He cupped his hand to his brow like a teller of the seasons, and called out, "Look quick! There's a twister headed in our direction. She'll be here within minutes!" I looked up to see an angry wild spiraling funnel cloud that looked like wheels within wheels, spinning at breakneck speed right toward us. We were all worried.

I always thought it was strange that natural disasters and furies of nature were always referred to as *she*. I pondered the subject briefly, maybe it was something like our neighbor woman, Rachel Sand, on the old Huggarude place, who could literally move mountains, while old Guerney, her husband, slumbered his way through life like Rip Van Winkle, content to let her take the lead. Ma said, "Men had their chance, now it's the womens' turn. When they intend it for good, there'll be miracles ya never even heard 'bout! All hell can't stop 'em either." *That's Ma*, I thought, *always coming up with something pretty good.*

That's the way the twister was. It may not have intended good, but it did intend to hit the mark. We had no time to get home. Pa hustled around throwing all small objects under the hayrack, mumbling something like: "Don't know why all hell breaks loose on us. S'pose God and the devil have a survival pact set up fer us, like fer Job, jus' to see if we'll come through it." Pa always blamed the gods for catastrophes in our lives, like crop failures, broken fences and low cash flow.

Pa's voice grew louder as his prophecy became a reality. "Give the horses more rope. Stick the pitchfork tines deep into the ground, an' grab a rope an' tie the rack to the mower wheel." Panic gripped our hearts. The dark angry twister was bearing down on us. We scrambled under the hay wagon. The tornado tore in, gyrated and whirled in a frenzy, as if it didn't want to miss anything. It suctioned the hay from the rack and the newly stacked hay mounds and sent it twirling up into the air. It uprooted small trees and sent tumbleweeds colliding into space, as if gravity had lost its hold on the planet.

The invisible spindle-like nothingness had forced blades of grass into the hides of the animals and into the boards of the hayrack like porcupine quills. Above our heads, the rack was heaving and lurching from side to side. "Quick!" Pa yelled, "Ferne, Gene, John, and all you hired hands, git to the windward side of the wagon. Grab on, hold tight and hang your body weight on the rack!"

I asked Pa if the horses would be taken up with us and the hayrack like chariots of fire. He didn't answer. Nature once again had a hammerlock on our emotions just as it had during previous catastrophes. Nature's fury wasn't new to us. Cyclones, blizzards, and dust storms had all waged war on us several times before.

It seemed like hours before the storm ended. The rain and hail continued to pelt the ground in sheets of white. The funnel cloud and severe winds left as quickly as they had come. We gathered up all that was left and headed for home. Although Pa appeared calm, he had a worried look about him. That was an unheard of characteristic for Pa. I'm sure he was worried about the safety of Ma and the younger kids at home. Our horses were cold, wet and tired. They acted the way we felt—nervous and shaken. Massive amounts of water, mud, hailstones and desolation was visible the entire way home.

We rounded the bend by the bog. Just over the rise we saw, to our horror, our full flock of more than 200 turkeys, drowned in a pool of water. They could easily have walked to higher ground. Instead, with no one to lead them, they huddled for safety and all died together. Pa swore, "Those stupid b$%@& turkeys could've walked out," then he cried. The flock was our livelihood. We had just lost several hundred dollars.

After seeing the turkeys, Pa became more worried about Ma and the kids. I wanted to ask about them, but I knew that at a time like this, silence was best. We pressed on through the lane, dreading the worst. Fear for the rest of the family seized our hearts. I swear we tried to look *through* the hills on both sides of the lane expecting complete devastation. We all held our breath. What would we see? Would the twister have destroyed everyone and everything?

Relief came as we sighted the first building, the granary. It leaned a bit more perhaps, and what few shingles remained had been greatly damaged. As we climbed the hill, a full view told us that the house and old barn were still standing. As we came closer we noted that the house was set a full inch and a half off the foundation. The yard was strewn with boards, chicken feathers, posts and tree limbs. Everyone was too numb to cry. Devastation reached as far as we could see.

Wind squalls had ripped the leaves from the poplars and cottonwoods. Leaves, grit and pieces of lumber had been flown great distances, winding up in a mangled mass in some places. Debris had been blown flat against the few wet window panes that remained.

Ma explained as we trooped toward her, "There was no time to crack the windows to relieve the pressure. The walls looked like they were breathing, they flexed in and out, and the glass cracked and blew out." Ma anxiously related the rest of the happenings: "The rain pelted in everywhere. It was powered by a fury that I hope never to see again. The d$#n thing ripped past the back door and cut a swath directly toward the Jenkin's place!"

Near the house, the wind had driven straw and grass blades through wooden posts. It had left some objects unharmed but completely destroyed others. Our one and only work truck was crushed, along with our new barn. Bodies of some of our livestock had been pierced through with two-by-fours. Others were riddled with splinters and shattered glass.

We heard later that the violently revolving funnel cloud, with its collection of dirt, debris, hail and 100 plus mph winds, had peeled the 600-pound cupola from the new barn at the Jenkins place. During its airborne flight, it traveled much distance, then lodged in a barbed wire fence a mile from the barn. By the grace of God my sister, Shirley, and our cousin, Gordon Mell were spared. They had been tending sheep that morning. Shirley said they could see the twister coming, so Gordon pushed her down, face-first in the mud of a cornfield. Each time she raised her head, he pushed her back down again, so the wind couldn't penetrate under her and perform a "lift-off". Meanwhile, they saw the cupola, dead turkeys, chickens and farmyard debris whizzing past over their heads, like missiles. It's a miracle that disaster was averted.

Ma's Magic Carpet Ride — The tornado had sent the children hustling into the dark cellar. Ma, bent on saving her precious piano, attempted to secure the doors by slipping table knives into the door jams. The minute or two that it took for the tornado to pass brought a change in the barometric pressure. It fell so rapidly that the raging wind sucked Ma, on her magic carpet—the front door—right out of the house, like Dorothy in the Wizard of Oz. Her semicircular flight pattern carried her skyward for 30 rods (165 yards) across the yard and over the clothesline, where she landed on the side hill. Bruised and breathless, she crawled back to the house. She was grateful that "Only one end of the piano got wet, and you kids are all safe." Then she asked of no one in particular, "This was a bad one, wasn't it?"

What destruction! Windows had blown out. We stared in disbelief at the gaping holes in the walls and the heaps of plaster on the floor. Wall decor had suddenly become just laths with no plaster. The only papered wall now resembled a venetian blind of twisted wet festoons, clinging only by a thread. Wind had thrown broken bits of glass from windows, along with dishes, pots and pans, house plants and knickknacks to the floor. Rain had drenched everything. The excessive winds had blown the long panel curtains out the window frames and had whipped them to shreds.

The storm had finally ended. The air had become calm and exhilarating. We gathered together on the back porch, looking out over the old dilapidated farmstead—the only place we knew as home. To the east, the arched crescent of a beautiful bright rainbow hung from the heavens. We counted on it to be a promise that things would get better. Ma spoke in hushed tones about the cyclones of the past, and about this twister that had given her a "magic carpet ride."

It took months to dig out and to replace the items that were mandatory for survival. Many never were replaced. Our melancholy but resigned attitudes, grew to accept situations such as this. Ma told us, "It's better to deal with the devil that ya know, than one ya don't know and can't see."

The Medicine Wagon
And The McNess Man

Back-Country Remedies — In late 1928 and early 1929 a quarantine sign hammered to our front door caused neighbor kids to fear and persecute me. I was bedridden, flat on my back for ninety days with five childhood diseases that had attacked me simultaneously. The diseases were measles, whooping cough, chicken pox, pneumonia, and diphtheria. It was difficult for Ma to know how to treat them because some required light for healing, and some needed darkness. Some of the diseases preferred cool, and some preferred warm.

Ma just wrung her hands in grief. The slightest provocation would ignite her nervous system. Once she got wound up, I thought she sure resembled our old talkin' machine. When left unattended, it too, would repeat the same old tune, over and over. After ninety days in bed, my muscles were like mush. I told Ma one day, "I feel better, I'm getting up." She said "You just stay in bed. You won't be able to walk." But I knew better, like all kids do. I climbed out of bed, and the next thing I knew I was flat on my rump on the floor. *I guess I'll listen to Ma from now on,* were my very thoughts.

My Ma's little gold-edged diary from the 1920s has this to say, "Prescription #15979, Medina Drug Company, December 31, 1928, for cough and pneumonia. It was listed next to Exema Salve and an ad for the Boote Ranch of

24,000 turkeys in Lyman County, and how to fashion belts from transparent wrappers from cigarettes, cigars, and candy that are smart, colorful, and shimmery.

The farmers' pharmacy, during my childhood, was not just a single place, it was almost every place. Medicine came from nettles in the draw, from garlic in the garden, from the mulberry bushes, the sage plants and from the red clover in the fields. The most regularly applied home remedy was plain salt. It was rubbed into the wound and rinsed away. Not only did it lift infection from the wound, but it lifted out a spontaneous flow of profanity caused by extreme pain.

Ma said, "Sufferin' from an attack of practical medicine is not all that bad. We kin always choose our own poison in any form we want: either from the travelin' medicine show or from natural sources." Country folks had their own philosophy about old wives' tales, remedies and curatives, and they used them whenever the need arose. People used mistletoe for anxiety attacks before Miss Lydia Pinkham's Formula became famous. A simple slab of dried salt pork wrapped in a piece of torn cloth, then tied around the neck seemed to cure sore throats and raspy voices. Old wives' tales have been handed down by almost every that has existed on this earth.

The Medicine Wagon — I shall never forget the day I saw the first traveling medicine show in our town. The small boxy Model T was painted a garish pink, purple and green, with letters outlined in black. The medicine wagon lurched to an abrupt stop in the wide street adjacent to the livery stable when the front end jackknifed into a pot hole. It was still spittin', sparkin' and rockin' when the hack bounded from behind the wheel into the hardpan street. If the jolt of landing on the packed dirt street had jarred the driver's innards, he didn't seem to notice. He flashed me a smile as he got out of the rig. As if set in mortar, the smile remained changeless until he left town.

The medicine show barker darted to the rear of the vehicle, dropped the tailgate and hopped up onto the makeshift platform. Through a megaphone, painted equally as bright as his rig, he began to hawk his wares. "Step right up folks! Get the elixir of a lifetime. Only 96 cents for a full pint. It will tighten down loose skin, soothe foot itch, treat aching muscles and rid you of the blues all at the same time."

Ma grunted, "Peddlers are like hoboes. They stake out the place to see if folks are gullible enough to buy." It was Saturday afternoon. Many people gathered around, listening to his flowery descriptions of yet another item from his medicinal cache of brown straight-sided flat bottles. He began his pitch. This time aimed at Ma. "How 'bout it little lady?" His tone was condescending. "I see you have a host of young'uns there. This fantastic formula will take the hacking cough out of the croup, take the swelling out of the mumps, and blast the blisters from the pox."

Ma snorted, "Probably ain't any better'n our own mixed-up sulfur and molasses spring tonic. Darn site more expensive too." My little sister Gladyce spoke up, "We learned about tycoons in school. Is this guy a tycoon, Ma?" "Hell no," Pa blustered in disgust, "He's just a huckster trying to make a fast buck."

The hawker saw Pa's attitude, and turned the volume of his hype to an escalated tone. As he pranced to and fro on the platform, he shouted out his banter. Much to my dismay, the entrepreneur had succeeded in taunting Pa. Not one to take ridicule lightly, Pa became *furious.* I could see he was struggling with his temper. Pa intensely resented hawkers who took advantage of poor folks, depleting them of their hard earned money when they had products on the farms that would do the same things.

The salesman continued his pitch, this one about beauty aids and all they could do for a woman's skin. Losing out to his temper, Pa spouted, "Hell, fella, I can do more for my woman's skin with the mineral-salt block out in my corral, than with yer whole cockeyed truck load of wares." I could see in the crowd's uneasiness that Pa, at this point, was becoming less than a great inspiration to them.

Turning a deaf ear—and his back side—to Pa, the vendor spoke to the crowd which had gathered on the other side of the wagon. He held up a bottle of tiny green pearls that he touted as being "the only antacid that works." Pa's lip began to quiver in anger and he bellowed, "We can do the same thing by cookin' down bones in vinegar and salt water, then drinkin' it."

With that, Pa was forced to spit the abundance of Peerless tobacco juice that had accumulated—partly because he was mad and partly because he appeared to be drowning in it. He spat the ugly brown juice on the hardpan street, where it imprinted a Rorschach-inkblot pattern over the dirt. It was times like this that Pa's unrelenting measure of honesty was embarrassing to me.

Without a doubt, the vibration was set up. Ma now suffered from a skirmish of the heart. "It's yer Pa that sets me off," she blamed. Muttering under her breath, she philosophized, "Yer Pa is on the threshold of character building—everyone else's character—that is!" And the barker, sure enough, had supplied the stimulus. Ma rapped out the D-word in disgust. She said, "Far as I'm concerned, this fool can take his patent medicine and go hang." Shortly after this episode, Ma went back to her original idea—suffering from an attack of practical medicine is not all that bad.

Bartering With the McNess Man — In those days, *our way was the McNess way.* The distributor, Ali Tim, traded staple groceries, pudding mixes, extracts, spices and potent patent medicines for spring chickens. His ancient truck resembled the medicine wagon, only it was decorated with crates of live chickens that he had received in payment for his wares. As the huckster of the henhouse drove into our yard, the rattle-trap was hitting on only three of its four cylinders. It chugged in, lurched forward a few leaps, the engine hissed and sputtered, then it died.

Ali Tim bounced off the running board, pad and pencil in hand to begin his spiel. Ma was a serious buyer. She listened intently and deliberated on which products would be essential. Us kids hung around like starving refugees from a prison camp, hoping for something we could eat immediately. Ma made her choices, which as usual, contained no *fast food.*

High on my Ma's priority list was the McNess answer to ExLax, products like Laxative Cold Tablets and Chocolate Flavored Laxative Wafers. But Ma said we couldn't afford them, so we had to buy Epsom salts in five pound bags which cost about one-third of Watkins or McNess brands. She overdosed us on Epsom salts regularly—and I knew, all too well, the results of Epsom salts! Ma's idea was that a lack of Carter's Little Liver Pills didn't cause liver problems, nor did the lack of Preparation H applications cause hemorrhoids.

The word *physics* had a laughable connotation for Ma. She told me it reminded her of a time in her high school days, when the teacher had written on the blackboard, "All who are taking physics, bring paper to class." We were given laxatives a lot, and needless to say, Ma would flip into the same old yarn about them. In his joking manner, Pa said, "Laxatives prevent us from having collie marbles of the gooseberry grinder!". In other words—constipation.

Other medicinals Ma usually purchased were sorghum, molasses, and sulfur. The question of Blue vitriol, Vaseline and vanity cream was out, they exhausted Ma's purchasing power. "Don't have enough chickens to spare this time, Ali."

Ma said reluctantly, "Pudding mix and nectar will have to wait."

No order was complete without Denver Mud. "This," Ma said, "is to heat and apply to boils and wounds, until all yer meanness comes to a head." Ma never had the slightest doubt about the curative powers of either mustard plasters or Denver Mud. "There isn't much difference between Watkins' Carbolated Saniscope and Denver Mud," Ma pointed out, "When each is applied to the flesh, it draws the meanness out." Bound to have the last word, I retorted, "Even both of 'em put together and heated up, couldn't hurt as much as the time you and Mrs. Ochsner suctioned the boil on my ankle with a beer bottle of hot steam from the teakettle."

As the shopping and visiting wound down, I was sent to the granary to fetch a can of chicken scratch. I scattered it in the center of the yard to attract the chickens that would be payment for Ma's purchases. Ali took the staff from his truck and walked to the circle of unsuspecting hens contentedly pecking at the feed. Ma loaded us kids' arms with the purchased wares and told us to take them into the house. As she crated the hens for Ali, he related the products that each had paid for. I suppose he was hoping that the number of products that each hen was worth might trigger Ma into purchasing more goods. But Ma held fast.

Us nosey kids quickly established that the majority of the provisions Ma had purchased turned out to be inedible. There were "icky" things like carbolic salve, Ma's answer to the "big-genie," Vaseline, and Bag Balm, which we used to heal cows' teats lacerated in the barbed wire fence. There was liniment for "haymaker's muscle twitch," and dry mustard powder for seasoning beans and making mustard chest plasters.

In response to our complaining, she justified her selections by giving us this to think about: "If you don't shut yer mouths, the next mustard plasters I put on will remove yer hide quicker 'n the time before." When the grippe caught our lungs, she used a mustard plaster on our chests to draw out the infection. If the flesh on the chest cavity stayed intact long enough, the cure was close behind.

The Sorceress And The Boil — I remember the incident very well. It was the last days of a long hot summer. We'd been haying for weeks, and everyone was too busy to notice my swollen ankle. It was only when it had festered to near grapefruit-size that it was noticed.

Though I could no longer hobble without pain and some semblance of gracefulness, Ma and Pa decided that the problem could wait until Saturday night. That's when the townsfolk would be gathering for their weekly visiting sessions. Surely *someone* would know how to treat my disorder.

Was it a boil? Ma said it was. Boils were a common condition on the prairie due to unsanitary conditions, farm injuries, and insufficient diets. Government commodities of canned foods, and home canned and preserved foods, combined with a diet made up of fifty percent white flour products lacked appropriate nourishment for our bodies.

Saturday, when we arrived in town, sure enough, Mrs. Ochsner and Ma decided to be the self-appointed surgical team. First they conferenced to determine how to attack the monster. When the determination was made, they stoked the potbellied stove to boil water. As they huddled over the teakettle collecting steam for the "genie" in a one quart beer bottle, they whispered in low tones. It made me feel that a couple of sorceresses were conspiring to draw hidden poisons from my very soul.

One enchantress held me to the mat while the other, using extreme pressure, administered the mouth of the hot bottle to the boil. As Martha clamped the steam-filled bottle over the core of my boil, the air inside the bottle cooled and contracted, forming a partial vacuum. In a loud voice, Ma directed Martha, "Prop the kid's leg up on the ten-gallon can, quick." Martha was definitely not a sister of mercy. She grabbed my leg at the ankle and let it drop unceremoniously onto the ten-gallon cream can, while pushing the steam filled bottle harder onto the infected area. The bottle filled rapidly with bacterial debris from the ulcer. Almost instantly, the core of the boil erupted into the bottle. When that occurred, Ma immediately yanked the bottle away from the half inch opening in my ankle, and cupped her hand over the wound. I was wrenched with pain and begging for mercy, but relieved that the initial ordeal was finally over.

The sterilization process followed. My misery continued. They dripped a teaspoon of salt dissolved in hot water into the hole in my flesh. The drip-drop method was not new to me. Ma once told me that it came from the "old Chinese torture method of dripping water, drop by drop on a convicted person's head until it bore a hole into his skull." I figured Ma and Martha were up to the same stunt with my ankle. The last step of the agonizingly painful process was Lysol water. They dripped it slowly into the cavity. Not until the "ace bandage" streamers, torn from old flour sacks, were secured around my ankle, did I feel freed from the fledgling surgeons.

My Ma And Old Wives' Tales — There were no doctors, clinics or pharmacies for us country folks. We relied on the knowledge and experiences of the old folks and old wives tale remedies to treat our conditions.

For instance, it was said that a needle heated to the red-hot branding iron stage could be thrust into the nerve of a tooth to kill any tooth affliction. Ma said she knew this to be true because, "Yer Pa did it one time on his own achin' tooth. It brought him to near faint. That tooth never ached again." Us kids weren't anxious for the experience, but we thought it might come in handy for the removal of slivers and wood ticks which plagued us on the farm.

Iodine, another reliable home remedy, gave birth to Ma's theory, "Burning the infection out is good fer what ails ya." The mere mention of iodine brings back my worst memory of adolescence. I had contracted ringworm from the farm animals. Its massive spreading ate into my flesh, covering the upper third of my face. It wrapped itself around one eye socket, turning my flesh into grotesque rough crocodile-like skin. Ma insisted that iodine would cure the severe blemish. She painted it with iodine, which turned my skin a nasty shade of brown. The iodine created a patch-like effect around my eye. I was sent to school once again looking like a pirate.

I can't remember which hurt me most—the physical pain that numbed my face, or the emotional pain caused by the kids who didn't want to play with me because I was scary looking, and they didn't want to catch ringworm. In any case, I finally recovered. What little vanity I had at that point in life ended. For several years, the only scar that remained with me was my memory of the episode. Ma scolded me, "Jus' forget it. As long as ya keep rememberin' it, the scar will stay."

Onion poultices, blue vitriol, and turpentine were other farm remedies that were favorites. They made good substitutes for antibiotics, compresses, and the like. For cuts and abrasions, the eggs of the banty hen supplied our Band-Aids. The inside air pocket membrane of a fresh hen's egg was our God-given suture for small lacerations. We cleansed and dried the cut, then applied the fresh egg membrane. As the membrane dried, it drew the edges of the wound together. The membrane was soaked off when the cut was healed.

Ma often used eggwhites as a facial mask. She would apply it to her face, allow it to dry, then rinse it off. The eggwhite mask left her face soft, smooth, and wrinkle free for a time. Eggwhite was even used to seal envelopes and secure postage stamps on letters.

Vitamin Enrichment Prairie-Style — Out on the prairie, miles from nowhere, householders shared their special techniques for supplementary nutrients. Though they knew little about the body's nutritional needs, they all raised gardens. Perhaps the economy dictated it, or perhaps it was an inherent characteristic of prairie people. In any case, a wide variety of greens from the garden, as well as prairie sweet grasses, such as dandelions, wild onions, chokecherries and other delicious items were served at meals.

I remember Ma telling us, "The ancients stuck a rusty spike into an apple in the evenin', and ate the apple in the mornin'. That way, they got all the iron they needed for the day." "Not only that", she rambled on, "I read where Jason and the Argonauts, in search of the Golden Fleece, used sword filings to furnish their daily iron supply."

As I look back, our daily sodium and trace mineral supply must have come from the iodized salt lick out in the barnyard. Us kids frequently licked it until our tongues looked like little red sponges.

Ma never ceased to amaze me. Although she wasn't the best cook in the world, she used facts gleaned from reading books to provide nourishment to her family. Most of her cooking had a hint of vinegar flavor. At the Ladies Aid Society, when asked about the flavor of her main dish, she was only too happy to twitter, "Why, the women in China have used vinegar and salt in sinewy meat and fibrous plant tissue cookery for centuries, in order to soften the connective tissue, and to leach out the nutrients from the ingredients." Her eyes sparkled with joy over being able to reveal her educational superiority to her peers. She always added, "The Boss likes it that way, too."

Flour Power — I have firsthand knowledge that bleached white flour was prairie country's rudimentary response to the need for blood coagulants. I speak with authority on this matter because of an incident that occurred one day when I chose to disobey orders from "headquarters"—headquarters being my Ma.

On her way out to the cornfield, Ma whizzed by me in the horse-drawn two-wheeled cart. Looking back over her shoulder, she yelled at me in an accusing tone, "Stay off the pighouse roof, ya hear?"

What better challenge to a defiant ten year old? Can I blame the entire incident on Ma? Afterall, with that single declaration, hadn't she just dared me to commit the forbidden act? The roof in question was the one on the tiny rock and mortar original homestead house that sat on the knoll east of the main house. Its current purpose was to house the pigs, but its old roof was in a weakened state because of missing undergirdings.

Us kids knew it was dangerous to jump on it, but we liked its trampoline effect as we bounced up and down and danced in the middle of it. It seemed to have more bounce to the ounce than a 250 count coil spring mattress. As I stood there contemplating my next move, my oldest sister's words came to me, "Stop being such a flibbertigibbet and use the sense God gave ya—one high-jump and yer either on yer way to the moon or into a fiery furnace of hog manure." Bea had admonished us younger kids time and again about the dangers of the roof.

As soon as the dust had settled on the road out by the cornfield, I pole vaulted to the roof. I'd discovered that if I jumped hard enough, I could see into the haymow. With a little more effort, I could see over the barn to the garden and the old Huggarude place! I jumped, bounced, romped, and squealed with glee in my Ma's absence. Needless to say, I was having so much fun that I hadn't noticed the time. I looked up from playing just in time to see a mini whirlwind of dust on the east road, reminding me that Ma was approaching at a fast pace. One last jump, I thought, and that will be it!

Well—that really was it! My one last trapeze-type flip sent my left leg crashing through the jagged shingles. My blood curdling, agonized shrieks brought Ma and the buckboard to a screeching halt. Ma was hustling toward the pighouse even before the cart could stop. Being a bit "thickset" her speed of approach was a bit compromised. By the time she reached me, Ma had had ample time to turn the air blue with profanity. She didn't dare walk on the roof. Instead she had to lie on her stomach and slither toward me.

I was never too sure whether Ma and Pa used profanity as a means of intimidation, or if it were the forerunner of out-and out rage. At any rate, Ma had to crawl very slowly to me, lest her bulk further stress the roof. If that had happened, both she and I would have fallen into the pig wallow below.

With each attempt to dislodge my leg, the splintered dirty shingles and a rusty spike gripped my bloody leg like a Venus Flytrap closes on its prey. The roof didn't release me until Ma could get a board to distribute her weight on the roof, which was becoming more sway-backed by the minute. She tugged, I screamed, and the spike and shingles retraced their path back out through the profusely bleeding furrow in my flesh.

By the time Ma had rescued me, others had gathered around. They carried me to the east porch, the emergency area where all other minor surgeries had been performed. This, like most of the others, was definitely not a bloodless surgery. Every available home remedy was rushed to the porch: hot water, salt, Lysol, torn bed sheet strips, and a dishpan filled with bleached white flour. Ma was so angry with me, she threatened to take my life herself—via the slow bleeding out process, no doubt.

When she finally finished purifying and sterilizing my wound with salt from the salt-brine solution, Ma dumped flour into the crevice of ragged flesh. She finished the procedure by tying torn strips of cloth around my upper leg.

Ma prowled, yelled and swore, "A 14-inch gash all the way to the bone! Serves ya right! Wait 'til yer Pa hears 'bout this. You know how many blankety-blank times you've been told to stay off that roof!" When Ma had stopped yelling at me, I whimpered with fright, "What if the flour and blood turn into a pancake?" Ma yelled back at me, "If it does, I'll fry it and you can eat it for blood sausage." I recoiled with the thought. When Ma had completely lost all patience with us kids she was apt to say most anything.

The crater in my leg took three months to heal. After a week of sitting out on the fly-infested back porch with my leg elevated on an apple crate, I tried to decide if the pighouse roof was really all that much fun.

Patent Medicine Ads And My Recovery — One day, Ma sensed my contemplative mood and finally broke the silence. "Well, I guess you've hurt long enough to do as yer told from now on. How would you like it if I read some stuff for curin' from this *Review Magazine*?" I consented. After all, it was rare that Ma took time to sit a spell, let alone read to me. She pulled up a rickety milking stool and thumbed quickly through the pages, looking for something to read that would cheer me up.

"Listen to this," she laughed, "This is something that you need. Its a cure for the deaf. It reads, 'Peck's Patent Improved Cushioned Ear Drums'—the contraption allows ya to hear all conversations, even whispers." We both laughed. "And listen to this, Short Stuff." she said, "Here's an ad that will make you taller overnight so you can see over the barn without jumping on the pighouse roof anymore." She read:

"Mr. Leon Minge's wonderful new discovery will make you grow taller overnight so you don't have to be embarrassed in public, and you can see over large crowds." "That would've come in handy at the medicine show in Pettibone, wouldn't it?" I questioned. She agreed.

"Oh look," she went on, holding the magazine toward me to look, "it's a picture of an old armchair like Grandpa Carter's, only his had a built in coil spring contraption between the seat and the leg platform." The advertisement read something like this: "The Health Jolting Chair has a power to cure disease and prolong life." Ma told me, "I don't know if we wanna get it for ya, though. If we try to prolong yer life, ya'd probably jus' go out and kill yerself anyway through some other disobedient act."

She continued on with the periodical advertisements. One of the nerve syrups, we decided, would be good for the kid up in Pettibone with St. Vitus' Dance. The young man had been struck with the disease, chorea. Ma explained to me that was one of the forms of the scourge of childhood rheumatism. Ma said, "I read 'bout it in a copy of my Dad's old doctor books. The disease, even a slight attack of it, could produce rheumatic heart disease.

Another ad was for *Dr. Guertin's Nerve Syrup.* It was said to be a valuable remedy for epilepsy, St. Vitus' Dance, convulsions, and hysteria. Ma said, "If nerve syrup is so all fired good, why don't they sell it to the people who are already in the crazy house down in Jamestown?" We had all witnessed first hand, the effects of epilepsy. Our McNess man, Ali Tim, had had an attack in our yard one day. Ma and Pa went into near hysterics trying to find something to place in his mouth. It so happened that a dirty pair of pliers was the only thing they could grab onto quickly. It was so scary to me. Pa told me that if they hadn't placed something in Ali's mouth while he was having a seizure, he might have chewed his tongue off. Pa sent us little kids into the house before Ali woke up. Pa didn't want him to be embarrassed.

Reading the last of the ads, Ma closed the magazine. She wasn't one to have too much faith in patent medicines. She did however, have faith in the healing powers of the old wives' tale remedies.

My First Trip to Town

Preparations For A Trip To Town — Us kids jumped for joy one day, when Pa dropped the hint that *maybe* we could *all* go to town. Ma told me that I "walked a foot above the ground for a week." *That's Ma,* I thought, *always exaggeratin' the truth.* She seemed to read my mind. "It don't hurt to slip a little flair on things now and ag'in," she said defensively.

After Pa's surprising announcement, I thought briefly about our clothes and our mode of transportation—now these were the things in need of flair—not to mention our need for supplementary cash. Money was so scarce during the '30s that one of the few times Ma got her hands on a dollar bill, she quickly mastered the exotic art of folding a "greenback" to pocket change purse-size.

On the prairie, a trip to town was considered no small feat even under the best of circumstances. Us kids knew that this would mean a lot of work for us, but we were too thrilled to care. The trip to town would require cleaning up the wagon, tightening the wheels, loading our bartering items, and packing the lunch to have along the way, as well as getting ourselves ready.

Pa decided that the dirt and manure-mottled wagon, which stretched from "here to kingdom come," would be the best choice for our excursion, since it had the best axles. The brindle "barge on wheels" was our summer supplement to the manure spreader. We were so accustomed to the barnyard smells from our daily association with them that it didn't dawn on us that our scent might not be the sachet of the day in Pettibone. The flatbed wagon was an embarrassment! Why—it even drew comments from bewhiskered old John Trowbridge. When us kids balked at the thought of it, Ma said, "The only way anythin' can make you embarrassed is if *you* think 'bout it too much."

For the wagon, our country style cleanin' compound was the same one that we used to clean everything else out on the farm—sand, dirt, tiny pebbles and lots of elbow grease. One time in the playhouse, under our clothesline quilt tent, my little sister Vonnie said, "This stuff makes the best mud pies I ever ate." I giggled to myself at the thought. Me and seven of my brothers and sisters proceeded with the job at hand. We called the method we used, the friction rub.

We didn't actually choose sides in relation to who was to perform each task, but those who weren't big enough to carry water, had to be the scrubbers. Getting water was difficult work. Sometimes the pump needed to be primed and took lots of strength to do it. As we pumped the handle, us kids made jokes about it sounding like somebody with the dry heaves.

Scrubbing the dirty wagon wasn't done with a brush, since we had none. We accomplished everything barehanded out on the farm. First we softened the dirt clods and manure with a few sloshes of water, then we performed the *rubba-dub-dub* song as we cavorted around and around the wagon. The hardest workers were the pumpers and the scrubbers, who had to use their arms and shoulders until their limbs fell like limp blobs to their sides in exhaustion. The water boys would take a run at the hulk, tossing thin splats of water on the "polished parts" from their buckets. Sometimes a kid or two got *accidentally* splashed to the wringing-out stage. *Accidentally?*—I was never too sure about that!

232

When the wagon had been scrubbed to our version of *sterile*, we put our shoulders to the wheels and rocked, pushed and pulled until we nudged it to a sunny spot in the yard to dry. Sometimes, to prove our Herculean prowess, us kids would crawl under the wagon box, place our backs to the underside of the box and lift. We got better at it as we grew taller.

The next step in preparing the wagon for our trip to town was to soak the wheels. Between uses, the wagon wheel rims and spokes would dry out and loosen. The only way to tighten up was to soak them in our big watering tank. We asked Pa if they could be secured with bailing wire, but he said traveling across open prairie with bailing wire on the rims would be too risky. The rocky one-track road would sever the wires, leaving the rim and spokes to fall from the hub of the wheel. "Besides," Pa said, " if we came to town *all wired up*, people would think we were hayseeds, for sure."

Before we could get the wheels off the wagon, we had to prop it up. We hunted old cream cans, chicken crates, and pieces of railroad ties, stacked them up, then placed them under the axles to prop up the wagon. We quickly loosened the nuts and dislodged the grease-packed wheels. It took us some time to unwind the bailing wire bands used to hold the rims in place.

Now it was time to take the wheels to the water tank—easier said than done for eight little kids. Picture four heavy cumbersome wagon wheels—each followed by two scampering tots—rolling down toward the water tank. The yard by the barn descended sharply, with a turn at the base of the knoll, then an incline to the water tank. As the wheels crested the knoll, they gained momentum, with each of us running alongside trying to keep up. The wheels took a sharp turn, leaped into the air and bounded in the opposite direction, right through the hog wallow into the cornfield!

Our speeding little legs couldn't stop in time, so we wound up in the watery black loam of the hog wallow. We managed to retrieve the wheels but didn't feel very good about being covered with what the pigs had left in their slushy wallow.

Eight drenched kids guided the wobbling wheels up the knoll to the horses' watering tank by the windmill. The sides of the tank were taller than most of us, so our midget crew had to improvise. How would we heave the wheels over the side of the tank? When isolated from everything but destitution, one learns to practice ingenuity. Us kids had seen Pa use a winch many times, so we decided we could construct one, as well. We knew that a real winch had a pulley, which increased the applied power. However, we didn't have one, so we did the next best thing.

My brother climbed up the windmill, tossed a homemade rope over one truss, and threaded the "winch roller" while we tied a slip knot to one wheel rim on the ground. That left one "shrimpy" kid—me—by the tank to guide the wheel over the side into the water. The remaining kids skirted the tank, laughing joyously, as if we had already accomplished the feat. The Carter kids were all great anticipators and optimists.

We set our tug-of-war game in motion. From short to tall, in that order, they grasped the opposite end of the rope. After much grunting and tugging, they finally got the wheel airborne, above the tank, so I could reach out to guide it. "Before ya could set yer mind to it"—Pa's expression—the rope broke my grasp, and the wheel lurched and spun with the fierceness of a wrecking ball at a demolition site. The wheel plopped into the tank, showering us with a geyser-like volley of water. The force hoisted the kids into the air, kicking and squalling over the water tank. One kid fell into the tank, but ultimately climbed to safety while we all stood around laughing.

When we had settled down from the episode, we realized we had forgotten one thing—the axle grease in the hub of the wheel—it had oozed out and was making paisley swirls on the surface of the water. The sapphire blue sky and the alabaster fleece clouds reflected on the water in the rainbow of colors.

When we finished hoisting the remaining wheels into the tank, we were drenched. Having a hilarious time splashing water on each other, we stomped our bare feet in the overrun, a goodly portion of which was draining down the hill into the pig wallow. We were so happy about going into town that this ritual of wheel dousing was like a real immersion into the higher joys of heaven.

The next day, we hoisted the wheels out of the tank the same way we had put them in. Only this time, because they now were twice as heavy, we threaded a real pulley. Even with the new rigging, we had to secure the rope by tying it to the tank. After we regained our strength, we changed our strategy. The troop, moving to the full length of the rope, strained their muscles to wrap the rope, in a half-hitch, around a large rock, which doubled for a foot brace.

While we took a breather, we leaned over the tank and watched the swirl of rainbow patterns which had been left by the axle grease. We worked the first wheel loose, laid it in the dirt beside the tank, then mustered strength to finish the other three wheels, using the same procedure. We were exhausted and wet, but determined to get the job done. We always worked hard to please Pa.

The muddy wheels were lifted to an upright position. We knew we had to be careful and employ techniques to keep them standing and to prevent them from changing course or toppling over. Keeping in mind that the hog wallow was just below the first rise, we took straight aim toward the left and started down the hill, hoping for enough velocity to make it up the steeper rise by the barn. As Pa would have said, "It was tough sleddin'." The wheels flopped over several times before we made it to the top. Each time a wheel landed on the ground it would flop from side to side, while the spokes turned round and round. Catching hold of the rim was hard, but we finally made it to the wagon.

We propped the wheels against the side of the wagon box to await mounting by Pa, Eugene and Bill. Pa let us open a new five-gallon pail of axle grease. Then each kid gouged into the shiny ebony lubricant with a stick, and placed a large smear inside a hub and onto an axle. Once Pa and the boys mounted and fastened the wheels, we all worked together to move the wagon off its foundation of crates and railroad ties.

My Debut As A Real Person — Anticipating my first trip away from the homestead, I decided that I must now be considered a real person, making my debut, as it were. I had just turned twelve. Pa saw me *parading*, as *he* said, in front of the old mirror. I had been trying on my new dress, black stockings, high buckle shoes, and thought I looked pretty "snazzy" for town. I was proud. Pa sternly said, "Ya won't be wearin' *that* dress town."

Not a hint had been divulged that my long taffy-colored curls needed trimming, not until Pa saw me in front of the mirror, and decided I was coming into the boy crazy stage. He, for reasons of his own, was always ready to break a child's will much the same as he broke that of our western horses. Only this time he took the sheep shears, because the scissors were too dull, and bobbed my hair like a boys. My pride quickly faded. All my beautiful curls were gone!

Pa really knew how to cover himself. After clipping my hair, he said, "You look much more sophisticated now." To make matters worse, he called me "funny face", a name which would stick with me forever. Trotting this label out in front of company was his greatest sport. His reason for calling me *funny face* was, "You have such quick unending wit." In his mind, calling me *funny face* was his way of apologizing. I didn't see it that way!

Pa pulled strings with us, much as we operated the strings of our marionettes on stage in the school program: Jerk this string and this will happen. To defer appropriately to Earl's demands always averted trouble. Ma said, "Only God knows why he acts that way." However, Pa's sister, my Aunt Eliza Swanson, said wisely, "It always shamed Earl to descend from a British royal blue-blood to blue jeans and overalls."

My First Trip To Town — After all the preparations, the loading of the wagon, and the packing of the picnic lunch, the time had finally come to go to town. With a snap of the reins, the wagon team lurched into motion, and we headed out. Accompanied by a menagerie of waddling ducks, clucking hens, peeping chicks, our barking sheep dog and the cats, we bounced along the path to the west gate. I was hoping their animal instinct wouldn't allow them to figure out the plight of the crated chickens that were strapped to the sides of our wagon box. We outdistanced them at the gate, bounced over the culvert washout, turned right, then headed out across the open prairie toward Pettibone, thirteen miles away. Pa told us, "It's six miles as the crow flies."

The first quarter-mile of the rutted wagon track road ran straight through a tall stand of scorched prairie grass and hay needles. There were great stands of purple buffaloberry flowers, tumbleweeds not yet ready to spin off across the acreage, patches of wild pink prairie roses, and a variety of multicolored wild flowers. Jack rabbits hopped out of sight, and gophers squeaked at each other and charged for the tall grass. The slippery snakes slithered away from the road into the tall brush as we came near. In the hollow, milkweed stalks with bulging smoke-blue pods stood like sentinels, as if guarding any moist area that felt like marshland to them.

I watched my brothers and sisters. A slight smile escaped their faces. I knew it was because Ma and Pa were letting all of us go to town. My smile faded somewhat when a blanket-like cloud of "pissy ants" swarmed over our heads. Their intentions were to suck the sweat beads from our brows. For some reason, these pesky gnats gravitated to water and heat. Not being irritated by such nuisances as gnats and mosquitoes was hard, but Ma said it was all part of life. "Ya always have to take the good with the bad, so jus' forget it." She was right. We all decided to play a game of pretend: pretend it isn't happening, then it won't bother us.

As our rig quaked along the road, I thought about our trip to town. I had anticipated going to town for so long, that hearing about it from others didn't mean much to me. It was hard for me to picture mere words. I could relate to sight and action much better. Ma told me my inability to picture by words could someday be my downfall. But today, my chance had come to go to town. I didn't have to worry about painting pictures with words anymore. I hoped everyone in town would like us. Pa had said that if we acted proper, used the good manners he had taught us, and didn't touch things unless we intended to buy them, people would think we were good folks.

The creaking brindle-colored wagon rumbled on, lurching from side to side. We felt amply justified in leaning heavily toward the passenger side, to the point of near toppling over the side of the wagon. The momentum of the clopping horses' hooves on the soft earth increased at the foot of Cobblestone Hill by the old Huggarude place. The Sand's place looked as windswept and desolate as the alkali lake. The house and buildings looked as if they had never seen a coat of paint, but had simply been splashed with Ma's lye water and bluing. The barn with its backdrop of

Toboggan Hill, was a lost cause. Beyond the Huggarude place to the east, below the slope, was the west hook of the lake with its quicksand bog.

As we passed to the west, the cadence of the horses' shod hooves shifted abruptly. Now on the incline of Cobblestone Hill, the pressure of the wagon and metal on the flint cobblestones shot sparks high in the air in every direction. The team bowed their backs and strained every muscle and sinew as they tugged the monstrous load over the sharp rise.

We broke the rise and saw the road meeting the skyline miles beyond as shimmering heat waves danced over the plains. There were no road signs, only landmarks, many of which were prairie rock piles referred to only as directional pointers for strangers. Pa gestured at a rock pile, saying "That far rock pile is on the corner of the Bunker place. We'll angle 'round that way." Even near large cities, the road signs weren't standardized, and people couldn't decipher many signs by small towns because juveniles used them for target practice.

The sweltering sun and the erratic stifling breeze showed no mercy to man or beast. Us kids all complained of the unrelenting heat. Ma answered us with, "Now you kin git a rough idea what the *fiery furnace* is all about." She added, "Or for that matter, what it means to be mummified." We felt like china dolls that had been baked in a 500 degree oven.

We crept along averaging about three miles per hour, sitting only a hand's breadth apart in the crowded wagon. A multitude of incompatible scents on the wagon load made it nearly impossible to get a breath of fresh air. The sun-scorched blend of Cameron's pomade hair dressing, raw sweat, Blanche's rose petal perfume that had turned sour, musty sheep lanolin, chicken crate debris, and an occasional whiff of skunk, made my lungs choose to inflate only when a direct breeze wafted pure air. Ma caught the sound of our irregular short breaths. With disdain, she said, "No wonder yer all slow of mind. Yer brains need oxygen to work good. Now breathe!" At Ma's incessant word pictures, I chose to close down my hearing, and to ignore her breathing instructions. Ma, however, was right most of the time.

The Toy of Terror — The joy of the venture wasn't enough to keep us from being restless. Cammie whipped out his much feared "buzzer," a simple toy made of a large button threaded in the center of a string hoop. He had made it himself, and operated it by slipping his hands through the string loops on either side of the button. Then, giving the string a few twirls, he wound it up. A few fast wide, outward tugs on the string sprung the "buzzer" like a whirligig, almost like a rubber band or a yo-yo. Once it made contact with its target, the impact was not lethal, yet it could cause bruises, as well as tempers to flare. Cammie cranked the buzzer to its full capacity and gave a quick tug. A quick pass over my head resulted in it the "toy of terror" tangling itself into a mass of my flaxen locks. The buzzer had burned in for a painful landing and had inextricably tangled my hair in the string of the "mean machine." I let out a great howling shriek, my body jerking toward Cammie in the crowded wagon.

Without a moment's hesitation, Pa pulled up the team, and spat out his tobacco along with a few bold blistering cuss words. He leaned over the spring board seat and removed the sheep shears from beneath it. Next thing we all knew, he was gouging away at the tangled blonde mass where the buzzer had landed. Clumps of hair and bits of string flew everywhere. As he hacked at my already short hair, he bellowed out another sequence of profanities, the likes of which most of us kids had never heard. The others averted their eyes and stole glances at each other. Glad, no doubt, that I was the one in trouble. When he was finished, a huge hole graced my sun-lightened hair. He issued both of us a swift swat. Pa's reprimands and swats always hurt my pride more than they did my flesh. I didn't cry, because I *so* wanted to arrive in town a proper lady. Pa warned, "Now you two straighten up, or I'll take away yer gopher-tail money!"

Oh, gosh! Not our gopher-tail money! We had lain belly-down beside the gopher holes on the parched prairie grass for what seemed like an eternity, waiting to snare each head that popped up. In those days, the flickertail gophers were destroying farmer's crops, and the state offered a penny per tail. Cammie and I each had a sugar sack full of tails that were eligible for bounty. Needless to say, we settled down after that little incident.

As we bumped along the road, the day started to look like the weather gods were against us. "Ole Sol" was blasting down on us, making us sweat profusely. We were all miserable, itching and scratching. The salty water trickled down my back, making me feel like I had the "creepie crawlies" under my hand-me-down gingham dress. Ma said it was likely that I hadn't splashed off after sudsing down with her homemade lye soap.

We were passing the time, counting rock piles strewn over the land, when Cammie reached down and snapped the innertube garter on my low slung bloomer leg. I dared not screech again or Pa would likely threaten us with getting out of the wagon and walking behind it. I didn't want to rile Pa. He had clearly spelled out the consequences after the buzzer fracas. Besides!—This was snake country! I decided to just keep a low profile, and when Pa wasn't looking I gave Cammie a vicious jab with my elbow to his ribcage. I hissed, "I'll fix ya! Jus' for that, you ain't gonna get a lick off my sucker when I git one, and ya better not use my toothbrush anymore!"

Picnic at Brock's Slough — The unyielding heat plagued us until we reached the pocket of hills called the Hawk's Nest. Ma became the orator since she was the one with the most education in our family. We hung on her every word as she told us about the history of the site. She said we lived on the great glacial terminal. Here, just across the Wells County line, Little Crow had massacred many in Minnesota in the middle 1800s. The North Dakota territory had been previously ravaged by a band of hostile Indians whose ancestors had migrated mostly from Asia Minor. It was said that they massacred an entire white settlement near Mandan, North Dakota. Their treacherous acts came to a close on July 4, 1863 at the Battle of Big Bend on the Cheyenne River, southwest of Lisbon, North Dakota. General Henry Hastings Sibley had followed the band to the Hawks Nest, northwest of our homestead, then on to the Big Mound, where a bitter battle ensued.

How like the Indians we are, I thought. *They lived in a wilderness, rode ponies or walked wherever they went. They foraged for food, just like us.* There were however, some differences, which I was thankful for. We had a team and wagon, but they had traveled on ponies using dogs and travois to transport women and children. In the late 1800s, some had used ox-drawn two-wheeled carts.

We came upon Brock's slough as we entered the trough of rolling hills. The place with its perfume of cool water and carpet of lush grass was like Paradise to us. Ma pointed out a spot. "We'll have our picnic lunch right here." Several trees shaded the area where we could unload for lunch and rest the horses. The reflection of the white fleecy clouds on the water, as they slowly drifted across the sky, remains indelible in my mind. The day was beautiful, the sound effects of the frogs croaking, the crickets chirping, and the birds singing to one another all combined to make my first trip to town more memorable.

242

We pulled up under the trees and piled out in turn, using the wheel spokes and hub for a ladder. The boys unhitched and watered the horses, then tethered them in the shade. We helped Ma and Pa unload the cream cans. Then we set them into the slough water to cool. The gunny sack covers were resoaked and draped over the cans. Ma spread quilts on the ground for us. The food and drinks were laid out for lunch. Before we ate, Ma read the Capper's Farmer while Pa stretched out on a wool sack in the shade of the huge cottonwood tree, and us kids waded in the water. A fifteen minute cat-nap always made Pa feel like a new man. We wouldn't eat until he awoke with a better frame of mind.

Ma called us for lunch. Wet, but not much refreshed, we sat down on our quilts and looked over the food. Our picnic was something else! The lunch consisted of three kinds of sandwiches. One was mashed potatoes, chopped onions and sour cream. Another was mashed boiled beans and meat bits from pig feet seasoned with vinegar, salt and sorghum. The third was Ma's most delicious sandwich, a thin slice of her homemade head cheese and tongue loaf. The vinegar tang in the loaf needed no condiments. There was little danger of the filling saturating the hard bread. I think the texture of our bread, in those days, may have been attributed to Ma's lack of interest in cooking, or the homemade farmer's yeast, or possibly cooking with wood in the range oven. Inventiveness and creativity in food preparation was Ma's long suit. Even so, she wasn't the best cook in the world. But it didn't matter because most of the time we were just too hungry to be critical of the food she provided. And furthermore, we didn't have anything else to compare her cooking to.

We had brought tin syrup pails filled with Watkin's nectar, accompanied by separate containers of soda, vinegar and a quart of Ma's homemade fermented chokecherry juice.

Each of us had fun stirring this country "soda fizzy" into our cup of nectar. We giggled spontaneously as the bubbly mass swept up our nostrils and foamed over the edge of the tin cup. We closed our eyes and drank through clenched teeth in an attempt to keep the pink fuzzy ferment out of our mouths. We were happier than *popaholics* in a bottling plant, and the soda fizzy was a real treat for us.

We wolfed down our sandwiches and slurped our fizzy water. After lunch we played tag and held a contest for skipping rocks on the surface of the slough. We were raised with a rough-and-tumble style of play, and we were skilled at it. But we were always very careful what we did around Pa. He wasn't one to save syllables or spare the switch if he felt things were getting out of hand. Ma told us many times, "Maybe it is because yer Pa was a heller in his day!"

Since there were no facilities for a "comfort and relief" break along the hot monotonous trek, we took turns with the "Monkey Ward's" catalog out behind the hedge of trees. Back in those days, there was never much privacy for the call of nature.

We came back to the quilts for more fizzy water and chokecherry juice. Chokecherries reminded us of the time our neighbor, Albin Rosselle, came to our house for dinner and ended up eating Ma's chokecherry sauce—seeds and all! Ever since then, we had called him "rock-crusher Albin". This thought made us all giggle. Pretty soon giggling turned into fits of laughter. When Ma had had enough, she stopped us, "You kids stop yer laughin' over folks who are slow." Her tone quieted us down.

As the heat of the day and the heavy lunch worked its magic in our bodies, us kids laid belly down in a secluded patch of cattails at the edge of the slough. Pa ate slowly, as usual. He was *always* a slow eater. He called us around him, and we gathered on the quilt, waiting for him to stop stirring his coffee. He was a great one for stirring, stirring and stirring his sugar and cream into his coffee. Ma said, "Yer Pa is like a tea-leaf reader. When he gets a cup and a spoon together, he goes into a trance." While he ate his sandwich, Pa retold a tale that we had heard many times before.

Pa The Storyteller — "See those duck blinds over there, kids? That's where hunters, Frank White, Wobbly Jost and Gabby Ingalls hunted ducks. They got drunk and went out in a boat, early in the fall in this here slough to shoot ducks. They dropped a new gun overboard into the mire, and never did find it."

That story reminded Pa of the time he nearly blew his thumb off when the 12-gauge backfired. Then he came back to the duck hunters, again. "Well the following spring the neighborhood's drifter and entrepreneur, better known as Pete Vardell, waited 'til the slough dried up an' he found the gun. He scrubbed an' oiled it, cleaned the trigger hammer an' the barrel an' refinished the wood. The neighbors were all scared that he would be asked to return the shotgun to its rightful owner. But it didn't happen, and Pete kept the gun."

By the time Pa finished his sandwiches and his stories, it was time to get underway. We loaded the cream cans and hitched the team once more. We "toed-in" on the wheel spokes and assembled in our allotted spaces atop the brindle hulk. Pa, now rested and in a jolly mood, intoned the "Giddyap" command in a rich, tranquil voice. The team stretched the tugs and we eased out. He allowed the horses to take their own pace in the heat.

Our eyes lifted to the geese flying overhead as we jerked along over the stony roadway. There they were, wings flapping in the precision of a perfect regiment. Us kids wondered how the lead goose was chosen. Though we were nonchalant about certain natural wonders, we were in awe of this flock of migrating geese. We wondered if they had that new craze of the airwaves called radar, invented by Robert Watson. If so, where did they carry their equipment?

We wondered about their instincts and asked Ma if we had it too. She grunted, "Jus' listen to yer Pa and his uncanny predications. You'll know we do."

Pa carried an aura of infallibility. If by chance his prediction didn't happen on time, all we had to do was wait a while. We asked Ma if the lead geese were elected like she and Pa elected FDR. "Do they train like airplane pilots?" my brother asked. Another kid piped up, does the Pa goose rule the roost, or does the Ma goose?"

We watched a small splinter group of the geese break from the flight pattern, honking and squawking. Ma said, "That's the way you kids act. You kin go along with the bunch jus' so long, then ya try yer own way." We decided to change the subject. After our burst of enthusiasm for nature, we settled into daydreaming and bickering. Taunts like these: "Betcha don't know what I got!" "Yer Pa's pet!" "Yeah, well, yer Ma's pet!" Suddenly, it became quiet in the wagon, we drew ourselves up. All eyes stared ahead. We had spotted the grain elevators at the Marstenmore spur. We knew the scene brought back haunting memories for Pa.

He interrupted our thoughts to cite: "The Carters have vested rights to sore backs, sweat, broken bones, tragedy, and death connected with this spur." He continued in a tone that revealed deep sadness. "It was near here, at the Marstenmore spur track, that my cousin Swan got blowed up in the steam engine. Near scalded all his flesh away, but he lived. His conductor was killed."

Us kids wondered which would be the worst of the two outcomes, death or being near scalded alive, but as Ma had told us before, "The choice is never yers to make." As if impervious to my thoughts, Pa was inclined to unburden his soul just when I was becoming a real person and going to town. The words tumbled forth, and his voice faltered. I looked toward Pa, it could've been the lurching of the wagon, I told myself. Things got quiet—hurt feelings for Pa and all.

Because the wagon track road ran parallel to the railroad tracks, we knew that Pa was going to meet the "enemy of grief" once again when we crossed the tracks into the town of Pettibone. Us kids began to feel nervous about our mode of dress and the way the old hulk of a wagon squeaked and groaned. Ma, in an attempt to bolster up our courage, began to prattle. Pa added his two cents worth when he sensed our embarrassment. He said in a somewhat haughty tone, "You don't have to be ashamed. We got our land by settlement, not by being squatters. We don't lie, cheat or steal, and we leave our betters alone." Ma nodded her approval, then burst in, "Cripes sakes, wasn't our family the first even dozen in Chase Lake Township? Why, we near filled the school by ourselves, and boarded the teacher, too!" Ma could be rather verbal at times, actually to the point of haranguing. She felt compelled to give us the whole rundown.

Ma Suffers From The Remember Whens — Ma turned toward the back of the wagon and asked no one in particular, "Remember when I played the lead in the community play? Remember, it was yer Pa's second cousin that went down on the Great Titanic? It was yer Pa, his brothers and his dad who worked the railroad in this very town. And wasn't it yer Grandpa Walters who started the first flour mill?"

She turned to me, the urchin of the group, and said, "Weren't you the softball pitcher? Wasn't it an honor for you to win the All-County Declamation contest, and the sewing prize at the County Fair? You played the female comic in the school plays and gave a good performance of the Charleston on stage. Besides that, you got promoted to the amateur contest after you practiced yer yodeling on the prairie while you herded the sheep. We got plenty to be proud of." Her

247

tone reflected a certain pride that only a mother can feel over the least of accomplishments.

I wasn't always proud of my academic record, and I never wanted it to be mentioned. Ma used to say to me, "If ya hadn't been born a natural comedian, maybe ya could of accomplished somethin' worthwhile." I always felt like a spectacle in public. I wasn't particularly chic. In fact, Ma said I was at that awkward age. My figure was beanstalk-straight—not a bend or a curve to the entire four foot two inches of me. And Pa had just bobbed my hair with the sheep shears. It made me feel ugly. I just knew I looked like a boy.

We rounded the bend by the Holstein cattle farm outside town to the southeast. A whiff of the corral when the wind stirred certainly wasn't the aroma of sweet cream butter! The country met the town directly behind the Holstein corral. Pa said they built the town on the land homesteaded by Mr. Minnekers. Our view of Main Street, all three blocks of it, was for me, the equivalent to strolling down the boulevard of a Shangri-la. We were on a pilgrimage to buy, sell, and barter for necessary provisions—everything from kerosene to coal, seeds to salt blocks, and sardines to sorghum.

Sure enough, we were about to cross the Great Northern Railroad tracks by the grain elevators, and I could see Pa had that distant look in his eyes, but not a tear broke the surface. He finally spoke, "Like a strike of lightnin', our dog, Carlos, bayed for three nights. Two days later a through passenger train hit my sister Libbie, her husband Edgar, their baby, and the local barber who were driving in a Tin Lizzy. Edgar once told me that when my sister Lib got the frights in the Tin Lizzy, she would just reach over and shut off the ignition. My guess is she got the frights, and he couldn't get the Tin Lizzy to spark. The brakeman, Clarence Swanson (her brother-in-law), and the engineer, Joe Carter (her brother), couldn't get the passenger train stopped in time."

The incident was a sad and tragic one. The young couple, their baby, and our local barber perished. Edgar and Libbie Mell left five children, our immediate cousins, who became foster children of their railroad worker uncles. Pa said, "It wasn't the best of solutions. Some wanted to come live with us, but that would have made nineteen living at the homestead. Times were just too tough for that." We watched Pa melt under the strain of yet another sad memory.

I had also heard Pa tell about our neighbor, Bill Jenkins, Pa's second cousin. One of Bill's brothers had gone down on the great Titanic. Pa found it hard to express his emotions over the loss of his cousin, so he just blurted out, "Don't know where the damn fool got the money to board her anyhow!" I felt bad for Pa, but this was my first trip to town, and I was going to enjoy it no matter what.

Our Invasion Of Town — We rumbled directly down Main Street in Pettibone. It looked as if a cattle drive had just gone through. The town was only thirteen years older than I was, yet it already looked all worn out. The storefronts were dingy and in need of repair. Some had broken or cracked windows and hadn't had a fresh coat of paint in years.

"Those buildin's are only thirteen years older than you, Funny Face," Pa smiled. I hoped he wouldn't use that insulting name in front of the townsfolk, but I knew better than to voice my feelings to *The Gentry*. Pa had a temper on him like a hand grenade with a pulled pin.

My attention was drawn from my musings as the wagon lurched over the railroad tracks. We crept toward the center of town and the cream station, past the place where the Dakota Land and Townsite Company had stood. We rolled slowly past the Farmers' Elevator, the Farmers' Oil

Company, and beyond the wind charger that was being mounted for electricity.

Beside the depot was the town's first two cylinder Maxwell, owned by Mr. Andrews, manager of the elevator. As Pa pointed out the new car, we all looked at it longingly and discussed how snazzy it was. We asked Pa if we could get one like it. If we did, we told him, we wouldn't have to ride to town in the "honey bucket" wagon ever again. Pa ignored the question. I knew he didn't care to answer for fear it would stir up his own longings for things he would never have.

The narrow three block street was lined with Dad Brown's Pool Hall, Hattie's Cafe, a shoe repair shop, Dalstrom's Butcher Shop, and last but not least, the cream station. Us kids gaped in amazement at the line of buildings. Pa pointed out the horse-powered well digger alongside of George Bellow's Livery Stable

"There's George Bellow's Livery Stable!" Cammie shouted. We all bellowed in unison for Bellows, then giggled. We passed Hattie's Cafe and Welch's Shoe Repair. The hotel, managed by Mrs. Tripp, looked to be a little larger than our farmhouse—but not by much. "Some hotel," I snorted in disgust, "Ain't no bigger 'n our barn. Looks like we saw the whole town already," I complained disappointedly. "Don't be dumb, kid Ya ain't even been in the buildin's, yet!" Ma snapped.

As our wagon continued down the center of town, I noticed women peeking curiously from behind soiled lace curtains. The sudden drop of the misshapen panels revealed that curiosity knew no class distinction. Passersby clustered at intervals along the weather-beaten boardwalk to have a look at us. They gave a quick glance, turned to their comrades, and laughed. Others stared, then brushed the air in a half-hearted mannerly salute. Ma snorted to Pa, "What're they rubber-neckin' for?" I knew it was our mode of transportation, which was anything but mint condition that shocked and horrified the crowd. We must have looked like the advance advertising rig for a circus. There wasn't one inch of space available inside, since it was packed an army of kids, crates of eggs, cans of cream, a sack of freshly sheared fleeces, and our copper wash boiler filled with picnic supplies. Crates of live cackling hens and restless crowing roosters were strapped to the tailgate and sides of the wagon box. Between the spectacle and the spectators, I decided it would be real good to discover the secret of making myself invisible.

After seeing the dress and demeanor of the townsfolk, I became a bit uneasy about appearing in homemade clothing with no idea of what the proper town manners were. I looked at the rest of the kids and wondered if they felt the same way I did.

The team's motion created a melodious clink and jingle of the harness hardware. White foam and lather had emerged on the horses' necks and flanks from the heat and strain of the heavy load. The tiny swarming flies collected, waiting for an opportunity to light. I hoped Pa would take the horses to the livery so they could rest in the shade, instead of making them stand at the hitching rail in the full sun, switching tails and stamping at the flies. We cruised through town at a snail's pace, up the street toward the cream station.

Ma warned, "Now don't ya go gawking, people'll think we're hicks." Shopkeepers peered from behind murky storefront windows. When we made eye contact with them, they stepped back quickly from view. A rotund stoop shouldered man wearing a half apron stepped out from Dad Brown's Pool Hall into the doorway. He spat a mushy wad of chewing tobacco six feet out onto the street in front of our team. Then he turned, scratched his greasy balding head with an equally grease-laden paw, cast another glance in our direction, and grabbed the screen door. Glancing back in our direction once again, he lumbered through the door and disappeared from sight.

Ma and Pa sat ramrod straight as we passed the curious onlookers. The two littlest kids sat between the folks on the spring seat in the front of the rig, just behind the team. The rest of us kids were crowded in on the spring seats that Pa had mounted in the back. The spring seats could be mounted to any of our wagons or flatbeds when more seating space was needed, which was usually the case in the Carter family.

After glancing down both sides of the street, Ma grunted her disapproval of the gawkers. In an insolent tone, she muttered, "They think we're dressed like hayseeds, or somethin'? 'Peers we're causin' more 'citement than the canonization of Joan of Arc by Pope Benedict, or her lead'n the French Army, for that matter!" Ma had an affinity for French history for some reason. Although she and Pa were proud of their British ancestry, they had given most of us kids first names or middle names that were French.

Our noisy wagon rocked slowly along the rutted road as we neared the jail. Pa said, "I better hurry up and get yer *jingles* for spending, so we don't look like vagrants and get tossed in the jug!" He laughed and continued on, "Beggars aren't really arrested, they jus' let 'em sleep in the jail overnight for shelter." We had been told that a farmer, whose farm had been foreclosed on, was retained there after he had shot the sheriff who served the papers.

To me, Pa was the pillar of security, although he had never come to the attention of the tax collector. He had nothing that anyone would have coveted—not unless hazard, hardship and hunger drew envy. He did come to the attention of our school nurse, though. After that we became the recipients of the State's supplemental food program.

Jingles From The Creamery — At last our rig eased up to the creamery station platform. Ma's nervous talk—Pa called it that—ceased. Pa, seeing the gents congregated on the platform, drew back on the reins and called "Whoa! Howdy gents!" in his most business-like manner. The wagon lurched to an abrupt halt.

"Ever'body pile out!" Pa ordered. Some of us in the back were already half in and half out. All of us tried to scale the wagon box at the same time. The scene was a conglomeration of flailing arms and kicking legs. Our flying pinafore skirts revealed the *Occidental Flour* lettering on the bottoms of our bloomers.

Ma wasn't too sympathetic when I skinned my leg vaulting over the side of the wagon box. She fumed, "Ya ought'a know by now that yer made breakable and shouldn't go flyin' through the air without a parachute!" She was next to step to the platform. Her every muscle strained to dismount the wagon gracefully. Though she was stout, she planted her sturdy scuffed shoes daintily on the platform, and pivoted to the walk in her swan-like manner. She had come to town wearing her standard serviceable dark blue dress which flared at the hips and had been sponged to threads. I wished that she could have had a new one.

Ma snapped open the well-worn black cowhide pocketbook that she had clutched tightly all the way across the prairie. She stored all her most treasured keepsakes in the valise style bag. I believe some of the items may have been Grandma Walters' pearl and gold brooch, Aunt Genevieve's emerald ring, Grandpa Walters' pipe, and an old tintype photo of her family. From a side pocket, she pulled a large piece of hand-hemmed flour sack.

Ma glanced about her surroundings before beginning the face cleaning ritual of each of us kids, using her famous *spit-wash method.* She spit on one corner—using fresh spit for each kid—of course—and made her way down the long line, wiping sweat, road dust, and runny hair pomade from our faces.

Ma shot a swift glance up and down the street then muttered to herself, "These biddies best not gossip 'bout the poor farmer's brood, or they might git the same lesson comin' to them somewhere down the road." In her own way, Ma had coined the axiom of modern-day vernacular: *What goes around, comes around.*

We lined up according to size and age, waiting patiently for the cream to be tested, so Pa could give each of us our promised spending money — or as Pa liked to say—our jingles. Standing there in the blazing sun, I noticed that the garter on my stocking had slipped and my sock was now at half-mast. Bending down, I gave the black ribbed sock a good yank back to its full height and tucked it under the lax elastic band of the leg of my black bloomers. I secured it with the one inch wide cutting of inner tubing. This type of garter was known as a poor man's leg cinch. It bore no resemblance to the electric blue garter with pink roses and lace that I had seen on the cover of a Rangeland Romance Magazine. I adjusted it, and like any underprivileged twelve year old would do—I just pretended it was the pretty blue garter. I rose to my full height and heaved a sigh, "Oh well. Outa sight outa mind."

I had heard Ma say many times, "Nothin' can hurt ya, if yer mind don't go to work on it." My Ma and Pa were country philosophers of the finest kind. At times, hardship turned their strife to meanness, but the hidden quality of greatness in their souls somehow found a time to shine through.

We heard Pa address the cream station owner, "Nice buncha kids I got. Don't ya think so, Mike?" Mike had no recourse—he was a captive audience. He responded with, "I ain't ever heard nothin' off color 'bout yer kids, Carter." This response brought a rare smile to the face of *The Gentry.* My

Pa was proud to hear the report, even though he had goaded Mike into the answer. Sometimes I wondered whether our good name rested on the shaky ground of Pa's ever-changing personality, or if people were just too kind to speak their minds. Like the house built on sand, Pa's good demeanor was inclined to slip from time to time. His better nature was reserved, for the most part, for those outside the Carter household. He vented his darker nature on people he didn't cotton to, and during situations which he, himself, hadn't initiated.

Mike was slow in processing our cream. The heat became almost unbearable while we stood there, waiting with anticipation under the sweltering sun. Us kids stood rigid with both feet planted on the boards of the platform. No shifting from one foot to another. In my Pa's eyes that showed impatience, and he wouldn't tolerate it in his kids. We knew better than to disobey *The Gentry*, so we continued to wait patiently. Pa's motto was, "Don't do what I do—do what I tell ya to do." Ma told us that Pa's attitude wasn't his real self. "Deep down he's got a soft spot, he jus' don't have much time to show it." she said.

Pa finally came out of the creamery with a big smile and a quick wink at us kids. He wasn't only pleasant—he seemed downright happy. With his very own natural aura of infallibility, he addressed us in the line, "Stick out yer hands," and began passing shiny copper pennies to all of us.

Pa issued strict instructions before we departed the cream station. "Stay away from the Pool Hall, and don't pick up nothin' ya don't intend to pay fer." Then Pa turned to Ma and said, "Guess I'll go see the boys," and headed down the street to the Pool Hall.

Midway up the boardwalk, us kids went into a huddle trying to decide where to go first. We settled on visiting the Mercantile, and headed down the road, each of us clutching our own sack of gopher tails in one hand, and our Bull

Durham pouches containing our three coppers in the other. Ma kept her eye on us the whole way down the boardwalk.

One Stop Shopping — The barter system was well in place even before the Great Depression had begun. Neighbors bartered with neighbors, traveling salesmen bartered with their customers, including the Watkins and McNess men, and the town merchants bartered with their customers.

In town, the merchants bartered with the farmers for crocks of butter, candled fresh eggs, and fresh milk and cream. Ma and Pa had made sure to candle the eggs they used for bartering. The process consisted of weighing each egg on a balance-beam type scale fitted with a very bright light. The light would shine through the egg and allow the buyer to see if there were any impurities or embryos inside the shell.

In payment for goods received from the farmer, some stores offered aluminum chips representing different denominations which could be traded for merchandise from the store at a later date, if desired.

Sometimes farmers bartered a small amount of meat, but most merchants purchased hanging carcasses of meat from the Swift Packing Company in St. Paul, Minnesota. A chopping block was usually located in the back of the store, where the store owner would cut up the meat at the time of the customer's request. The meat would be wrapped in butcher paper, with no attention paid to the flies buzzing around or the lack of refrigeration.

The Mercantile was a literal hodgepodge of barrels, crocks, bushel baskets, hundred pound gunny sacks of grains, flour, sugar, and potatoes. Two and five pound bags of table salt were stocked in the same area as rock salt blocks for the livestock. The rock salt would have been better for us than our table salt because it contained several minerals that our bodies needed. Little did we know! We also had no idea that the huge bags of chicken scratch that we tripped over would have served our bodies better than the food we lived on. It contained such nutritional elements as sunflower seeds, flax, millet, corn, wheat, rye, oats, and barley.

Though the store shelves were stocked with Fels Naptha, P&G (Proctor and Gamble), and Crystal White soap bars, most farm women didn't include it on their grocery lists because they usually made their own from rendered pork fat, lye, and cold water. The 99 and 44/100ths percent pure Ivory Flakes didn't come until several years down the road.

To the men of the plains, the tobacco counter was like a candy store is to a tiny tot. The country grocer went to great lengths when it came to stocking the mens' favorite brands of tobacco. There were small round cardboard boxes with tin lids that contained Copenhagen for ten cents a box, small cloth bags cinched with yellow string containing Bull Durham, paper packages of Peerless Chewing Tobacco, and Duke's Mixture and Plug Chewing Tobacco for five cents. At the customer's request, the proprietor would cut up the bulk tobacco with a plug cutter to the desired size. Roll-your-own cigarette papers and a small machine were available for making your own cigarettes at home. Us kids all took turns rolling cigarettes for our big brother, Bill. We also fought over who would grind the Peerless for making Pa's chewing snuff. As I recall, the recipe for making the snuff was a pinch of salt, a pinch of baking soda, plenty of ground Peerless and enough strong black coffee to moisten the tobacco.

Benny Stern's Mercantile — Us kids rushed the door of the old store, all trying to enter simultaneously. The rickety fly-laden screen door creaked and sagged a bit as we hustled through the door all at once, pushing, shoving, and elbowing each other to keep from getting stuck in the door jamb.

Benny Stern's store had evolved from the early mercantile building which had burned down some years before. For a few years a chicken hatchery had operated in the basement. Now, even after being rebuilt, the store still carried the malodorous overlay of brooder-house stench.

Once inside, we saw a perfect example of an "uptown" butcher was in those days. Benny's huge midriff was wrapped tightly with an apron that had once been white, but was now covered with blood stains from cutting meat, dark smudges from stoking the coal stove, and brown smears and stains from cutting plugs of tobacco. Sanitation and hygiene certainly weren't Benny's strong suits. My little sister Gladyce, not knowing any better, pointed at him and said, "Oh look, his belly's bleedin' and it got to us before he did!" Tittering with delight, the rest of us kids tried to hide our faces and ducked behind the counter. Ma snapped at us to calm down.

Benny nodded at Ma, and set about measuring a "nose to fingertip" yard of rick rack for her. Looking around the store, my brother Cammie poked me and said, "Look, the Belle Flour Company copied your pinafore print. There's the same one as yer school dress." I looked over to where he was pointing. I said excitedly, "And look, the price tag says $2.39 for fifty pounds of flour."

There were great bolts of paisley fabric, muslin and multicolored gingham; some soiled, and some faded. The bolts were carelessly stacked and *squeahawed* over long counter. Above were spools of whip cord, rick rack, and blocks of beeswax. I noticed the pair of scissors that dangled from a dirty string nearby was missing the tip of one blade. Ma caressed the pretty colored fabrics, yearning I expect, for the day she could buy a few yards.

The store owner finished with Ma, and returned to the butcher block to hack away at the huge cut of meat he had been working on when we came in. I saw twine-tied roasting hens lying on one corner of the block.

We roamed around for a considerable amount of time. The store was big and barn-like. Benny's General Store boasted the new lighting system that had just arrived in the territory. Dangling on a cord from the ceiling over the antiquated cash register was a single light bulb glowing in the dimness. For the most part, a mile high pile of cash-and-carry receipt books upstaged the old cash register.

There was so much stuff to see. I had never come in contact with anything like it in all my life. The store smelled of mingled aromas of fermented sauerkraut, pickles in barrels, briny tubs, pungent spices, herbs, and coffee. A breeze wafted the smell of new leather harnesses into my nostrils. Added to that were the smells of smoked sausages, hams and slabs of bacon that were hanging from the rafters of the ceiling.

Arranged in no particular manner on the opposite wall of the store were shovels, rakes, hoes, and other types of farm and garden tools, horse collars and barnyard supplies. It looked like a dimensional mural to me.

Ma seemed to be in one of her Humph moods. "This store looks like it's practicin' that new gimmick that I read 'bout in the Ladies Home Companion. It's called merchandisin'—that means that stores put things they want to sell directly in your path so that you'll grab the stuff before you buy what's really on yer list. But they have to git up pretty darn early in the mornin' to fool me." *Please don't talk so loud, Ma, people are lookin'*, I thought.

Over the register, a clothesline was strung with red and black licorice ropes—*more of Ma's merchandisin'*, I thought. The heat of the electric light bulb and the sugar in the candy had attracted swarms of flies. After seeing that the flies had discovered it, we decided not to indulge. Benny had slung a few strips of flypaper over a long string, in hopes that it would deter flies from the tantalizing sweets. "Bet they come from the Livery," my sister Marian said. We all tittered. We had often heard Ma say our fly problem had come from the cow barn.

It was obvious that Benny didn't consider pint-size patrons his priority of the day. After he'd waited on all the adults first, he finally peered over his tiny oval gold rimmed glasses and said, "S'pose you kids brought gopher tails for trade." I was embarrassed by the insinuation that we were poor and needed to barter. I dug one toe into a crack in the floor where sweeping compound had lodged in the patches made of tin cans. Shyly but proudly I held up the Bull Durham tobacco pouch and said, "Pa gave us real money." Benny didn't seem real impressed by this, but he counted our gopher tails, filled out credit slips for each of us, and handed Ma our gopher tail bounties.

"What'll it be ladies and gents?" Benny asked us. We were so bashful, we all diverted our eyes to the dingy cracked glass candy containers of horehound hard candies, jelly beans and all-day suckers. We scuffed our feet and toed the wide cracks in the floor, while trying to decide what we wanted. Each of us took our time selecting which candy would be the best buy for the least price. It was difficult because Benny wasn't inclined to post price tags on the merchandise. Pa and Ma had agreed that no prices were posted because the shop owner could choose to reduce the price "If they took a likin' to ya," or "Hike the price," Pa said, "for the shift eyed folks."

As my brothers and sisters made their decisions, Benny began dipping into the huge jars for their candy. When it was my turn to choose, Ma became impatient with me and said, "Stop snoopin' 'round and make a decision." "I'll take the raspberry all-day sucker, for now," I assured Benny. I chose one that would last a long time so I could hold onto my remaining coppers longer. I reached in to my pouch and pulled out some of the money. With a bashful smile, I held my money out to Benny. He said, "Thank you, little lady," and turned to help my little brother with his purchase. Ma looked my way and said, "Maybe we can git some ankle socks over at the drygoods store."

Now that I had my candy, things were becoming a bit boring for me. I slowly moseyed toward the back of the store, dragging my free hand lightly over the merchandise on each shelf, holding the sucker in my other for quick licks. When I neared the back of the center aisle, I heard male voices muttering, accompanied by a few curses and the sound of cards slapping the table. I was startled to find the old timers' hangout in a niche in the rear of the store.

The community card sharps and cronies gathered here daily around the potbellied stove, to play Whist, and spit in spittoons. I thought the spittoons should have been sitting closer to each spitter. In the dimness of the hanging light bulb, it was difficult to make out their faces. One old man saw me and smiled after spitting in the spittoon and wiping the tobacco juice from his chin. I remember thinking that his brown stained teeth looked like the teeth of the dead badger in our winter kitchen. I got out of there quick while Ma was making the last of her purchases. Besides, I had places to go and things to do!

Guess I'll Go See The Boys — Meandering down the boardwalk, sucking on my all-day sucker, I slapped the rough iron pipes of the hitching rails with my Bull Durham bag of pennies. It made a clinking sound that penetrated my daydream.

Suddenly the memory of Pa's last words to us, "Guess I'll go see the boys!" came to me. I decided, *I'm all dressed up, guess I'll go see the boys, too!* The cobbler's shop was the first shop I came to. I peeked in. The cobbler had the shoe last between his knees, and was spitting nails into his palm, then driving them into the shoe sole with a small hammer. I snorted to myself, *Huh, that's nothin' my Pa can do that blindfolded.* I was proud of Ma and Pa. They could do lots of stuff.

I sauntered on a bit further until I came to Hattie's Cafe. I flattened my nose to the glass in order to view the layout. The tables were pretty, all neatly arranged and covered with red and white checkered oilcloths. Some patrons were eating and some were just moving about. I guessed it was like some country club that folks like me were not privy to. Pa had said it was a place to "Drink a spot of java and shoot the rag."

The next scarred and dirty old storefront establishment caught my attention. It needed no neon lights in the window and no advertisement at all for me to know what kind of place it was. The decrepit door stood open. Judging from the noise and the aroma that escaped out to the boardwalk, I would have said no one could mistake what it was. According to Rachel Sand, anyone who had half a brain in their heads could tell who ruled the lot in there! "It's dat ol' devil drink dat come ta rule da menfolk on da prairie."

Once I realized how close I was to the door, I backed up a few steps. I stopped at the window, now opaque with smoke and grime, and put my face up to it, cupping my hands at the sides of my eyes. I could see enough to make out the brass rail and the bar. Some men were standing with one foot on the rail, and others were seated on rickety stools in front of it. The once highly polished spittoons had deteriorated into sloppy swamps, and hand-rolled cigarette butts were scattered around the floor. At a nearby card table, a few men were gambling for a pouch of Bull Durham. Colorful language and uproarious laughter filled the bar room and floated out into the street.

Suddenly my eyes fell on a scuffed old pair of barnyard soiled shoes. They widened in surprise. *Oh my gosh! Are those Pa's shoes?* I found out very quickly!—They were!

Just then, some farmer casually turned toward the window. He spotted me, touched Pa's arm, and roared in a not-so-sober voice, "Hey Carter! Ain't that one of yer girls out there?"

Pa wheeled around and flew from his place at the bar. Dashing through the open doorway, he grabbed me by the arm and gave me a boot in the posterior with the flat of his foot that would have sent me near a mile, if he hadn't been holding onto my arm. He pulled me toward the livery stable so fast that my feet were only fanning the air. Ma told me later, "For good reason, too, if he woulda opened his mouth when he had a mad on, the profanity that came out woulda numbed the ears of the whole town, includin' the horses at the livery!"

Pa scooped me up in his arms and bounced me hard on the back spring seat of our rig. The jolt knocked the raspberry sucker from my grip. It shot through the air like a skeet at a trap shoot and landed amidst the hay and manure on the floor of the hulk. Pa chastised me, "You sit right there 'til it's time to go home. Maybe that'll teach ya to do what yer told!"

It seemed like *hours* before the rest of the family came straggling back to the wagon where I sat alone and forlorn. Some of my siblings felt sorry for me, but others believed I had gotten what I deserved because I was always Testing Ma and Pa's patience. I ignored their comments and "I told ya so" attitudes, and decided to retrieve my sucker. I spit on it, wiped it on my pinafore and slipped it into my mouth. I slid it back and forth over my tongue, tasting the wonderful sweetness, like a baby with a sugar teat. I recalled making sugar teats for the babies at our house by wrapping sugar in a rag and tying it off with string. It kept them quiet between meals. The baby usually dropped it on the floor at intervals, and with no regard to cleanliness, stuffed it back into its mouth.

About the time Ma climbed into the wagon, she began to rankle, "Yer never satisfied 'til you git what you deserve, are ya?" I remembered what my school teacher had said, "Nothing ventured, nothing gained." Deep down I questioned, *how can ya tell how much courage ya have if ya never been tested?* At least now I knew that people were the same everywhere. They all had a healthy balance of good and not so good points. I secretly hoped that the townsfolk would remember me for my good points—*this bein' my big debut 'n all.*

We all waited a while, then Pa finally came. I could tell he felt sorry for me over the harsh punishment, but he kept it to himself. As our wagon rumbled home the other kids dug deep into their candy bags and taunted me, "Betcha don't know what else I got!" I thought to myself that my raspberry pacifier and my two remaining copper pennies balanced out the scale, but I kept it to myself.

The Homestead Lives On In My Memory

Hard Times On The Prairie — Earl and Lillian raised twelve of us kids while trying to scratch a living out of the soil and coax crops to grow in the undernourished soil on the prairie. We were poor, and Ma and Pa took desperate measures to provide food, clothing, and shelter for their brood. I'm certain that to Ma and Pa the job must have seemed equivalent to the twelve labors of Hercules. Perhaps Ma and Pa never had to kill the lion by thrusting their arms down its throat, or capture a wild Arcadian stag, but they did have to slaughter animals, which oftentimes were our pets. My parents also had to trap, kill, or capture wild dogs, badgers, and coyotes to prevent them from killing our sheep. Us kids knew they did this so we could eat.

I recall Ma telling me that at one point times were so hard, that Ma's sister, Emma, became concerned that my parents couldn't winter over both livestock and a large family. She made an offer to pay for some of the children so they wouldn't starve. Ma said, "No matter how hard times git, I could never be forced to give up one of my kids."

We were unforgiving when Ma sometimes turned into an irritable and boisterous haranguer because of her rambunctious brood and the monumental breakdowns on the farm. She was a woman who found her marriage to be less than perfect, but she was willing to stick it out for the sake of us kids. My Ma didn't smoke or drink, although she did use occasional profanity exclaiming, "This d$#n farm is enough to make a preacher cuss!" I knew that if I dared to blaze the air with profanities, she would scrape the lye soap across my teeth. "And if that don't work," Ma reprimanded, "there's more where that came from!"

For some selfish or inconsiderate reason, I had the unrealistic expectation that Ma and Pa should be infallible; even while fighting to near death to keep clothes on our backs and food in our mouths. When my expectations weren't met, I had one choice—to become that which I expected them to be. Although I expected many more miracles than they could perform, incredible empathy overtook me each time I was witness to the strife my parents endured in bringing their large family to adulthood.

Pa and Ma taught me many great things: integrity, honesty and perseverance. Pa scolded me that if I should "fall into adversity, don't limp"; and that if I failed or lost out on something, "stand up straight, hold yer head high, get movin', and try again." I believe that us Carter kids are all that we are today because of the mold that my Ma and Pa created.

The Homestead Lives On In My Memory — Although my only tangible reminders of Ma and Pa are a lace tablecloth that Ma crocheted for me, and a barometer that Pa won on a punchboard, I do have fond memories of the times we shared, the sacrifices they made, and the values they passed on to me.

Many years after the death of my parents, my brothers, sisters, and myself celebrated a Carter Family reunion near the original site of the old homestead in the vicinity of Medina, North Dakota. Under the guidance of our brother, Eugene, we located the three trees that had been on the hill southwest of the house. Using the trees as our compass, we trudged around in search of some reminder of what had been our home. The buildings were all gone, and the cowpath road that ran by the front of the house had long since been overgrown with grass, brush, and wild roses. After much searching, we came upon the concrete slab that had been the entrance to the old chicken house. Emotions ran high, for there on the concrete slab, were the roughly scrawled initials W.H.C.—the initials of our Pa, William H. Carter. A monument to *The Gentry*, who had long ago left his stamp of approval for all of us to see. It was here, at this place where Ma and Pa had worked so hard and suffered so much tragedy. I'm not sure what thoughts my brothers and sisters had as we each stared down at the slab, but I'm sure we all came to realize that the lives of William and Lillian had not been in vain—their legacy still lives on in their children, their grandchildren, their great grandchildren, and their great great grandchildren. These are the people that will carry on the values and principles that William and Lillian practiced so many years ago out on the North Dakota prairie farm.

It was there, at the old chicken house entrance, looking down at the initials on the concrete slab, that each of us made a silent decision never to allow the memories we shared at the homestead to be extinguished. Nor would we continue to allow the memories that were less than good, lest they deter the growth of our very own souls.

Appendix A

Sour Cream Coffee Cake With Crumb Filling

1 1/2 cup sugar	1 3/4 cup all-purpose flour
1/4 cup brown sugar	1 1/2 t. baking powder
2 eggs	1/4 t. salt
2 t. almond flavoring	

Filling:

1 T. almond paste	3 T. bread, cake or cookie crumbs
1/2 t. almond flavoring	1 T. butter
1 t. cinnamon	3 T. brown sugar

Cream together the butter and two sugars. Beat in eggs, one at a time. Add almond flavoring and sour cream. Stir together the flour, baking powder, and salt. Spoon half the batter into a well greased tube pan.

In a separate bowl, combine the almond paste, nuts, almond flavoring, and butter. Work in the crumbs, cinnamon, and brown sugar. Sprinkle one half of the crumb mixture over the batter in the tube pan.

Add the remaining batter to the top of the crumb mixture, then sprinkle remaining crumb mixture on top of the batter. Bake at 350 degrees for 55 minutes. Cool cake in the pan. Remove from pan on to a plate. Note: 3 T of coconut blended with 1 T sour cream can replace the almond paste.

Sour Cream Raisin Pie

2 eggs	1/2 cup sugar
2 t. cornstarch	1 1/2 t. lemon extract
1/2 cup whole milk	1/2 cup sour cream
1/2 cup heavy cream	2 egg whites
3/4 cup raisins (chop if desired)	1/4 cup sugar

Blend the eggs, sugar, cornstarch, lemon extract, sour cream, milk, and heavy cream together. Scatter raisins into an unbaked pie crust. Pour filling over the top of raisins.

Bake at 350 degrees 35-40 minutes. Remove from oven. Beat egg whites and 1/4 cup sugar together, forming meringue. Spoon meringue on top of warm pie and return to the oven for approximately 10 more minutes, or until meringue is light brown.

Fresh Liver Sausage Spread

1 large liver, about 5 lbs, cut up   1/2 pounds fat, chopped
1 1/2 pounds lean pork, cubed   2 onions, sliced
2 T. vinegar   1 clove garlic
Salt and Pepper to taste   Sage or any choice of herb

Cook meats in boiling water with vinegar and garlic. When cooked, strain and run all meats through a meat grinder. Mix well with hands. Season with salt, pepper, and sage or any other herb of your choice. Pack in an oiled loaf pan. Cover with melted rendered fat. Cover with plastic wrap and chill. Cut into slices and spread as needed.

Ma Carter's Favorite Egg Mustard Dressing
(As written in 1926 in the Dakota Farmer)

Take 1 egg in a granite saucepan, add 1 level tablespoon flour, 3 tablespoons ground mustard, 2 tablespoons sugar, 1 teaspoon salt and 1/8 teaspoon pepper. Beat well, add 1 cup of vinegar very gradually so as to prevent it from curdling. Cook 10 minutes. After it is removed from the heat, add a piece of butter, the size of an egg. Beat well. When making deviled eggs, mix a couple tablespoons of the mustard with ¼ cup sour cream, a bit of horseradish and a sprinkle of sugar, to enhance the flavor. Blend with one dozen hard-boiled egg yolks. Add 1 tablespoon of minced onion and fill the cooked egg whites.

Cranberry Relish

Take one pound or one quart of cranberries, two cups sugar, one and one-half oranges. Wash berries, peel oranges.

Take all of white membrane off them. Grind berries and oranges with rind of one orange in food chopper, add sugar and mix well. Then pour in glasses and cover with hot paraffin. Do not cook this relish. Very good with meat or fowl.

Prepared Mustard

Mix ground mustard with water, which has been boiled and allowed to cool to a smooth paste. Let stand at least one hour, then add sugar, salt, and vinegar. Flour may be added if a milder mixture is desired. To avoid bitterness, do not add vinegar until the mixture of water and mustard has stood for one hour.

Norwegian Rommegrot (Pudding)

1 cup butter *	1/3 cup sugar
3/4 all-purpose flour	1/2 t. salt
4 cups whole milk, scalded	1 t. vanilla flavoring
Cinnamon and sugar to taste	

Melt butter in a heavy saucepan. Stir in the flour until its well blended and smooth. Bring the mixture to simmer. Cook for one minute, stirring constantly. Stir slowly while adding the hot milk. Bring the mixture to a boil. Add salt and sugar. Serve immediately with cinnamon and sugar, or cover to keep warm. * Ma substituted cream for the butter. We ate ours topped with milk and sugar.

Rhubarb Bread Pudding

3 cups day-old bread, buttered	3 eggs
3 cups rhubarb, diced	2 t. sugar
1 cup sugar	1/2 t. salt
1 t. vanilla	1/2 t. nutmeg
3/4 cup cream	2 egg whites

Dice the rhubarb and marinate in sugar overnight.

Butter the bread and cut into cubes. Stir in the rhubarb. Put mixture into oiled baking dish. Beat the eggs well, Add sugar, salt, vanilla, nutmeg, and cream. Bake 40 minutes at 350 degrees. Reduce heat to 325 degrees and bake another twenty minutes. Beat eggwhites with 2T sugar until stiff peaks are formed. Spread mixture over hot bread pudding, and return to the oven. Bake until meringue is lightly browned. Currants and raisins may be used as a rhubarb replacement.

Grandma Walters' Lemon Cake

1 cup freshly churned butter
2 3/4 cups sugar
5 fresh eggs, separated
1 1/4 t. baking soda
4 egg whites, stiffly beaten

3/4 t. salt
4 cups white flour
1 lemon
1 cup whole milk

Beat together egg yolks, butter, and sugar until thick and creamy. In a separate bowl, whip the flour until fluffy, then measure. Combine the baking soda, flour and salt. Grate the lemon peel and squeeze the juice from the lemon. Add milk, lemon juice, and grated rind to the egg mixture. Stir in the dry ingredients.

In a separate bowl, beat the egg whites until stiff, but not dry. Fold them into the cake batter. Spoon batter into two greased and floured 11x4x3 loaf pans. Bake at 350 degrees for 50 minutes or until toothpick comes out clean when inserted in center of cake. Cool. Remove from pans. Dust with confectioners sugar.

* Lemons were not readily available, so Ma used Watkins' Lemon Flavoring, 2 teaspoons to 1 tablespoon as desired. The cake may be lightly brushed with lemon juice, then dusted with confectioners sugar. We used the Watkins Queen of Puddings over our Lemon Cake.

Buckwalter Hotel Lemon Dessert

1 qt. fresh whole milk
3 cups dry bread crumbs
1/2 t. salt
1 cup sugar
1/4 cup butter, or a piece of
butter the size of a large egg

4 eggs, separated
Juice and rind of
of 1 large lemon, or
2 t. lemon flavoring
1/2 cup heavy cream

Topping: 4 egg whites   3 T. confectioners sugar
        1 t. lemon juice

Heat milk and pour over bread crumbs. Stir in butter and salt, allowing butter to melt. Beat egg yolks with sugar, and fold into bread crumbs. Add lemon juice and rind, or lemon flavoring and cream. Blend together. Bake in lightly buttered 8x8x2 baking pan at 325 degrees for 30 minutes.

Beat egg whites to stiff, but not dry. Slowly add confectioners sugar and lemon juice. Return to hot oven and bake until meringue is lightly browned on top. Serve with lemon sauce or whipped cream.

Lillian's Canned Carrot Pudding

1 cup grated carrots
1 cup flour
1 cup grated raw potato
1 cup sugar
1/2 cup raisins
1/2 cup currants

1/2 cup fresh butter, melted
1/2 t. cloves
1/2 t. nutmeg
1 t. cinnamon
1 t. baking soda

Rinse raisins in hot water, then drain. Stir baking soda into the grated potatoes. Combine all ingredients in a large bowl, adding the potatoes last. Mix well. Spoon mixture into pint jars to one-half full. Seal jars. Steam for three hours or at ten pounds of pressure for 25 minutes. Serve hot or cold with ice cream or orange sauce.

Carter Family Favorite Pasty

3 cups flour
1 t. salt
3/4 cup lard, or rendered pork fat
1/4 to 1/3 cup ice water
Filling:

1/2 lb. thinly sliced pork	1/2 cup sliced potatoes
2 slices salt pork, simmer	1/2 cup thinly sliced onion
in 1 cup water, then dice	1/2 cup cubed carrots
1/4 cup peas or corn	1/2 cup sliced rhutabaga,
salt and pepper to taste	or turnip

In a medium bowl, cut lard into flour and salt to size of coarse meal. Sprinkle in the ice water. Toss with a fork. Form a ball. Wrap and refrigerate for one hour.

Meanwhile, prepare the vegetables and mix with salt and pepper. At this point, individual pasties can be made by dividing the dough into four equal pieces and rolling into eight inch circles. Place 1/2 cup of the filling on one-half of the circle, then fold over opposite side of circle and pinch edges together to seal. Then bake.

For one large dish pasty, place the vegetables in the pan. Roll the dough out large enough to fit the top of the pan or baking bowl. Place over top of vegetables and seal dough over the edges of the dish. Cut several small slits for air vents. Bake until vegetables are cooked. If the crust browns too quicly, place a top over the dish. Foil, baking parchment, or brown paper bag works well.

Dutch's Mutton Stew

This dish was served when our dignified and placid Aunt Cora Carter came to visit on the farm. After dinner, Cora always announced that it was the best meal she had ever eaten. Mutton, not lamb, was eaten at the Carter household.

3/4 cup flour	3 medium tomatoes, diced
1 t. salt	2 rhutabagas, cubed
1/2 t. pepper	3 medium potatoes, cubed
1 t. mixed herbs,such as thick	3 large carrots, sliced 1/2"
thyme, rosemary, bayleaf	3-4 cups meat broth
1/4 t. cayenne pepper	1/4 cup rendered fat
2 large onion, chopped	3 1/2 -4 lbs mutton or lamb, cubed in 1/2 to 3/4" squares

Blend first five ingredients together, then dredge the lamb cubes in the mixture. Brown dredged meat and onions in fat over medium heat, small amounts at a time. Remove each batch of browned meat and onions to a platter. Set aside. Place meat broth and vegetables in a 12x14x2 baking dish or pan. Stir. Cover and bake at 350 degrees for 1 1/2 hours.

 * If preferable, rather than covering with a lid or a piece of foil, the covering can be made from a variation of pasty dough:

3 cups all-purpose flour	3/4 cup lard
1/4 cup cornmeal	1/3-1/2 cup shredded cheese
1 t. salt	1/4 -1/3 cup ice water

Cut lard into flour, cornmeal, and salt until mixture resembles pea-sized balls. Stir in cheese. Add ice water a little at a time. Chill in refrigerator. Roll out on lightly floured board to the slightly larger size than the baking dish or pan. Place dough over the top of the pan and seal edges. Cut 6-8 1/2" slits for air vents. Bake. If crust begins to get too brown, cover with parchment or foil.

Scrapple

Since my Ma was a descendant of Pennsylvania Dutch, scrapple was considered the entree at our meal. Pann Haas was a popular breakfast and dinner meal on the plains. It was made from meat scraps gathered at butchering time, much the same as headcheese. The liquid from the meat cookery was thickened with cornmeal, farina, or other cereal.

Bring the meat broth and chopped meat scraps to a boil. Slowly stir in the meat, stirring constantly to prevent lumps. The ratio for our family's meal was approximately 2 pounds of meat scraps to a couple quarts of water and 2 1/2 cups of cornmeal. It was seasoned with 2t. sage, 2t. salt, onion flakes, a dash of cayenne pepper and sweet marjoram. When the mixture begins to leave the sides of the pan, pour it into a loaf pans. Chill quickly. When set, slice the loaf. Roll the slices in flour, and fry until golden brown.

Farmers Cottage Cheese

Making cottage cheese has a certain mystique surrounding it, yet if you have ever done it, you know its relatively easy. Unless you're a farmer, it can be expensive to make your own cottage cheese from scratch.

For every 1 1/4 pounds of cottage cheese to be made, four quarts of milk are needed. Fresh raw milk, pasturized or homogenized milk can be used. Always use fresh milk as opposed to milk that is three or four days old.

An activator such as buttermilk, yogurt, or Rennet contains the correct bacteria to start the clabbering process. The milk can be ripened first, by adding 1/4 cup cultured buttermilk to each quart of milk and allowing it to set, covered for 24 hours at room temperature. This will produce a quart of buttermilk which may be used for other purposes if one doesn't wish to make cottage cheese.

Warm the milk to 86-90 degrees F. over very low heat for about 1 to 2 hours. At this point, 1/8 of a rennet tablet may be used for each gallon of milk used. Stir rennet into 1/2 cup of cold water, then add to milk. My Ma didn't use rennet

Allow milk to stand until a finger inserted in the milk, comes out clean, with milk making a clean break like yogurt. Return milk to a very low heat. With a long knife, cut through the clabber several times to break it up. When the milk reaches 105 degrees F. the whey will begin to separate. Stir to prevent scorching.

When the cheese curds form, they will be rubbery. Pour most of the whey off. Set aside to reserve it for cooking purposes later. When you use it, don't add more salt to it because whey is already a good source for natural sodium. My Ma used it in soups, stews, and breadmaking.

To strain more whey from the curds, double or triple a cheesecloth, or use a clean tea towel. Tie the curds in the cloth and secure with a string. Fasten the cloth bag to a cabinet door handle with a dishpan under it to catch the remaining whey. When the curds have dripped to near dry, place them in a bowl and add a small amount of sweet cream, salt, and pepper. It's the very best cottage cheese you could ever hope to eat. My family consumed it by the dishpanfuls. It was our major source of protein out on the prairie.

Country Bread Pudding

4 1/2 cups cubed firm white bread   1/3 cup sugar
2 cups whole milk   1/2 t. cinnamon
2/3 cup strong black coffee   1 cup raisins
1/4 cup brown sugar or sorghum   3 large eggs

Simmer the coffee until slightly reduced. Cool to warm. Beat in the eggs, sugars or sorghum, and cinnamon. Add milk and raisins or currants. Arrange bread cubes in a large baking dish. Spoon milk mixture over the bread cubes. Let stand for 20-25 minutes. Bake 20 minutes at 325 degrees, then increase oven temperature to 375 degrees. Bake for 10 minutes longer, or until custard is formed and lightly browned.

*If the Watkins man had come, we would serve butterscotch sauce over this dish, but if he hadn't come, we would eat it with milk and sugar. If company was coming, and Ma could spare the egg whites, she made a meringue for the top of it.

Homestead Headcheese

Another name for headcheese was "Souse". In old country cooking, food preservation was quite unique since there were no refrigerators and freezers. On butchering day a use was found for every part of the animal. Nothing went to waste on our farm during the Depression, or for that matter, anytime. With twelve children, my folks were forced to use every morsel available. The feet were used for pickling, the tail was used in stew, and the fat was cut from the skin and rendered for cooking lard. The tongue was boiled and pickled.

Headcheese, scrapple and liversausage were all made from the head, skin, ears, organs, and bones of the animal. The eyes were removed from the head, and the head was quartered and soaked overnight in salted fresh well water. This was one way of sterilizing the meat and drawing out the remaining blood. The head portions were then rinsed well and cooked in a large kettle along with other meat scraps, bits of skin, and feet, if they hadn't been previously pickled separately. The cooked meat was removed from the bones and chopped. The meat was then returned to the pot and all manner of spices and herbs were put in with the meat along with enough water to cover the meat plus one-half inch.

To each batch of headcheese, Ma added almost any Watkins or McNess savory herbs she had available. A tablespoon each of savory, garlic, onion, and sweet marjoram was added. Some cloves , 1/4 - 1/2 t. of red pepper, a tablespoon or two of black pepper, 2 tablespoons of salt, 1/4 cup of vinegar, and a crushed bay leaf were added. The mixture was brought to a boil, and allowed to boil for five minutes.

Loaf pans were lined with a heavy white cloth, or a double layer of cheesecloth, but this step was not mandatory. The meat was then dipped from the liquid with the fatty portions going into the pans first. Next, the lean bits of meat went into the pans. Then some cooked liquid was poured over the meat in the pans.

If a cloth wasn't placed in the pans first, then a strip of cloth should be placed over the loaf, and weight it down with a clean rack on top of a saucer, or a sturdy piece of wood. This action causes the meat to form a compact-shape loaf for slicing after the loaf of meat has set up.

In our family, the headcheese didn't last long enough to require preserving, but the following two methods were commonly used by other families on the prairie: The loaf was tightly wrapped in cloth, secured with a string, and allowed to soak in salt brine for 48 hours. The second method was spooning the meat mixture into jars before molding it, and processing it at 15 pounds of pressure for 90 minutes in a pressure cooker. The liquid in which the meat is cooked jells the loaf.

Souse and Sylte, a Swedish veal and pork loaf with allspice, bay leaves, onions and black pepper were our favorite treats on the farm.

In Colonial Times, one of the congealing agents was isinglass, which in its purist form was the best gelatine known at that time. Calves feet and pigs feet were also used for congealing. The isinglass was broken into small pieces and cooked in the broth along with the meals. The isinglass was soaked in hot water overnight, then cooked with the other ingredients. In those days, blancmange was made into a delicate jelly made opaque by the addition of almond paste, cream and sugar.

Farmhouse Coffee Cake
The vanilla, chocolate pudding mix, baking powder, and baking soda were usually Watkins or McNess products that Ma traded with the salemen for our live chickens.

3 cups all purpose flour, or half whole wheat pastry flour
1 1/2 t. baking powder   1 1/2 baking soda
1/3 cup buttermilk (from home-churned butter)
3/4 t. salt   1 teaspoon vanilla
1/2 cup butter, softened   1 cup sour cream
1/4 cup stewed prunes, minced   3 eggs
Filling: 1 cup chopped walnuts or peanuts
    1/2 cup brown sugar
    1/4 cup white sugar
    1 t. cinnamon
    2 t. chocolate or vanilla pudding mix

Blend the filling ingredients together, set aside. In a separate bowl, whisk together flour, baking powder, baking soda, and salt. Set aside. In a large bowl, beat the softened butter, sugar, and eggs until slightly thickened. Add the sour cream, prunes and buttermilk. Blend. Add the flour mixture, one half at a time, scraping sides of bowl often. Sitr in vanilla.

Place half the batter in a greased and flour-dusted 10 inch tube pan, or two loaf pans. Sprinkle the filling mixture over the batter. Add remaining batter to top of filling. Bake at 350 degrees for 50-55 minutes, or until toothpick inserted in center comes out clean. Since toothpicks were not available to us, and matchsticks were too large, we just popped a straw from our kitchen broom. This worked just fine for us. But if your thoughts are on sanitation, this is not the way to go. Walnuts were only available to us at Christmas time, but we used peanuts instead. If the prunes are omitted, add 1/4 cup more of sour cream.

Prune Supper Cake

Ma used eggshells to measure small amounts of ingredients. Two half eggshells would be equal to approximately 1/4 cup of liquid. One-half cup of butter would be equal to a piece the size of two large eggs or a tea cup full.

1/2 cup freshly made butter	1/4 c. strong coffee
1 cup sugar	1 c.sour cream
3 eggs	3/4 t. salt
1/4 cup prune juice	1/2 c. chopped nuts
1 t. baking powder	2/3 c. snipped prunes
1/2 c. fresh buttermilk	3 cups flour
1 t. black walnut flavoring	

Beat together first three ingredients. Set aside. In a separate bowl, blend together the baking powder, baking soda, salt, prunes, and flour. Set aside.

Add the sour cream, prune juice, coffee, and buttermilk. Mix well. Add dry ingredients in two parts. Blend in the black walnut flavoring.

If desired, sprinkle the top of the cake with a mixture of dry sweet bread crumbs, 1/4 cup sugar, and 1/2 t. cinnamon before baking. Bake at 350 degrees for 35-40 minutes in a 9x13x2 pan or two loaf pans.

Appendix B

MEMORIES FROM MY BROTHERS & SISTERS

My Brother Eugene Shares This — In hunting season 1931, two of Pa's friends from Jamestown, Frank White and Gabby Ingalls, came to hunt ducks on the pass by Chase Lake. In them days, they would shoot all the ducks and other game they wanted, so there was no limit enforcement.

They brought a boat along, and one day were out in the boat on the slough. Gabby stood up to shoot, lost his balance, and fell overboard. Lost the gun in six or seven feet of water. Pa, Pete Vardell, and the two unhappy hunters with home designed grappling tools, scraped the bottom, but no luck. The gun remained in the water.

The early thirties were drought years, and the slough went dry in 1936. Pete remembered where the gun was lost, went back, and found it. It was badly rusted. The barrel was so rusted it had holes clear through, but Pete got the mechanism loosened up and fired it, but it wasn't safe to hunt with after that. Pete was the most mechanical person I have ever known. He could fix just about anything you had to fix.

Gene Also Had This To Say — Of my CCC experience June 15, 1935 to October 1937: In March, 1935, after the deaths of our brothers, Cameron and Duane and sister Blanche, and the hospitalization of Winfred and Gladyce for some time, it was a very hard blow to our parents and the whole family.

The folks were forced to move, as there was friction between Uncle Joe, the owner of the homestead, and Pa. In the later part of April, Pa and I moved over to the Challman Farm, and put the crop in. The rest of the family and the livestock moved later.

281

By the first of June, the crop wasn't doing well. The folks had lots of bills, hospital and burial expenses, so it was decided that I would go into the CCCs, as brother Bill had the year before. Bill and I each received $5.00 a month, and the folks got $50.00 a month. A good income along with the income from the farm. It was the Depression years, and times were very hard.

On June 17, 1935, we left Jamestown on two Pullman cars, about eighty of us, all teen-aged boys. It took a day, a night, and another half day to go less than a hundred miles, as we had to change trains twice. Today, as the crow flies, its only about seventy-five miles, a little over an hours drive.

Our first camp was a tent company with approximately 240 boys. We spent the summers building small dams. A lot of rocks were hauled to do the stone work on the dam surfaces.

In the fall of 1935, late in September, we moved to Camp Crook, South Dakota, where we had a permanent shelter for the winter months. The barracks were heated with wood. It was a very cold winter, and it wasn't very pleasant. Our camp was in Custer National Forest, part of the Black Hills area. We built fire trails, thinned the timber so that it would grow into better logging trees, and built line fences on the forestry land for the benefit of the ranchers.

At Christmas time in 1935, we got leave to go home, the first time in six months. Getting home was a problem, as the railroad connections weren't too good. About fifteen of us got lined up with a potato trucker from Minnesota who had just delivered a truck load of potatoes, and was going back empty. So for $6.00 a piece, we could ride to Jamestown, approximately 350 miles. We rode all night and about 10:00 a.m. I got off at Medina. That was some ride. Can you imagine a 1934 truck on gravel washboard roads in a truck van going 40 to 50 miles per hour for that length of time. The dust rolled in, and we about choked. There were no blacktop roads in them days, but anyway, I got home for Christmas. Pa was in Medina to pick me up. The weather had been fine, no snow. On the way home, it started to snow and storm and it snowed all the time I was home.

On January 3rd I was to catch a bus at Medina to go back. After the storm, all the roads were all blocked, and it was real cold. I borrowed a saddle horse from Dan Voth to ride to Medina. The snow banks were so hard, the horse could walk on top of them. At one place, I rode right over the telephone pole. It was about a sixteen mile ride, and very cold. I stopped at Pete Vardell's and left the horse in his barn for Pa to pick up later. I slept at Pete's that night, in his cook car. When we woke up in the morning, everything was white, as the snow had blown in through the cracks. I made it to the bus that day to return to Camp.

The first part of 1936 was one of the coldest for North Dakota. I spent most of my CCC days in South Dakota, and got home only twice in twenty-seven months. The last two months I got promoted to Forestry work as a machine operator. I was a bulldozer operator, and it was the most pay and quite a jump in pay. One day I was getting $5.00 a month, the next day $140.00 a month. I felt pretty good about that, only three guys out of 240 to get promoted.

In the later part of October 1937, the job completed, the Forest Service moved their machinery to Red Lodge, Montana. I was supposed to go there and work, but I wanted to go home and visit first.

When I got home, Pa talked me into staying to work around home on the section for others, Don Williams, Cliff Gunderson, Fred Bitz, Bill Wutzke, and Bill Hinger. Then courting and marriage. My wife and I were married about a year and a half before the draft, so I didn't serve in the military. I spent twenty-five months of CCC life, earned $125.00 and the folks got $625.00. An experience I do not regret, and will always remember. Signed: Eugene A. Carter, third of twelve in the Carter Family

Eugene A Carter

Marian Has This To Say — Well, Marian Murriel Carter was born August 13, 1919. Black curly hair and brown eyes. My folks cut my curls off when I was around three. I was then nicknamed Bobby. Mom saved a curl for me, also one for Gene.

I remember when I was about four, Pa put me on top of a table to do the Charleston for our company. As I grew up, I had to herd sheep and cattle. We had a Billy and Nanny goat in the sheep herd. When the sheep were ready to rest they would lay by the water in the old bog over the hill. We had a couple buggy wheels put together with a reach in between, and we rolled it down the hill and watched old Billy hammer it. When it wiggled, he would hit it again.

Blanche and I were the hired men after the boys joined the CCC's. We plowed, hayed, milked, cultivated, and anything else that needed doing. After a while, all these chores were passed on down the line as everyone grew up.

One day we were catching lambs to put in for fattening. We kept one eye on old Jiggs (sheep buck) as he would get you if he could. To Uncle Joe's dismay, he was going to show us how to do the job. He stooped over to grab a lamb, and Jiggs hit him square in the behind. Uncle Joe went belly-flop in the musky corral. We started to giggle, but Pa put a stop to that.

One day while haying, Pa yelled, "Tie the horses to the rack, and get by the hay stack." That was the day the tornado struck. On the way home we saw Ma's flock of turkeys in piles gasping their last breaths. The front door was gone, and Ma had gone with it. Shirley had been herding cattle, and Ma had sent Gordon Mell to run to her. They were to lay in a ditch and hold tight to whatever they could grab onto. Well, they panicked and started home. As they crossed the fence, they heard a big noise. The cupola off the Jenkins' barn had hit the fence about a yard behind them. They also saw the tornado hit the big lake and saw the a large funnel of water.

Nothing else that I know that was different in our lives. It was just passed from one to the other, like our clothes and our shoes!. Signed: Marian M. Carter Holmes

Marian M. Carter Holmes

Shirley Contributes Memories Of The Past—She itemizes: Remember the little gray kettle we fought over with the German girls next door in Medina?

Remember picking corn by the wagon loads, shucking it and cutting it off the cob so Ma could cold pack it in the wash boiler?

Remember the walks across the lake to school when one of us would go through the ice into a spring and our stockings would be frozen to our legs when we got there?

Remember when the Halverson and Sand boys would pile up behind the wood stove at school like so many pigs to get warm?

Remember the community picnic at Crystal Springs when Pa got Ma out in a rowboat to fish?

Remember the hurt pelican we locked in the granary so he would have food until he could fly—not knowing that they ate fish instead of grain?

Remember snaring gophers so we could get a penny for their tails?

Remember the baby skunks Bill kept in the underground silo until trapping season so he could sell their pelts?

Remember how Pa used to climb the windmill to check on us when we were late bringing in the cattle and sheep?

Remember Pa going to Pettibone for a load of coal shortly before Christmas so we would all have an orange in the toe of our Christmas stockings?

Remember Bill carving toy bobsleds and Ma making rag dolls from mens' work socks for our Christmas presents?

Remember the snowdrifts that made our hilly trip to school a flat run?

Remember the chokecherry picking? Chopping ice from the straw or manure pile to make ice cream for July Fourth? The walk from Crystal Springs after a Fourth of July doings and getting caught in a freak snowstorm?

I remember the time Dan and Pet ran away from me on the hayrake. The time the same pair and a hayrack on a trailer with a loose hitch tipped me upside down in the ditch south of the Gunderson Place.

I remember my first trip home after I was married. Pa hid all the beer. The first thing Julius did was stop up town for beer. From then on, Julius was great.

I remember the cyclone that went through our place. Gordon Mell held me face down in the mud of the cornfield, and the cupola from the Jenkins' barn flew over our heads and hit the fence across the road from us. Signed: Shirley Ione Carter Zimmerman.

Shirley Ione Carter Zimmerman

Brother Winfred On Early Life—When asked of his memories of early childhood, my Brother Winfred responded with: "Farm work, older sisters, and sickness at a very young age. Hospital stay with Catholic nun nurses, and older and younger brothers leaving our family for the Heavenly Family. Later on, three younger sisters arrived in the Carter family making a unique situation—one boy between six sisters. As the younger sisters appeared on the scene, the older ones moved on to jobs, careers, and marriage.

Childhood went fast. My playtimes seemed scarce, and pretty much resembled chores and farm work. Grade school and school friends was a time of fun, for me, even though it was sandwiched into the farm life and war years of the 1940s.

We all remember the events of the years. With everyone moving on with their own lives, I soon became the oldest child on the farm. I was responsible for some of the activities on the farm. Regular chores of herding the animals, cleaning barns, feeding, milking. Up at daylight and to bed at dark. This was the pre-indoor plumbing and electricity era. Running water was defined as *run to the pump and get it!* Kerosene lanterns were used in doors at times, and always out in the barns in all types of weather. Winters on the plains of North Dakota seemed very severe to a young man and frost bitten noses, cheeks, fingers and toes proved to be a way of life.

After the War years my folks, tired of fighting the elements on the farm, migrated to Puyallup, Washington. Relocating, getting settled, and working new jobs was the agenda. Mom, Dad, and I all worked at the Brew Manufacturing Company, which was a sawmill and lumberyard. This type of work proved to be a real change of vocation for us all.

During and after World War II, manpower was hard to come by, as the men were in the Armed Forces. The young men and women of high school age were hired to fill in the labor gaps, picking up the slack in production output.

The sawmill was an important time in the life of this seventeen year old farm boy. I met a blonde, blue-eyed, five foot two high school senior working on the other side of a large rip saw. Ethel M. Balch was to be my wife in 1947.

Seeking higher education, my wife and I moved to Seattle, Washington near Simpson Bible Institute. Working at Boeing Aircraft on the night shift, and going to school during the mornings lasted for seven and a half years. During this time, my son, Walter L. was added to our family, and a couple years later, Ruth Marie, our daughter, was born.

The early 1950s was an important time of transition for us. The college I was attending relocated in San Francisco, California. I was hired to repair and repaint the new facilities. After our move to San Francisco, I continued my morning study classes, working at the college during afternoons and working the nightshift at Pan American Airlines. I finished my education in the early 1950s with a major in missions and a minor in Theology.

I failed my missions physical exam due to a bad heart valve from having Rheumatic fever during childhood. This created a change in plans, and we were led to a small community church in Lynnwood, Washington. I served as Pastor builder there for several years. To supplement my income, I started a painting contracting business, which has lasted thirty-five years.

Later years have gone by very quickly. We are very glad we relocated back to the State of Washington to be near our parents. We spent many hours with them, and our children got to know both of their grandmas and grandpas very well during their later years. Signed:Winfred L. Carter

Winfred L. Carter

Robinson Crusoe Times Four From Gladyce —
One time Winfred, and myself, along with our friends, Laura
Belle and Harry Williams, went over to our brother Eugene's
property to play. We had decided to adopt his unused
granary as a fort. In our enthusiasm to play Robinson
Crusoe, the two boys labored to cut a man-sized hole in the
roof of the granary for use as a lookout. Using a handcrafted
ladder, they pulled an old door up to the roof, cut a hole,
and installed hinges on the door. It was to be used as a trap
door and a lookout. The best part was that it camouflaged
the hole in the roof. When the installation was complete,
they nailed the front door of the granary shut, so no one
could get into our lair.

We enjoyed our secretive hide-out for a while—that is,
until Pa decided to use the old granary to store some grain.
At the time, Pa didn't realize that the roof had been
modified. When the rains came, the roof leaked like a sieve,
and the grain was totally destroyed. Needless to say, the rest
was history for the four Robinson Crusoe *wannabes.*

Gladyce Reminds Us—Around 1932 or 1933, the
grasshoppers were so thick they looked like clouds and
blotted out the sun. Then in 1938 or 1939 the "army of
worms" came. They were about an inch long and went over
or through everything in their paths, eating anything that
was available. They covered houses, gaining entry through
cracks or got on clothes and the bodies of anyone entering
the house. The ground moved like waves of gray-green
water. When you walked, it was like walking on ice.

Gene was working on the railroad section crew. The
worms were so thick, he said, their railroad cart would spin
out. They had to put a broom on each track in front of them
to sweep the rails so the cart could move.

The "army" was over ten miles wide, and it took them
two weeks to pass through our area. And then there were
the little frogs. They were so thick on the roads that cars

289

would slip and slide. No one knows where they came from. Maybe they were dropped by a big rain storm?

Gladyce adds this postscript—Just writing about those worms is enough to give me nightmares. I can still see them in my bed. We may be a little off on what year they came through, but it's close.

Gladyce Tells About Vonnie And A Rooster — While we were living in Alderton, Washington, Yvonne usually walked down the railroad tracks, and sneaked into the yard from the other side to avoid the rooster that patrolled the property. The rooster, Ben, was not above flying onto your back to claw you. Being a quick learner, it only took one attack for Vonnie to get smart. Pa didn't feel that her complaints about the rooster were valid, until Ben decided to pounce on him! It looked like a stand-off, with Ben squawking, flapping, and jumping around while Pa flailed a broom in all directions. After some time, the rooster lost the battle, and became the main ingredient in our chicken and dumplings dinner!

The Buck Sheep Perspective From Gladyce — When we were little, Winfred and I rode Mike, the buck sheep, like he was a horse. Over time, Pa noticed that Mike, who followed the cows around in the pasture, was getting sway-backed. He told Ma, "I cogitated the matter, then decided to sit behind the rock pile and watch for the sly little shepherds to drive the herd home. Sure enough, there they were, riding double on the old buck sheep!"

Gladyce And The Hay Hole — The chore of feeding the animals required pitching hay down through holes in the loft floor. The hay holes were strategically placed so that if you were on target, you could pitch it equally to each feed bin without much effort. As easy as it sounds, it could sometimes be very challenging—and a little painful!

Such was the case one evening when, my brother, Winfred, a neighbor boy named Fritz, and myself attempted to carry out the task. In our exuberance to complete our chores we pitched too much hay into a hay hole, clogging it up. To resolve the quandary, Fritz volunteered to jump into the stuck pile of hay. He got stuck in the hole waist-deep. Us kids panicked—I climbed down the ladder and yelled up to Winfred, "I'll swing on his legs, you jump on his shoulders." The swinging and jumping went on, it seemed, forever—but Fritz stayed stuck! We finally decided that the only way to free Fritz and the stuck hay was to remove clumps of hay from around him. Alas, poor Fritz fell through to the floor below. Needless to say, he was scared, and slightly bruised and banged up.

Gladyce Adds This — We played hide and seek in the tall pigweeds. We also used the leaves as fans in the mosquito-infested heat.

When there was water in the slough, we would go swimming. That consisted of walking on our hands and letting our legs float...that is about all you could do in a foot of water.

We used to tie a rope to the rafters of the barn. Then we would swing and drop in to the hay below. Sometimes we would over-shoot and land on the bare boards below.

Pa bought Queen, a quarter horse. She was a one-stepper and wouldn't let any horse get ahead of her. Yvonne and I rode her to school. The neighbor boys used to race and Queen would take off. Being only ten or eleven, I couldn't hold her back, and we really had the ride of our lives, especially when it was wet and slippery. We still won the races.

Once, after a big storm, Yvonne and I were on our way to school when the horse got stuck. She fell through the snow up to her chest. Pa heard on the radio, the wind chill factor was 52 below zero, and came looking for us. Its a good thing he did. We were trying to shovel the horse out with our hands and weren't making much headway.

In the winter, Pa would fasten one end of the rope to our sled and the other on his saddle horn, and give us a ride. He always made sure we were dumped off a few times.

Ma was fixing a skirt for me, when I was in high school and noticed I have a flat hip. She said it must have happened when I fell out of the hayloft on the manger when I was three years old. She said I didn't walk too good for a long time. They couldn't afford the doctor, like when I pushed a bead up my nose (I finally sneezed it out!): when I was straddling the chair and rocking it until I tipped it over, pinning my chin to the floor: or when I got a roll of rusty barbed wire imbedded in my leg. They did take me to the doctor when I was caught eating potatoes that had been treated to kill bugs. Winfred wouldn't own up to eating them too, until he found out how sick I got.

Pa's favorite punishment was a kick in the behind with the side of his foot. One day he got mad at me and sent me to the house. I saw his shadow sneaking up on me. When he raised his foot to kick, I jumped and he missed and almost fell down. I never did figure out why I got away with it. One thing we knew, was that you always stood and took your punishment. Signed: Gladyce Erling

Gladyce Erling

My Sister Yvonne Writes — Being one of the younger Carter kids, my memories of the hard life is a shorter version since some of us Carters moved to the State of Washington when I was seven.

One of my most vivid memories of the North Dakota prairie life was the day I almost drown in the slough while getting the cattle. Pa and Ma were in the field on the hill, and I was sent with Old Daisy, the lazy horse, out to get the cows. Naturally, they found it very convenient to be on the other side of the slough, way in the corner where the good grass grew. I started to go around the water, when I heard Pa hollering to me to go across the slough where the cows were so it didn't take me all d$#n night! I think Old Daisy decided she was too hot and a little water would cool her off. I remember Pa running down the hill yelling just as Daisy started to lay down and roll over. That's all I remember about that day, but I never had to get those cows again.

Another memory of mine was when I was in the first grade. Since we only lived a couple miles from school, I got to ride horseback each day. Either behind my sister, Gladyce or Brother Wynn (Winfred). On one particular day, Pa was going to be in town getting feed, and said I could have the privilege of riding home with him in the truck. Well, it was common knowledge that Pa liked to catch a few at the local bar when he got to town. I sat on the street corner waiting for him until almost dark. Along came Mr. Schnider, driver of the local gas delivery truck, and since I went to school with his daughter, he convinced me to go home with him until Pa was ready to go home. Well, Pa not only forgot the time when he got to swapping stories with the locals...he even forgot his own daughter! About 10 P.M.. that evening, my brothers Gene and Wynn scouted the town for their little lost sister. Was it ever a surprise to me when we got home and I received the spanking of my life with the old razor strap.

Life was pretty normal for us little kids. The older children did the chores, and they were the ones to battle the elements outside each day. The only times I remember were when I had to babysit my little sister, Maridelle, while everyone was in the fields. One time, she cried so hard I had to get the old horse out, pull him up to the porch rail and boost Maridelle up on his back. Since I was only five at the time and Maridelle was about three and a-half, I had to lead the horse to the field. No shoes, just a lot of stickers and grain stubble to go through. I bet you know who got the dickens from Pa for that trip. I always seemed to be doing the wrong thing at the wrong time!

The most memorable time for me was the day sister Ferne came to visit. We had already moved to the State of Washington. I was in the third grade. She brought dolls for Maridelle and me that had eyes that opened and closed. They even had hair. Mine had a blue dress and Maridelle's had a pink one. We also received presents. I was dressed in a navy blue pleated skirt and light blue sweater that buttoned up the front, and Maridelle was in pink. My hair was curled in long curls, and we had our picture taken. Ferne in her fur coat, and Mama, Gladyce, Maridelle and me. I know that was the first store bought clothes I had ever owned, and I was very proud. I remember twirling around so the skirt would flare out, thinking I looked like a princess.

Maridelle was the spoiled one at our house. Anything she wanted to play with, she got. I remember the day I came home from school to find she had cut my doll's hair. She was saving her doll, so she practiced on mine. Mama said, "Don't scold her, she's little." I remember crying myself to sleep and vowing to "get even." The time never came, though, as all through my grade school years, Maridelle was there to tattle on me, and I remained in the doghouse for most of my early years.

I spent the early years babysitting for brother Bill's stepdaughter and later for Ferne's children. When I was in the fifth grade, the folks purchased a berry farm outside of Orting, Washington. My sister, Gladyce, and I were farmed out right away to the Japanese truck farm across the road. We worked from 6 A.M. until 6 P.M. (or until Pa came home, whichever was first). All of our wages went to help support the family.

My high school years were spent both in the berry fields, and by that time my folks had purchased a country store outside the gates of the First World War Veterans Home. Every day after school until 9 P.M. my job was tending the store.

I married a service man from Wisconsin and have resided there ever since. I am single, although I have had two husbands. Because of my strong upbringing, I seem to be a workaholic and have trouble accepting anything less from myself. I have nine beautiful and gifted children, and twenty-one fantastic grandchildren. I am proud to be a Carter. Signed: Yvonne LaPorte

Yvonne
LaPorte

Appendix C

Carter Family In The Armed Forces — My brothers, Bill and Eugene joined the CCC, Community Conservation Corps, where each learned many skills that enriched their lives. My brother, Bill, also joined the Army and served in the Philippines.

I joined the Spars, the Womens' Coast Guard, and became one of the youngest Chief Petty Officers ever promoted. While I was in the Spars, I met and married my husband of forty years, Jack Alfred Chapman. He was an infantryman in the 268th Army Air Force, serving under General George S. Patton during the Battle of the Bulge. Jack was an expert rifleman and mortar gunner. He was honored with American Theatre ribbons, three Bronze Stars and Victory Medals.

My mother's brother, Archie Walters spent a lifetime in the service of his country, as well as serving in the military of several other countries. Many of the Carter families' sons, daughters and other relatives followed suit, joining the armed forces.

It's been fifty-three years since this country danced in the streets, when Germany surrendered and all of the fathers, husbands, sons, boyfriends, fiancées, and daughters returned home from the War. It was VE Day, April 1945. Along with the town's people, we Spars whose barracks were in Cleveland, crowded into trolley cars, and headed downtown to celebrate in the streets. Every branch of the service was represented. Everyone grabbed someone—some perfect strangers—and kissed, and hugged and danced with jubilation. Everyone talked of mustering out.

We celebrated again in August, on VJ day, victory over Japan. There would be no more V-mail, where a single sheet was mailed, passed through the U.S. Army Examiner, and oftentimes censored so much that it blacked out most of the letter.

Wages for employees outside the service were about eleven dollars a week. The government rationed many items like sugar, meat, and gasoline, so that the soldiers could have more of the products.

Recycling was a reality on the homestead long before we began saving the fuzzy material of the milkweed pods for the construction of life jacket lining for Navy personnel. During the war, we did our patriotic duty and recycled for the war effort.

At the homestead we saved bits of string, paper bags, zippers, old buttons, aluminum foil, tin cans, rubber tires, even the old tubes from toothpaste, because we didn't have enough money to buy more. Little did any of we Carter kids know that our food and necessities would once again be rationed, only this time, not because we were poor, but because it was our privilege to serve our country.

Top photo is the Conrad Lutz family, Circa late 1800s, possibly in Minnesota. The woman standing in the upper left corner is Mary Anne Lutz, my grandmother, who would later marry Alfred Eugene Walters and one of their babies would be my mother, Lillian Blanche Walters Carter.

Bottom photo is the Josiah Carter family, Circa 1892? From left to right, back row: Annie Carter, my grandmother on my father's side; Dahl; Alfred; Josiah, Jr. and Josiah Carter, Sr., my grandfather. Front row: Eliza Ellen; Libbie; and the baby on Josiah's knee is my father, William Harlow Carter.

From top of page, left to right:
1. My Grandma, Mary Ann Lutz Walters.
2. My Grandpa and Grandma Walters standing in a field of oats, circa 1925.
3. My grandfather Josiah Carter, Sr.
4. The only known photo of my baby brother, Duane Willard Carter, circa 1933.
5. 1912 wedding photo of my mother and father, Lillian Blanche Walters and William Harlow Carter.
6. My mom, Lillian holding brother Bill w/ Blanche in front of her, circa 1916/1917.
7 Carters: Marian; Blanche; Lillian (Ma); Eugene, Cameron; Winfred; Shirley; Ferne; and William H. Carter, Sr. (Pa) is holding Gladyce. Circa about 1933.
8. Carters: William H. Jr.; Blanche Mae; Lillian (Ma) holding Ferne; Marian Murriel; Eugene Albert; and the little girl in the front is Shirley Ione. Circa 1912.

Starting at the top from left to right.

1. Chase Lake School: Back row: Clifford Halverson; Lloyd Halverson; Edwin Ocshner; Gordon Halverson; Bill Carter; Anna Carter; teacher Rachel Thorsness. Middle row: Marian Carter; Esther Ocshner; Ethel Ocshner; Ruby Ocshner. Front row: Stanley Halverson; Ferne Carter. Circa 1929-1930.
2. School a few years later: Back row: Shirley Carter; Jay Eisinger; Ferne Carter; Allen Crombie. Front row: Zola Reardon; Donna Reardon; and the two youngest girls are possibly Reardons.
3. Grandpa Alfred Eugene Walters and unknown duck hunter.
4. Blanche Mae Carter, by the old garage and Cousin Ione Carter with Mary's chicken coop behind her on the right.
5. The homestead with Eugene on horseback, Mama Lillian and Aunt Cora on the porch, and Blanche and Shirley in the yard, dated 1929.
6. Carters: Marian; Ferne; Shirley; Bill and Cameron.

From the top, left to right.
1. Wedding photo of Jack Alfred Chapman and Ferne Ladelle Carter, 1945. #2 also.
3. Ferne Carter at age 17 on the farm in No. Dakota just prior to leaving.
4. Lillian Carter (Ma) on the porch of the farm house.
5. Photo of the barn, truck and tractor. Earl Carter (Pa) and others.
6. William Carter as a soldier while in the Philippines.
7. Eugene Albert Carter while in the CCC's.
8. A more modern day photo of the Carter Kids taken in 1988. From left to right:
   Gladyce; Ferne; William, Jr.; Shirley; Marian; Winfred; Yvonne; Eugene.

50th wedding anniversary of my mom and dad, circa 1962. Upper photo, left to right: Back row: Eugene; Winfred; William. Center: Maridelle; Marian; Yvonne; Ferne. Front row: Shirley; Lillian; William H. (Earl); Gladyce.

Bottom photo taken at the same time showing all the generations of the Carter Family: Starting in the back row L to R: Raymond Zimmerman; Dennis Carter; Willard Carter; George Zimmerman; Donald Zimmerman; Jack Chapman; Donald Wolfe; William Holmes. 2nd row: Julius Zimmerman; Edna Carter; Eugene Carter; Ethel Carter; Winfred Carter; Anne Carter; William H. Carter, Jr.; Lynda Chapman; Richard Zimmerman. 3rd row: Maridelle Carter Stallone w/son Anthony; Gladyce Carter Erling; Shirley Carter Zimmerman; Lillian; Earl; Marian Carter Holmes; Ferne Carter Chapman; Yvonne Carter Laporte; Dale Wolfe. Front row: Verne Carter; Ruth Carter; Julius Zimmerman; Shirley Zimmerman; Sharon Zimmerman; Cheri Carter; Billy Carter; Paul Carter; Lisa Carter; Lenice Wolfe; Sandra Wolfe

From upper left to right:
1. Ferne Carter with Virginia Wallenberg at boot camp in Palm Beach, Florida.
2. Ships cook Ferne Carter.
3. United States Coast Guard mess line, Washington, D.C.
4. Ferne Carter with Virginia Wallenberg still at boot camp.
5. Ferne Carter, Ships Cook 2nd Class and Jane Ferabec, Ships Cook 2nd Class.
6. Honor Guard, Palm Beach, Florida.
7. Cook and Bakers at Captain of Port Cleveland, Ohio. Back row: Milly Bishop; Walt Dingle, Ships Cook 1st Class; Virginia Wallenberg; Instructor Reardon; Ferne Carter, Ships Cook 1st Class; Sally Wright; Minsloff, Ships Cook 1st Class; Sara Lynch, fresh out of boot camp.
8. Regimental Review at Palm Beach, Florida.